THE BIG BOOK OF QUOTES

FUNNY, INSPIRATIONAL AND MOTIVATIONAL QUOTES ON LIFE, LOVE AND MUCH ELSE

By M. Prefontaine

Published by MPPublishing

INTRODUCTION

The essence of the best quotes are that they express a truth or an insight in a short and often amusing way. The Big Book of Quotes is selected by the author and is a collection of quotations from some of the greatest minds that ever existed.

This is a book which you can just pick up anytime and carry on where you left off last time. It is for those who want to pep up a speech, a presentation or an email and for those who just want to jump start their brains with thought provoking or amusing quotations.

Thoughts expressed succinctly have tremendous power. They can inspire and motivate, they can get a message across and they can provide insight.

I hope this book will prove useful, amusing and the quotes will resonate with you.

TABLE OF CONTENTS

CHAPTER 1 POWER

POLITICS

Politics is the art of looking for trouble, finding it, misdiagnosing it, and then misapplying the wrong remedies.
-*Groucho Marx (1890 – 1977)*

He who seeks equality amongst unequals seeks the absurd.
-*Spinoza (1632 – 77)*

Peron had a wise saying. In politics, you can recover from anything except looking like a fool.
-*Alma Guillermoprieto (1949 -)*

The art of leadership is saying no, not saying yes. It is very easy to say yes.
-*Tony Blair (1953 -)*

There is a thin line between politics and theatricals.
- *Julian Bond (1940 -)*

Politics is the art of postponing decisions until they are no longer relevant.
-*Henri Queuille (1884 – 1970)*

Politics: "Poli" a Latin word meaning "many"; and "tics" meaning "bloodsucking creatures".
-*Robin Williams (1951 – 2014)*

When you give food to the poor, they call you a saint. When you ask why the poor have no food, they call you a communist.
-*Archbishop Helder Camara (1909 -99)*

A politician needs the ability to foretell what is going to happen tomorrow, next week, next month, and next year. And to have the ability afterwards to explain why it didn't happen.
-Winston Churchill (1874 – 1965)

Everything is changing. People are taking their comedians seriously and the politicians as a joke.
-Will Rogers (1879 – 1935)

Politicians are like diapers. They both need changing regularly and for the same reason.
-Mark Twain (1835 – 1910)

Political language is designed to make lies sound truthful and murder respectable, and to give an appearance of solidity to pure wind.
-George Orwell (1903 – 1950)

Ninety percent of the politicians give the other ten percent a bad reputation.
-Henry Kissinger (1923 -)

The most successful politician is he who says what the people are thinking most often in the loudest voice.
-Theodore Roosevelt (1858 – 1919)

Bad politicians are sent to Washington by good people who don't vote.
-William E. Simon (1927 – 2000)

The magician and the politician have much in common: they both have to draw our attention away from what they are really doing.
-Ben Okri (1959 -)

My choice early in life was either to be a piano-player in a whorehouse or a politician. And to tell the truth, there's hardly any difference.
-*Harry S Truman (1884 – 1972)*

The ability to change one's views without losing one's seat is the mark of a great politician.
-*Morris K. Udall (1922 – 1998)*

It is hard to imagine a more stupid or more dangerous way of making decisions than by putting those decisions in the hands of people who pay no price for being wrong.
-*Thomas Sowell (1930 -)*

Politicians never accuse you of 'greed' for wanting other people's money - only for wanting to keep your own money.
-*Joseph Sobran (1946- 2010)*

For a politician to complain about the press is like a ship's captain complaining about the sea.
-*Enoch Powell (1912 – 98)*

Talkers are usually more articulate than doers, since talk is their specialty.
-*Thomas Sowell (1930 -)*

There exists no politician in India daring enough to attempt to explain to the masses that cows can be eaten.
-*Indira Gandhi (1917-84)*

He knows nothing; he thinks he knows everything - that clearly points to a political career.
-*George Bernard Shaw (1856 – 1950)*

If you tell a lie big enough and keep repeating it, people will eventually come to believe it. The lie can be maintained only for such time as the State can shield the people from the political, economic and/or military consequences of the lie. It thus becomes vitally important for the State to use all of its powers to repress dissent, for the truth is the mortal enemy of the lie, and thus by extension, the truth is the greatest enemy of the State.
-Joseph Goebbels (1897 – 1945)

The first panacea for a mismanaged nation is inflation of the currency; the second is war. Both bring a temporary prosperity; both bring a permanent ruin. But both are - the refuge of political and economic opportunist.
-Ernest Hemmingway (1899 – 1961)

The best political weapon is the weapon of terror. Cruelty commands respect. Men may hate us. But, we don't ask for their love; only for their fear.
-Heinrich Himmler (1900 – 45)

Political correctness does not legislate tolerance; it only organizes hatred.
-Jacques Barzun (1907 – 2012)

History suggests that capitalism is a necessary condition for political freedom.
-Milton Friedman (1912 – 2006)

Political power grows out of the barrel of a gun.
-Mao Tse-tung (1893 – 1976)

There is no maxim, in my opinion, which is more liable to be misapplied, and which, therefore, more needs elucidation, than the current one, that the interest of the majority is the political standard of right and wrong.

-James Madison (1751 – 1836)

Reader, suppose you were an idiot. And suppose you were a member of Congress. But I repeat myself.

-Mark Twain (1835 – 1910)

Never believe anything in politics until it has been officially denied.

-Otto von Bismarck (1815 – 98)

Every decent man is ashamed of the government he lives under.

-Henry Louis Mencken (1880 – 1956)

Man will never be free until the last king is strangled with the entrails of the last priest.

-Denis Diderot (1713 -84)

People never lie so much as after a hunt, during a war or before an election.

-Otto von Bismarck (1815 -98)

A statesman is a successful politician who us dead

-Thomas Brackett Reed (1839 – 1902)

You campaign in poetry. You govern in prose.

-Mario Cuomo (1932 -)

The poor object to being governed badly, while the rich object to being governed at all.
-GK Chesterton (1874 – 1936)

The radical of one century is the conservative of the next. The radical invents the views. When he has worn them out the conservative adopts them.
-Mark Twain (1835 – 1910)

Bureaucracy is a giant mechanism operated by pygmies.
-Balzac (1799 – 1850)

We have the best government that money can buy.
-Mark Twain (1835 – 1910)

Illegal aliens have always been a problem in the United States. Ask any Indian.
-Robert Orben (1927 -)

My concern is not whether God is on our side; my greatest concern is to be on God's side, for God is always right.
-Abraham Lincoln (1809 -65)

The last thing I ever wanted was to be alive when the three most powerful people on the whole planet would be named Bush, Dick and Colon.
-Kurt Vonnegut (1922 – 2007)

Politics is the art of looking for trouble, finding it everywhere, diagnosing it incorrectly and applying the wrong remedies.
-Groucho Marx (1890 - 1977)

What difference does it make to the dead, the orphans and the homeless, whether the mad destruction is wrought under the name of totalitarianism or in the holy name of liberty or democracy?
-Mahatma Gandhi (1869 – 1948)

All war is a symptom of man's failure as a thinking animal.
-John Steinbeck (1902 -68)

The smallest minority on earth is the individual. Those who deny individual rights cannot claim to be defenders of minorities.
-Ayn Rand (1905 -82)

I'm completely in favor of the separation of Church and State... These two institutions screw us up enough on their own, so both of them together is certain death.
-George Carlin (1937 – 2008)

In politics, stupidity is not a handicap.
-Napoléon Bonaparte (1769 – 1821)

The first duty of a man is to think for himself.
-José Martí (1853 -95)

The only difference between Hitler and Bush is that Hitler was elected.
-Kurt Vonnegut (1922 – 2007)

Government exists to protect us from each other. Where government has gone beyond its limits is in deciding to protect us from ourselves.
-Ronald Reagan (1911 – 2004)

Too bad that all the people who know how to run the country are busy driving taxicabs and cutting hair.
-George Burns (1896 – 1996)

The rights of every man are diminished when the rights of one man are threatened.
-John F. Kennedy (1917 – 63)

The oppressed are allowed once every few years to decide which particular representatives of the oppressing class are to represent and repress them.
-Karl Marx (1818 – 83)

A nation of sheep will beget a government of wolves.
-Edward R. Murrow (1908 -65)

Absolute power does not corrupt absolutely, absolute power attracts the corruptible.
-Frank Herbert (1920 -86)

An appeaser is one who feeds a crocodile, hoping it will eat him last.
-Winston S. Churchill (1874 – 1965)

You show me a capitalist, and I'll show you a bloodsucker.
-Malcolm X (1925 -65)

If you want to rebel, rebel from inside the system. That's much more powerful than rebelling outside the system.
-Marie Lu (1984 -)

If our Founding Fathers wanted us to care about the rest of the world, they wouldn't have declared their independence from it.
-Stephen Colbert (1964-)

If an injury has to be done to a man it should be so severe that his vengeance need not be feared.
-Niccolò Machiavelli (1469 – 1527)

As government expands, liberty contracts.
-Ronald Reagan (1911 – 2004)

Bad men need nothing more to compass their ends, than that good men should look on and do nothing.
-John Stuart Mill (1806 -73)

Politics, it seems to me, for years, or all too long, has been concerned with right or left instead of right or wrong.
-Richard Armour (1906 – 89)

Politicians and diapers should be changed frequently and all for the same reason.
-José Maria de Eça de Queiroz (1845 – 1900)

We live in a world in which politics has replaced philosophy.
-Martin L. Gross (1925 – 2013)

There are many men of principle in both parties in America, but there is no party of principle.
-Alexis de Tocqueville (1805 -59)

We'd all like to vote for the best man, but he's never a candidate.
-Kin Hubbard (1868 – 1930)

In order to become the master, the politician poses as the servant.
-Charles de Gaulle (1890 – 1970)

Those who are too smart to engage in politics are punished by being governed by those who are dumber.
-Plato (427 -347 BC)

Politicians are the same all over. They promise to build a bridge even where there is no river.
-Nikita Khrushchev (1894 -1971)

When I was a boy I was told that anybody could become President; I'm beginning to believe it.
-Clarence Darrow (1857 – 1938)

Truth is not determined by majority vote.
-Doug Gwyn

We have, I fear, confused power with greatness.
-Stewart Udall (1920 – 2010)

A conservative is a man who believes that nothing should be done for the first time.
-Alfred E. Wiggam (1871 – 1957)

Don't vote, it only encourages them.
-Billy Connolly (1942 -)

Any American who is prepared to run for president should automatically, by definition, be disqualified from ever doing so.
-Gore Vidal (1925 – 2012)

Politics is the gentle art of getting votes from the poor and campaign funds from the rich, by promising to protect each from the other.
-Oscar Ameringer (1870 – 1943)

Members of Congress should be compelled to wear uniforms like NASCAR drivers, so we could identify their corporate sponsors.
-Caroline Baum (1958-)

Some men change their party for the sake of their principles; others their principles for the sake of their party.
-Winston Churchill (1874 – 1965)

The most intense hatreds are not between political parties but within them.
-Phillip Adams (1939 -)

Nearly all men can stand adversity, but if you want to test a man's character, give him power.
-Abraham Lincoln (1809 – 65)

When we are sick, we want an uncommon doctor; when we have a construction job to do, we want an uncommon engineer, and when we are at war, we want an uncommon general. It is only when we get into politics that we are satisfied with the common man.
-Herbert Hoover (1874 – 1964)

In war, you can only be killed once, but in politics, many times.
-Winston Churchill (1874 – 1965)

BUSINESS

Give a man a fish and he will eat for a day. Teach a man to fish and he will eat for a lifetime. Teach a man to create an artificial shortage of fish and he will eat steak.
-Jay Leno (1950 -)

You can fool all the people all the time if the advertising is right and the budget is big enough.
-Joseph E. Levine (1905 -87)

When you're out of quality you're out of business. - Anon
Hire character. Train skill.
-Peter Schutz (1930 -)

Music is spiritual. The music business is not.
-Van Morrison (1945 -)

Think P.I.G. - that's my motto. P stands for Persistence, I stands for Integrity, and G stands for Guts. These are the ingredients for a successful business and a successful life.
-Linda Chandler

Perpetual devotion to what a man calls his business, is only to be sustained by perpetual neglect of many other things.
-Robert Louis Stevenson (1850 – 94)

In the end, all business operations can be reduced to three words: people, product and profits. Unless you've got a good team, you can't do much with the other two. –
-Lee Iacocca (1924 -)

The greatest ability in business is to get along with others and to influence their actions.
-John Hancock (1737 – 93)

I don't pay good wages because I have a lot of money; I have a lot of money because I pay good wages.
-Robert Bosch (1861 – 1942)

Profit in business comes from repeat customers, customers that boast about your project or service, and that bring friends with them.
-W. Edwards Deming (1900 -93)

The golden rule for every business man is this: Put yourself in your customer's place.
-Orison Swett Marden (1850 – 1924)

Make the workmanship surpass the materials.
-Ovid (43 BC – 17 AD)

The competitor to be feared is one who never bothers about you at all, but goes on making his own business better all the time.
-Henry Ford (1863 – 1947)

You can't expect to meet the challenges of today with yesterday's tools and expect to be in business tomorrow.
- Raina Chapman

Your most unhappy customers are your greatest source of learning. –
-Bill Gates (1955 -)

A business absolutely devoted to service will have only one worry about profits. They will be embarrassingly large.
-Henry Ford (1863 – 1947)

It is an immutable law in business that words are words, explanations are explanations, promises are promises but only performance is reality.
-Harold Geneen (1910 -97)

Good business leaders create a vision, articulate the vision, passionately own the vision, and relentlessly drive it to completion.
-Jack Welch (1935 -)

In business the man who engages in the most adventures is surest to come out unhurt.
-Karl Marx (1818 – 83)

If you don't do it excellently, don't do it at all. Because if it's not excellent, it won't be profitable or fun, and if you're not in business for fun or profit, what the hell are you doing there?
-Robert Townsend (1920 -98)

It is difficult, but not impossible, to conduct strictly honest business.
-Mahatma Gandhi (1869 – 1948)

The purpose of business is to create and keep a customer.
-Peter F Drucker (1909 -)

Do what you love to do and give it your very best. Whether it's business or baseball, or the theater, or any field. If you don't love what you're doing and you can't give it your best, get out of it. Life is too short. You'll be an old man before you know it.
-Al Lopez (1908 – 2005)

A business like an automobile, has to be driven, in order to get results.
-BC Forbes (1880 – 1954)

Whenever you see a successful business, someone once made a courageous decision.
-Peter F Drucker (1909 – 2005)

The success combination in business is: Do what you do better... and: do more of what you do.
-David Joseph Schwartz (1927 – 87)

Objectives are not fate; they are direction. They are not commands; they are commitments. They do not determine the future; they are means to mobilize the resources and energies of the business for the making of the future.
-Peter F Drucker (1909 – 2005)

To succeed in business it is necessary to make others see things as you see them.
-John H Patterson (1844 – 1922)

A businessman is a hybrid of a dancer and a calculator.
-Paul Valery (1871 – 1945)

It is unfortunate we can't buy many business executives for what they are worth and sell them for what they think they are worth.
-Malcolm Forbes (1919 – 90)

If you had to identify, in one word, the reason why the human race has not achieved, and never will achieve, its full potential, that word would be meetings.
-Dave Barry (1947 -)

Advertising is legalized lying.
-*H.G. Wells (1866 – 1946)*

The superior man understands what is right; the inferior man understands what will sell.
-*Confucius (551 – 479 BC)*

Price is what you pay. Value is what you get.
-*Warren Buffett (1930 -)*

A man of business may talk of philosophy; a man who has none may practise it.
-*Alexander Pope (1688 – 1744)*

There's no luck in business. There's only drive, determination, and more drive.
-*Sophie Kinsella (1969 -)*

Business is a game, played for fantastic stakes, and you're in competition with experts. If you want to win, you have to learn to be a master of the game.
-*Sidney Sheldon (1917 – 2007)*

I insist on a lot of time being spent, almost every day, to just sit and think. That is very uncommon in American business. I read and think. So I do more reading and thinking, and make less impulse decisions than most people in business. I do it because I like this kind of life.
-*Warren Buffett (1930 -)*

The results of quality work last longer than the shock of high prices.
-*Anon*

Business, you know, may bring money, but friendship hardly ever does.
-Jane Austen (1775 – 1817)

A business has to be involving, it has to be fun, and it has to exercise your creative instincts.
-Richard Branson (1950 -)

When developing and designing products that invite people to use them, just do it right from the start and put your heart into it. It's harder and it takes longer, but everyone wins in the end.
-Michael D. Harris (1946 -)

A business that makes nothing but money is a poor business.
-Henry Ford (1863 – 1947)

Success in business requires training and discipline and hard work. But if you're not frightened by these things, the opportunities are just as great today as they ever were.
-David Rockefeller (1915 -)

Entrepreneurs average 3.8 failures before final success. What sets the successful ones apart is their amazing persistence.
-Lisa M. Amos

Always back the horse named self-interest, son. It'll be the only one trying.
-Jack Lang (1939 -)

A man may be a tough, concentrated, successful money-maker and never contribute to his country anything more than a horrible example.
-Robert Menzies (1894 – 1978)

In the business world, everyone is paid in two coins: cash and experience. Take the experience first; the cash will come later.
-Harold Geneen (1910 – 97)

Business is a combination of war and sport.
-André Maurois (1885 – 1967)

The absolute fundamental aim is to make money out of satisfying customers.
-John Egan (1939 -)

Corporation: An ingenious device for obtaining profit without individual responsibility.
-Ambrose Bierce (1842 – 1914)

It is not the employer who pays the wages. He only handles the money. It is the product that pays the wages.
-Henry Ford (1863 – 1947)

Experience taught me a few things. One is to listen to your gut, no matter how good something sounds on paper. The second is that you're generally better off sticking with what you know. And the third is that sometimes your best investments are the ones you don't make.
-Donald Trump (1946 -)

The entrepreneur in us sees opportunities everywhere we look, but many people see only problems everywhere they look.
-Michael Gerber (1936 -)

Be fearful when others are greedy. Be greedy when others are fearful.
-Warren Buffet (1930 -)

There is a tide in the affairs of men which, taken at the flood, leads on to fortune;

-Shakespeare (1564 – 1616)

Economics

There ain't no such thing as a free lunch.
-Robert A. Heinlein (1907 – 88)

It is no crime to be ignorant of economics, which is, after all, a specialized discipline and one that most people consider to be a 'dismal science.' But it is totally irresponsible to have a loud and vociferous opinion on economic subjects while remaining in this state of ignorance.
-Murray N. Rothbard (1926 – 95)

There's class warfare, all right, but it's my class, the rich class, that's making war, and we're winning.
-Warren Buffett (1930)

If you are rich, you have to be an idiot not to stay rich. And if you are poor, you have to be really smart to get rich.
-John Green (1977 -)

We have always known that heedless self-interest was bad morals, we now know that it is bad economics.
-Franklin D. Roosevelt (1882 – 1945)

The time to repair the roof is when the sun is shining.
-John F. Kennedy (1917 – 63)

If you owe your bank a hundred pounds, you have a problem. But if you owe a million, it has.
-John Maynard Keynes (1883 – 1946)

The United States spends over $87 billion conducting a war in Iraq while the United Nations estimates that for less than half that

amount we could provide clean water, adequate diets, sanitations services and basic education to every person on the planet. And we wonder why terrorists attack us.
-John Perkins (1945 -)

People were poor not because they were stupid or lazy. They worked all day long, doing complex physical tasks. They were poor because the financial institution in the country did not help them widen their economic base.
-Muhammad Yunus (1940 -)

1 billion people in the world are chronically hungry. 1 billion people are overweight.
-Mark Bittman (1950 -)

Economics was like psychology, a pseudoscience trying to hide that fact with intense theoretical hyperelaboration.
-Kim Stanley Robinson (1952 -)

Just as a poetic discussion of the weather is not meteorology, so an issuance of moral pronouncements or political creeds about the economy is not economics. Economics is a study of cause-and-effect relationships in an economy.
-Thomas Sowell (1930 -)

The first lesson of economics is scarcity: There is never enough of anything to satisfy all those who want it. The first lesson of politics is to disregard the first lesson of economics.
-Thomas Sowell (1930 -)

Economics is the painful elaboration of the obvious.
-Friedrich von Hayek (1899 – 1992)

The curious task of economics is to demonstrate to men how little they really know about what they imagine they can design.

-Friedrich von Hayek (1899 – 1992)

I can't imagine economists admitting how little they actually know. If they admitted to themselves, it would hurt their ego. If they admitted to others, it would hurt their job prospects.
-Joseph Mattes

The use of mathematics has brought rigor to economics. Unfortunately, it has also brought mortis.
-Robert Heilbroner (1919 – 2005)

A study of economics usually reveals that the best time to buy anything is last year.
-Marty Allen (1922 -)

Economic statistics are like a bikini, what they reveal is important, what they conceal is vital.
-Professor Sir Frank Holmes (1924 – 2011)

Doing econometrics is like trying to learn the laws of electricity by playing the radio.
Guy Orcutt (1917 -)

The First Law of Economists: For every economist, there exists an equal and opposite economist. The Second Law of Economists: They're both wrong.
-David Wildasin (1952 -)

An economist is someone who, when he finds something that works in practice, tries to make it work in theory.
-Walter Heller (1915 – 87)

The purpose of studying economics is not to acquire a set of ready-made answers to economic questions, but to learn how to avoid being deceived by economists.

-Joan Violet Robinson (1903 – 83)

An economist is an expert who will know tomorrow why the things he predicted yesterday didn't happen today.

-Laurence J. Peter (1919 -1990)

Economics is the only field in which two people can get a Nobel Prize for saying exactly the opposite thing.

-Anon

When an economist says the evidence is "mixed," he or she means that theory says one thing and data says the opposite.

-Richard Thaler (1945 -)

Inflation is the one form of taxation that can be imposed without legislation.

-Milton Friedman (1912- 2006)

I don't think you can spend yourself rich.

-George Humphrey (1890 – 1970)

A major source of objection to a free economy is precisely that it ... gives people what they want instead of what a particular group thinks they ought to want. Underlying most arguments against the free market is a lack of belief in freedom itself.

-Milton Friedman (1912 – 2006)

The most important single central fact about a free market is that no exchange takes place unless both parties benefit.

-Milton Friedman (1912 – 2006)

The only thing worse than being exploited by capitalism is not being exploited by capitalism.
-*Joan Violet Robinson (1903 – 83)*

If an exchange between two parties is voluntary, it will not take place unless both believe they will benefit from it. Most economic fallacies derive from the neglect of this simple insight, from the tendency to assume that there is a fixed pie that one party can only gain at the expense of another.
-*Milton Friedman (1912 – 2006)*

It is because it's prohibited. See, if you look at the drug war from a purely economic point of view, the role of the government is to protect the drug cartel. That's literally true.
-*Milton Friedman (1912 – 2006)*

All models are wrong but some are useful.
-*George Box (1919 – 2013)*

I'd rather be vaguely right than precisely wrong.
-John Maynard Keynes (1883 - 1946)

There is an entirely leisure class located at both ends of the economic spectrum.
-*Anon*

An economist is a man who states the obvious in terms of the incomprehensible.
-*Alfred A. Knopf (1892 – 1984)*

There can be no real individual freedom in the presence of economic insecurity.
-*Chester Bowles (1901 - 1986)*

If all economists were laid end to end, they would not reach a conclusion.
-*George Bernard Shaw (1856 - 1950)*

Economics is extremely useful as a form of employment for economists.
John Kenneth Galbraith (1908 - 2006)

Isn't it interesting that the same people who laugh at science fiction listen to weather forecasts and economists?
-*RAJ Phillips*

As a scholarly discipline, economics has always suffered from physics envy.
-*Robert Kuttner (1943 -)*

It [economics] is a method rather than a doctrine, an apparatus of the mind, a technique of thinking which helps its possessor to draw correct conclusions.
-*John Maynard Keynes (1883 - 1946)*

A society that puts equality before freedom will get neither. A society that puts freedom before equality will get a high degree of both.
-*Milton Friedman (1912 – 2006)*

The great virtue of a free market system is that it does not care what color people are; it does not care what their religion is; it only cares whether they can produce something you want to buy. It is the most effective system we have discovered to enable people who hate one another to deal with one another and help one another.
-*Milton Friedman (1912 – 2006)*

Many people want the government to protect the consumer. A much more urgent problem is to protect the consumer from the government.
-Milton Friedman (1912 – 2006)

The long run is a misleading guide to current affairs. In the long run we are all dead.
-John Maynard Keynes (1883 - 1946)

Capitalism is the astounding belief that the wickedest of men will do the wickedest of things for the greatest good of everyone.
-John Maynard Keynes (1883 - 1946)

The avoidance of taxes is the only intellectual pursuit that carries any reward.
-John Maynard Keynes (1883 - 1946)

When you combine ignorance and leverage, you get some pretty interesting results.
-Warren Buffett (1930 -)

Every man lives by exchanging.
-Adam Smith (1723 – 90)

What is prudence in the conduct of every private family can scarce be folly in that of a great kingdom.
-Adam Smith (1723 – 90)

Money

When I was young, I thought that money was the most important thing in life; now that I am old, I know it is.
-Oscar Wilde (1854 – 1900)

The easiest way to teach children the value of money is to borrow some from them.
-Anon

We have the best government that money can buy.
-Jim Rohn (1930 – 2009)

A man is usually more careful of his money than he is of his principles.
-Ralph Waldo Emerson (1803 – 82)

Time is more valuable than money. You can get more money, but you cannot get more time.
-Jim Rohn (1930 – 2009)

Don't lend people money, it gives them amnesia.
-Anon

No matter how little money and how few possessions you own, having a dog makes you rich.
-Louis Sabin

When it's a question of money, everybody is of the same religion.
-Voltaire (1694 – 1778)

Virtue has never been as respectable as money.
-Mark Twain (1835 – 1910)

Whoever said money can't buy happiness simply didn't know where to go shopping.
-Bo Derek (1956 -)

All riches have their origin in mind. Wealth is in ideas - not money.
-Robert Collier (1885 – 1950)

Borrow money from a pessimist - they don't expect it back.
-Anon

To give real service you must add something which cannot be bought or measured with money, and that is sincerity and integrity.
-Douglas Adams (1952 – 2001)

It is a wise man who lives with money in the bank, it is a fool who dies that way.
-French proverb

Money will buy you a fine dog, but only love can make it wag its tail.
-Kinky Friedman (1944 -)

Money will not make you happy, and happy will not make you money.
-Groucho Marx (1890 – 1977)

You aren't wealthy until you have something money can't buy.
-Garth Brooks (1956 -)

The rich would have to eat money if the poor did not provide food.
-Russian proverb

Don't tell me where your priorities are. Show me where you spend your money and I'll tell you what they are.
-James W Frick (1924 – 2014)

When I chased after money, I never had enough. When I got my life on purpose and focused on giving of myself and everything that arrived into my life, then I was prosperous.
-Wayne Dwyer (1940 -)

You have not lived a perfect day, even though you have earned your money, unless you have done something for someone who will never be able to repay you.
-Ruth Smeltzer

If you want to feel rich, just count the things you have that money can't buy.
-Proverb

Some people think they are worth a lot of money just because they have it.
-Fannie Hurst (1889 – 1968)

Many people take no care of their money till they come nearly to the end of it, and others do just the same with their time.
-Johann Wolfgang von Goethe (1749 – 1832)

Money never made a man happy yet, nor will it. The more a man has, the more he wants. Instead of filling a vacuum, it makes one.
-Benjamin Franklin (1706 – 90)

Every sale has five basic obstacles: no need, no money, no hurry, no desire, no trust.
-Zig Ziglar (1926 – 2012)

Money without brains is always dangerous.
-Napoleon Hill (1883 – 1970)

Money never starts an idea. It is always the idea that starts the money.
-Owen Laughlin (1951 -)

Being rich is having money; being wealthy is having time.
-Margaret Bonnano (1950 -)

The rich man is always sold to the institution which makes him rich. Absolutely speaking, the more money, the less virtue.
-Henry David Thoreau (1817 -62)

If women didn't exist, all the money in the world would have no meaning.
-Aristotle Onassis (1906 -75)

The art is not in making money, but in keeping it.
-Proverb

The safe way to double your money is to fold it over once and put it in your pocket.
-Kin Hubbard (1868 1930)

Money often costs too much.
-Ralph Waldo Emerson (1803 – 82)

I'd like to live as a poor man with lots of money.
-Pablo Picasso (1881 -1973)

Money is like love; it kills slowly and painfully the one who withholds it, and enlivens the other who turns it on his fellow man.
-Kahlil Gibran (1883 – 1931)

Blood's not thicker than money.
-Groucho Marx (1890 – 1977)

Money can't buy friends but it can get you a better class of enemy.
-Spike Milligan (1918 – 2002)

I think the person who takes a job in order to live - that is to say, for the money - has turned himself into a slave.
-Joseph Campbell (1904 -87)

The use of money is all the advantage there is in having it.
-Benjamin Franklin (1706 – 90)

A good reputation is more valuable than money.
-Publilius Syrus (49BC – 29AD)

So you think that money is the root of all evil. Have you ever asked what is the root of all money?
-Ayn Rand (1905 – 82)

Cocaine is God's way of saying you're making too much money.
-Robin Williams (1951 – 2014)

While money can't buy happiness, it certainly lets you choose your own form of misery.
-Groucho Marx (1890 – 1977)

I don't pay good wages because I have a lot of money; I have a lot of money because I pay good wages.
-*Robert Bosch (1861 – 1942)*

Don't marry for money; you can borrow it cheaper.
-*Scottish proverb*

Most people work just hard enough not to get fired and get paid just enough money not to quit.
-*George Carlin (1937 - 2008)*

Money, it turned out, was exactly like sex, you thought of nothing else if you didn't have it and thought of other things if you did.
-*James Arthur Baldwin (1924 -87)*

When money speaks, the truth is silent. Russian proverb
Money, if it does not bring you happiness, will at least help you be miserable in comfort.
-*Helen Gurley Brown (1922 – 2012)*

Money doesn't talk, it swears.
-*Bob Dylan (1941 -)*

I've got all the money I'll ever need; if I die by four O'clock.
-*Henry Youngman (1906 – 98)*

Government always finds a need for whatever money it gets.
-*Ronald Reagan (1911 – 2004)*

Successful people make money. It's not that people who make money become successful, but that successful people attract money. They bring success to what they do.
-*Wayne Dyer (1940 -)*

A fool and his money are soon elected.
-Will Rogers (1879 – 1935)

Money is related to class only in the minds of people who have too much of the former, too little of the latter or none of either.
-Doug Robarchek (1943-)

Why is it inflationary if the people keep their own money, and spend it the way they want to, [but] not inflationary if the government takes it and spends it the way it wants to?
-Ronald Reagan (1911 – 2004)

You are always a valuable, worthwhile human being -- not because anybody says so, not because you're successful, not because you make a lot of money -- but because you decide to believe it and for no other reason.
-William Dyer (1940 -)

Lend money to an enemy, and thou will gain him, to a friend and thou will lose him.
-Benjamin Franklin (1706 – 90)

Money isn't everything - but it's a long way ahead of what comes next.
-Edmund Stockdale (1903 – 89)

Money is not required to buy one necessity of the soul.
-Henry David Thoreau (1817 – 62)

The glow of one warm thought is to me worth more than money.
-Thomas Jefferson (1762 – 1826)

Rule No.1: Never lose money. Rule No.2: Never forget rule No.1.
-Warren Buffet (1930 -)

If you want to see what God thinks of money, just look at all the people He gave it to.
-Dorothy Parker (1893 1967)

Advertising is the art of convincing people to spend money they don't have for something they don't need.
-Will Rogers (1879 – 1935)

Money, not morality, is the principle of commerce and commercial nations.
-Thomas Jefferson (1762 – 1826)

Money will come when you are doing the right thing.
-Mike Phillips (1946 -)

Knowledge is like money: the more one gets, the more one craves.
-John Billings (1818 – 65)

Three groups spend other people's money: children, thieves, politicians. All three need supervision.
-Dick Armey (1940 -)

I have no money, no resources, no hopes. I am the happiest man alive.
-Henry Miller (1891 – 1980)

Never spend your money before you have earned it.
-Thomas Jefferson (1762 – 1826)

The lack of money is the root of all evil.
-George Bernard Shaw (1856 – 1950)

No one in this world has ever lost money by underestimating the intelligence of the great masses of the plain people. Nor has anyone ever lost public office thereby.
-Henry Louis Mencken (1880 – 1956)

Run for your life from any man who tells you that money is evil. That sentence is the leper's bell of an approaching looter.
-Ayn Rand (1905 – 82)

The highest use of capital is not to make more money, but to make money do more for the betterment of life.
-Henry Ford (1863 – 1947)

One difference between a liberal and a pickpocket is that if you demand your money back from a pickpocket, he won't question your motives.
-Anon

A bank is a place that will lend you money if you can prove that you don't need it.
-Bob Hope (1903 – 2003)

I wish I had a dollar for every time I spent a dollar, because then, Yahoo!, I'd have all my money back.
-Jack Handy (1949)

A rich man is nothing but a poor man with money.
-WC Fields (1880 – 1946)

Money won't make you happy... but everybody wants to find out for themselves.
-Zig Ziglar (1926 – 2012)

I hope that after I die, people will say of me: "That guy sure owed me a lot of money".
-Jack Handy (1949 -)

It will be a great day when our schools have all the money they need, and our air force has to have a bake-sale to buy a bomber.
-Robert Fulghum (1937 -)

Money is neither my god nor my devil. It is a form of energy that tends to make us more of who we already are, whether it's greedy or loving.
-Dan Millman (1946 -)

The best way to help the poor is not to become one of them.
-Lang Hancock (1909 – 92)

Love lasteth long as the money endureth.
-William Caxton (1422 – 91)

GOVERNMENT

I don't tell jokes, I just look at government and report the facts.
-*Will Rogers (1879 – 1935)*

Strange women lying in ponds distributing swords is no basis for a system of government!
-*Monty Python (1975)*

Nothing is so permanent as a temporary government program.
-*Milton Friedman (1912- 2006)*

Government is the people's business and every man, woman and child becomes a shareholder with the first penny of tax paid.
-*Ronald Reagan (1911 – 2004)*

We have the best government that money can buy.
-*Mark Twain (1835 – 1910)*

Sometimes I wonder whether the world is being run by smart people who are putting us on or by imbeciles who really mean it.
-*Laurence J. Peter (1919 – 90)*

You can't give the government the power to do good without also giving it the power to do bad - in fact, to do anything it wants.
-*Harry Browne (1933 – 2006)*

All government is an ugly necessity.
-*GK Chesterton (1874 – 1936)*

The heaviest penalty for declining to rule is to be ruled by someone inferior to yourself.
-*Plato (427 – 347 BC)*

It is dangerous to be right when the government is wrong.
-Voltaire (1694 – 1778)

The art of government is to make two-thirds of a nation pay all it possibly can pay for the benefit of the other third.
-Voltaire (1694 – 1778)

A nation of sheep will beget a government of wolves.
-Edward R. Murrow (1908 – 65)

War is when the government tells you who the bad guy is. Revolution is when you decide that for yourself.
- Anon

It is not the function of our Government to keep the citizen from falling into error; it is the function of the citizen to keep the Government from falling into error.
-Robert H Jackson (1892 – 1954)

The problem with socialism is that you eventually run out of other people's money.
-Margaret Thatcher (1925 – 2013)

The best government is a benevolent tyranny tempered by an occasional assassination.
-Voltaire (1694 – 1778)

I was ecstatic they re-named 'French Fries' as 'Freedom Fries'. Grown men and women in positions of power in the U.S. government showing themselves as idiots.
-Johnny Depp (1963 -)

As government expands, liberty contracts.
-Ronald Reagan (1911 – 2004)

The government is us; we are the government, you and I.
-Theodore Roosevelt (1858 – 1919)

It's easy being a humorist when you've got the whole government working for you.
-Will Rogers (1879 – 1935)

The most dangerous man to any government is the man who is able to think things out for himself, without regard to the prevailing superstitions and taboos. Almost inevitably he comes to the conclusion that the government he lives under is dishonest, insane, and intolerable.
-Henry Louis Mencken (1880 – 1956)

Only a government that is rich and safe can afford to be a democracy, for democracy is the most expensive and nefarious kind of government ever heard of on earth.
-Mark Twain (1835 – 1910)

I am sometimes a fox and sometimes a lion. The whole secret of government lies in knowing when to be the one or the other.
-Napoleon Bonaparte (1769 – 1821)

The greatest patriotism is to tell your country when it is behaving dishonorably, foolishly, viciously.
-Julian Barnes (1946 -)

The worst government is the most moral. One composed of cynics is often very tolerant and humane. But when fanatics are on top there is no limit to oppression.
-Henry Louis Mencken (1880 – 1956)

Government does not solve problems; it subsidizes them.
-Ronald Reagan (1911 – 2004)

When they call the roll in the Senate, the Senators do not know whether to answer 'Present' or 'Not Guilty'.
-*Theodore Roosevelt (1858 – 1919)*

The primary function of the government is - and here I am quoting directly from the U.S. Constitution - "to spew out paper".
-*Dave Barry (1947 -)*

One way to make sure crime doesn't pay would be to let the government run it.
-*Ronald Reagan (1911 – 2004)*

Freedom is the recognition that no single person, no single authority or government has a monopoly on the truth, but that every individual life is infinitely precious, that every one of us put in this world has been put there for a reason and has something to offer.
-*Ronald Reagan (1911 – 2004)*

The state is that great fiction by which everyone tries to live at the expense of everyone else.
-*Frédéric Bastiat (1801 – 50)*

Which is the best government? That which teaches us to govern ourselves.
-*Johann Wolfgang von Goethe (1749 – 1832)*

A little rebellion now and then... is a medicine necessary for the sound health of government.
-*Thomas Jefferson (1762 – 1826)*

I want the US government to dispense with all the "red tape," and start using Caution tape.
-*Jarod Kintz (1982 -)*

Government always finds a need for whatever money it gets.
-Ronald Reagan (1911 – 2004)

Can America get back to a point where politicians are honest? Not unless that point is the tip of a sword.
-Jarod Kintz (1982-)

We must not look to government to solve our problems. Government is the problem.
-Ronald Reagan (1911 – 2004)

Government, even in its best state, is but a necessary evil; in its worst state, an intolerable one.
-Thomas Paine (1737 - 1809)

Empires do not suffer emptiness of purpose at the time of their creation. It is when they have become established that aims are lost and replaced by vague ritual.
-Frank Herbert (1920 – 86)

Inflation is like sin; every government denounces it and every government practices it.
-Frederick Leith-Ross (1887 – 1968)

I consider trial by jury as the only anchor ever yet imagined by man, by which a government can be held to the principles of its constitution.
-Thomas Jefferson (1762 – 1826)

Were it left to me to decide whether we should have a government without newspapers or newspapers without government, I should not hesitate a moment to prefer the latter.
-Thomas Jefferson (1762 – 1826)

When one gets in bed with government, one must expect the diseases it spreads.
-*Ron Paul (1935 -)*

Public servants say, always with the best of intentions, "What greater service we could render if only we had a little more money and a little more power." But the truth is that outside of its legitimate function, government does nothing as well or as economically as the private sector.
-*Ronald Reagan (1911 – 2004)*

Good government is no substitute for self-government.
-*Mahatma Gandhi (1869 – 1948)*

I believe there is something out there watching us. Unfortunately, it's the government.
-*Woody Allen (1935 -)*

The universe never did make sense; I suspect it was built on government contract.
-*Robert A Heinlein (1907 – 88)*

We must not confuse dissent with disloyalty. When the loyal opposition dies, I think the soul of America dies with it.
-*Edward R. Murrow (1908 – 65)*

Liberty has never come from Government. Liberty has always come from the subjects of it... The history of liberty is a history of limitations of governmental power, not the increase of it.
-*Woodrow T Wilson (1856 – 1924)*

The strongest reason for the people to retain the right to bear arms is, as a last resort, to protect themselves against tyranny in government.
-*Thomas Jefferson (1762 – 1826)*

Writing laws is easy, but governing is difficult.
-Leo Tolstoy (1828 – 1910)

I think people need to be educated to the fact that marijuana is not a drug. Marijuana is an herb and a flower. God put it here. If He put it here and He wants it to grow, what gives the government the right to say that God is wrong?
-Willie Nelson (1933 -)

A government that robs Peter to pay Paul can always depend on the support of Paul.
-George Bernard Shaw (1856 – 1950)

We are imperfect. We cannot expect perfect government.
-William Howard Taft (1857 – 1930)

Today, if you invent a better mousetrap, the government comes along with a better mouse.
-Ronald Reagan (1911- 2004)

In the absence of justice, what is sovereignty but organized robbery?
-St. Augustine (354 – 430 AD)

That government is best which governs the least, because its people discipline themselves.
-Henry David Thoreau (1817 – 62)

Giving money and power to government is like giving whiskey and car keys to teenage boys.
-P.J. O'Rourke (1947 -)

Under a government which imprisons any unjustly, the true place for a just man is also a prison.
-Henry David Thoreau (1817 – 62)

Government exists to protect us from each other. Where government has gone beyond its limits is in deciding to protect us from ourselves.
-Ronald Reagan (1911 – 2004)

No man is good enough to govern another man without that other's consent.
-Abraham Lincoln (1809 – 65)

The amount of time required to complete a government project is precisely equal to the length of time already spent on it.
-Anon

Any people anywhere, being inclined and having the power, have the right to rise up, and shake off the existing government, and form a new one that suits them better. This is a most valuable - a most sacred right - a right, which we hope and believe, is to liberate the world.
-Abraham Lincoln (1809 – 1865)

Government is an association of men who do violence to the rest of us.
-Leo Tolstoy (1828 – 1910)

The oppressed are allowed once every few years to decide which particular representatives of the oppressing class are to represent and repress them.
-Karl Marx (1818 – 83)

Congress is so strange. A man gets up to speak and says nothing.
Nobody listens — and then everybody disagrees.
-*Boris Marshalov (1898 – 67)*

The government of the United States is not in any sense founded
on the Christian Religion.
-*George Washington (1732 – 99)*

A great revolution is never the fault of the people, but of the
government.
-*Johann Wolfgang von Goethe (1749 – 1832)*

Ask not what the government can do for you. Ask why it doesn't.
-*Gerhard Kocher (1939 -)*

Talk is cheap — except when Congress does it.
-*Cullen Hightower (1923 – 2008)*

A government is the most dangerous threat to man's rights: it
holds a legal monopoly on the use of physical force against legally
disarmed victims.
-*Ayn Rand (1905 – 82)*

History shows that when the taxes of a nation approach about
20% of the people's income, there begins to be a lack of respect
for government. . . . When it reaches 25%, there comes an
increase in lawlessness.
-*Ronald Reagan (1911 – 2004)*

The Constitution is not an instrument for the government to
restrain the people, it is an instrument for the people to restrain
the government - lest it come to dominate our lives and interests.
-*Patrick Henry (1736 – 99)*

Government is not reason, it is not eloquence, it is force; like fire, a troublesome servant and a fearful master. Never for a moment should it be left to irresponsible action.
-*George Washington (1732 – 99)*

A patriot must always be ready to defend his country against his government.
-*Edward Abbey (1927 – 89)*

The business of government is to keep the government out of business - that is, unless business needs government aid.
-*Will Rogers (1879 – 1935)*

It's a good thing we don't get all the government we pay for.
-*Will Rogers (1879 – 1935)*

The best minds in government? If any were, business would hire them away.
-*Ronald Reagan (1911 – 2004)*

The greatest purveyor of violence in the world today - my own government.
-*Martin Luther King, Jr. (1929 – 68)*

Must a government be too strong for the liberties of its people or too weak to maintain its own existence?
-*Abraham Lincoln (1809 – 65)*

Make the people sovereign and the poor will use the machinery of government to dispossess the rich.
-*C. Northcote Parkinson (1909 – 93)*

Remember that a government big enough to give you everything you want is also big enough to take away everything you have.
-Barry Goldwater (1909 -98)

All government, of course, is against liberty.
-Henry Louis Mencken (1880 – 1956)

Men whose lives are doubtful want a strong government and a hot religion.
-Elbert Hubbard (1856 – 1915)

Nothing is more destructive of respect for the government and the law of the land than passing laws which cannot be enforced.
-Albert Einstein (1879 – 1955)

It is a very sobering feeling to be up in space and realize that one's safety factor was determined by the lowest bidder on a government contract.
-Alan Shepherd (1923 – 98)

The philosophy of the school room in one generation will be the philosophy of government in the next.
-Abraham Lincoln (1809 – 65)

We are fast approaching the stage of the ultimate inversion: the stage where the government is free to do anything it pleases, while the citizens may act only by permission; which is the stage of the darkest periods of human history, the stage of rule by brute force.
-Ayn Rand (1905 – 82)

If human beings are fundamentally good, no government is necessary; if they are fundamentally bad, any government, being composed of human beings, would be bad also.
-Fred Woodworth

Whenever you have efficient government, you have a dictatorship.
-Harry S Truman (1884 – 1972)

Government's view of the economy could be summed up in a few short phrases: If it moves, tax it. If it keeps moving, regulate it. And if it stops moving, subsidise it.
-Ronald Reagan (1911 – 2004)

Whenever the people are well-informed, they can be trusted with their own government.
-Thomas Jefferson (1762 – 1826)

Government is not the doctor. It is the disease.
-H. S. Ferns (1913 – 92)

DEMOCRACY

Democracy must be something more than two wolves and a sheep voting on what to have for dinner.
-James Bovard (1956-)

The twentieth century has been characterized by three developments of great political importance: the growth of democracy, the growth of corporate power, and the growth of corporate propaganda as a means of protecting corporate power against democracy.
-Alex Carey (1922 -)

The people have spoken but it is going to take a little while to determine exactly what they have said.
-Bill Clinton (1946 -)

Without God, democracy will not and cannot long endure.
-Ronald Reagan (1911 – 2004)

Democracy means simply the bludgeoning of the people by the people for the people.
-Oscar Wilde (1854 – 1900)

Only a government that is rich and safe can afford to be a democracy, for democracy is the most expensive and nefarious kinds of government ever heard of on earth.
-Mark Twain (1835 – 1910)

Without God democracy will not and cannot long endure.
-Ronald Reagan (1911 – 2004)

Democracy arises out of the notion that those who are equal in any respect are equal in all respects; because men are equally free, they claim to be absolutely equal.
-*Aristotle (384 – 322 BC)*

A democracy is nothing more than mob rule, where fifty-one percent of the people may take away the rights of the other forty-nine.
-*Thomas Jefferson (1762 – 1826)*

Democracy is a pathetic belief in the collective wisdom of individual ignorance.
-*Henry Louis Mencken (1880 – 1956)*

Democracy is a process by which the people are free to choose the man who will get the blame.
-*Dr. Laurence J. Peter (1919 – 90)*

Democracy encourages the majority to decide things about which the majority is ignorant.
-*John Simon (1826 – 1904)*

Democracy is also a form of worship. It is the worship of Jackals by Jackasses.
-*Henry Louis Mencken (1880 – 1956)*

People shouldn't be afraid of their government. Governments should be afraid of their people.
-*Alan Moore (1953 -)*

In a room where people unanimously maintain a conspiracy of silence, one word of truth sounds like a pistol shot.
-*Czesław Miłosz (1911 – 2004)*

Freedom in capitalist society always remains about the same as it was in ancient Greek republics: Freedom for slave owners.
-Vladimir Ilich Lenin (1870 – 1924)

Our great democracies still tend to think that a stupid man is more likely to be honest than a clever man, and our politicians take advantage of this prejudice by pretending to be even more stupid than nature made them.
-Bertrand Russell (1872 – 1970)

I am a firm believer in the people. If given the truth, they can be depended upon to meet any national crisis. The great point is to bring them the real facts, and beer.
-Abraham Lincoln (1809 -65)

Propaganda is to a democracy what the bludgeon is to a totalitarian state.
-Noam Chomsky (1928 -)

I do not know if the people of the United States would vote for superior men if they ran for office, but there can be no doubt that such men do not run.
-Alexis de Tocqueville (1805 – 59)

Democracy consists of choosing your dictators, after they've told you what you think it is you want to hear.
-Alan Coren (1938 – 2007)

The ballot is stronger than the bullet.
-Abraham Lincoln (1809 -65)

The great thing about democracy is that it gives every voter a chance to do something stupid.
-Art Spander

Democracy is the recurrent suspicion that more than half of the people are right more than half the time.
-EB White (1899 - 1985)

In democracy it's your vote that counts; In feudalism it's your count that votes.
-Mogens Jallberg

It's not the voting that's democracy, it's the counting.
-Tom Stoppard (1937-)

WAR

In preparing for battle I have always found that plans are useless, but planning is indispensable.
-Dwight D. Eisenhower (1890 – 1969)

God created war so that Americans would learn geography.
-Mark Twain (1835 – 1910)

It is not enough to conquer; one must also know how to seduce.
-Voltaire (1694 – 1778)

War is what happens when language fails.
-Margaret Atwood (1938 -)

All war must be just the killing of strangers against whom you feel no personal animosity; strangers whom, in other circumstances, you would help if you found them in trouble, and who would help you if you needed it.
-Mark Twain (1835 – 1910)

The true soldier fights not because he hates what is in front of him, but because he loves what is behind him.
-G.K. Chesterton (1874 – 1936)

I am not only a pacifist but a militant pacifist. I am willing to fight for peace. Nothing will end war unless the people themselves refuse to go to war.
-Albert Einstein (1879 – 1955)

Older men declare war. But it is youth that must fight and die.
-Herbert Hoover (1874 – 1964)

The real and lasting victories are those of peace, and not of war.
-*Ralph Waldo Emmerson (1803 – 82)*

I have no doubt that we will be successful in harnessing the sun's energy... If sunbeams were weapons of war, we would have had solar energy centuries ago.
-*Sir George Porter (1920 – 2002)*

It is forbidden to kill; therefore all murderers are punished unless they kill large numbers to the sound of trumpets.
- *Voltaire (1694 – 1778)*

There are causes worth dying for, but none worth killing for.
-*Albert Camus (1913 – 60)*

In time of war, when truth is so precious, it must be attended by a bodyguard of lies.
-*Winston Churchill (1874 – 1965)*

If you win, you need not have to explain...If you lose, you should not be there to explain!
-*Adolf Hitler (1889 – 1945)*

Love is like war; easy to begin but very hard to stop.
-*Henry Louis Mencken (1880 – 1956)*

Never think that war, no matter how necessary, nor how justified, is not a crime.
-*Ernest Hemingway (1899 – 1961)*

The supreme art of war is to subdue the enemy without fighting.
-*Sun Tzu (544 – 496 BC)*

What difference does it make to the dead, the orphans and the homeless, whether the mad destruction is wrought under the name of totalitarianism or in the holy name of liberty or democracy?
-*Mahatma Gandhi (1869 – 1948)*

We used to wonder where war lived, what it was that made it so vile. And now we realize that we know where it lives, that it is inside ourselves.
-*Albert Camus (1913 – 60)*

Listen up - there's no war that will end all wars.
-*Haruki Murakami (1949 -)*

It is only the dead who have seen the end of war.
-*Plato (428 – 324 BC)*

All war is a symptom of man's failure as a thinking animal.
-*John Steinbeck (1902 – 68)*

One cannot simultaneously prevent and prepare for war.
-*Albert Einstein (1879 – 1955)*

There is no flag large enough to cover the shame of killing innocent people.
-*Howard Zinn (1922 – 2010)*

Men are at war with each other because each man is at war with himself.
-*Francis Meehan*

Sometimes you have to pick the gun up to put the Gun down.
-*Malcolm X (1925 – 65)*

An inglorious peace is better than a dishonorable war.
-*Mark Twain (1835 – 1910)*

When the rich wage war it's the poor who die.
-*Jean-Paul Sartre (1905 – 80)*

The object of war is not to die for your country but to make the other bastard die for his.
-*General George S. Patton (1885 – 1945)*

If everyone fought for their own convictions there would be no war.
-*Leo Tolstoy (1828 – 1910)*

I know not with what weapons World War III will be fought, but World War IV will be fought with sticks and stones.
-*Albert Einstein (1879 – 1955)*

How is it possible to have a civil war?
-*George Carlin (1937 – 2008)*

The only real diplomacy ever performed by a diplomat is in deceiving their own people after their dumbness has got them into a war.
-*Will Rogers (1879 – 1935)*

You can have peace. Or you can have freedom. Don't ever count on having both at once.
-*Robert A. Heinlein (1907 – 88)*

There has never been a protracted war from which a country has benefited.
-*Sun Tzu (544 – 496 BC)*

It is foolish and wrong to mourn the men who died. Rather, we should thank God that such men lived.
-*George S. Patton Jr. (1885 – 1945)*

A prisoner of war is a man who tries to kill you and fails, and then asks you not to kill him.
-*Winston Churchill (1874 – 1965)*

A wise man gets more use from his enemies than a fool from his friends.
-*Baltasar Gracián (1601 – 58)*

War does not determine who is right - only who is left.
-*Bertrand Russell (1872 – 1970)*

The war against terrorism is terrorism.
-*Woody Harrelson (1961 -)*

Do you think it's possible for an entire nation to be insane?
-*Terry Pratchett (1948 – 2015)*

Peace is more than the absence of war. Peace is accord. Harmony.
-*Laini Taylor (1971-)*

In war, there are no unwounded soldiers.
-*Jose Narosky (1930-)*

The choice is not between violence and nonviolence but between nonviolence and nonexistence.
-*Martin Luther King Jr. (1929 – 68)*

War is a poor chisel to carve out tomorrow.
-*Martin Luther King, Jr. (1929 – 68)*

In times of war, the law falls silent.
-*Cicero (106 – 43 BC)*

War is fear cloaked in courage.
-*Gen William C. Westmoreland (1914 – 2005)*

No one won the last war, and no one will win the next war.
-*Eleanor Roosevelt (1884 – 1962)*

We make war that we may live in peace.
-*Aristotle (384 – 322 BC)*

It is not enough to win a war; it is more important to organize the peace.
-*Aristotle (384 – 322 BC)*

Those who can win a war well can rarely make a good peace and those who could make a good peace would never have won the war.
-*Winston Churchill (1874 – 1965)*

In wars, boy, fools kill other fools for foolish causes.
-*Robert Jordan (1948 – 2007)*

Americans play to win at all times. I wouldn't give a hoot and hell for a man who lost and laughed. That's why Americans have never lost nor ever lose a war.
-*General George S. Patton (1885 – 1945)*

Like Alexander the Great and Caesar, I'm out to conquer the world. But first I have to stop at Walmart and pick up some supplies.
-*Jarod Kintz (1982 -)*

To wage a war for a purely moral reason is as absurd as to ravish a woman for a purely moral reason.
-Henry Louis Mencken (1880 – 1956)

The nuclear arms race is like two sworn enemies standing waist deep in gasoline, one with three matches, the other with five.
-Carl Sagan (1934 – 96)

Cry 'Havoc', and let slip the dogs of war, that this foul deed shall smell above the earth with carrion men, groaning for burial.
-William Shakespeare (1564 – 1616)

You ask, what is our aim? I can answer in one word. It is victory, victory at all costs, victory in spite of all terror, victory, however long and hard the road may be; for without victory, there is no survival.
-Winston S. Churchill (1874 – 1965)

If war is ever lawful, then peace is sometimes sinful.
-CS Lewis (1898 – 1963)

Nations have recently been led to borrow billions for war; no nation has ever borrowed largely for education... no nation is rich enough to pay for both war and civilization. We must make our choice; we cannot have both.
-Abraham Flexner (1866 – 1959)

War is the trade of kings.
-John Dryden (1631 – 1700)

I find war detestable but those who praise it without participating in it even more so.
-Romain Rolland (1866 – 1944)

If you think of humanity as one large body, then war is like suicide, or at best, self-mutilation.
-Jerome P Crabb (1940 – 2013)

Don't talk to me about atrocities in war; all war is an atrocity.
-Lord Kitchener (1850 – 1916)

All war is deception.
-Sun Tzu (544 – 496 BC)

War makes rattling good history; but peace is poor reading.
-Thomas Hardy (1840 – 1928)

Vietnam was the first war ever fought without any censorship. Without censorship, things can get terribly confused in the public mind.
-General William Westmoreland (1914 – 2005)

Politics is war without bloodshed while war is politics with bloodshed.
-Mao Tse-Tung (1893 – 1976)

War is like love, it always finds a way.
-Bertolt Brecht (1898 – 1956)

War will disappear only when men shall take no part whatever in violence and shall be ready to suffer every persecution that their abstention will bring them. It is the only way to abolish war.
-Anatole France (1844 – 1924)

We love peace, but not peace at any price. There is a peace more destructive of the manhood of living man, than was is destructive of the body. Chains are worse than bayonets.
- Douglas Jerrold (1803 – 57)

War is only a cowardly escape from the problems of peace.
- Thomas Mann (1875 – 1955)

All delays are dangerous in war.
-John Dryden (1631 – 1700)

There was never a good war or a bad peace.
-Benjamin Franklin (1706 – 90)

In war, truth is the first casualty.
-Aeschylus (525 – 456 BC)

Men like war: they do not hold much sway over birth, so they make up for it with death. Unlike women, men menstruate by shedding other people's blood.
-Lucy Ellman (1956 -)

It's funny how those who are most pro-war are almost always the guys who never had to fight in one.
-Jerome P Crabb (1940 – 2013)

He who sweats more in peace, bleeds less in war.
-Proverb

Wars do not end wars any more than an extraordinarily large conflagration does away with the fire hazard.
-Henry Ford (1863 – 1947)

War is so unjust and ugly that all who wage it must try to stifle the voice of conscience within themselves.
-Leo Tolstoy (1828 – 1910)

After a long, hopeless war, people will settle for peace, at almost any price.
-*Salman Rushdie (1947 -)*

You can't say civilization don't advance... in every war they kill you in a new way.
-*Will Rogers (1879 – 1935)*

War is a severe doctor; but it sometimes heals grievances.
-*Edward Counsel (1849 – 1939)*

As long as war is regarded as wicked, it will always have its fascination. When it is looked upon as vulgar, it will cease to be popular.
-*Oscar Wilde (1854 – 1900)*

A mind at peace does not engender wars.
-*Sophocles (496 – 405 BC)*

War is an instrument entirely inefficient toward redressing wrong; and multiplies, instead of indemnifying losses.
-*Thomas Jefferson (1762 – 1826)*

Wars of pen and ink often lead to wars of cannon and bayonets.
-*Edward Counsel (1849 – 1939)*

War is not an adventure. It is a disease. It is like typhus.
-*Antoine de Saint-Exupery (1900 – 44)*

No catalogue of horrors ever kept men from war. Before the war you always think that it's not you that dies. But you will die, brother, if you go to it long enough.
-*Ernest Hemmingway (1899 – 1961)*

War seldom enters but where wealth allures.
-John Dryden (1631 – 1700)

When music and courtesy are better understood and appreciated, there will be no war.
-Confucius (551 – 479 BC)

Peace is not the absence of war but the presence of justice.
-Harrison Ford (1942 -)

I hate war as only a soldier who has lived it can, only as one who has seen its brutality, its futility, its stupidity.
-Dwight David Eisenhower (1890 – 1969)

Give me an army of West Point graduates and I'll win a battle. Give me a handful of Texas Aggies, and I'll win the war.
-General George S. Patton (1885 – 1945)

You say it is the good cause that hallows even war? I tell you: it is the good war that hallows every cause.
-Friedrich Nietzsche (1844 – 1900)

Only the winners decide what were war crimes.
-Gary Wills (1934 -)

Once we have a war there is only one thing to do. It must be won. For defeat brings worse things than any that can ever happen in war.
-Ernest Hemmingway (1899 – 1961)

Making peace, I have found, is much harder than making war.
- Gerry Adams (1948 -)

War is just when it is necessary; arms are permissible when there is no hope except in arms.

-*Niccolo Machiavelli (1469 – 1527)*

War is evil, but it is often the lesser evil.

-*George Orwell (1903 – 50)*

There is no avoiding war; it can only be postponed to the advantage of others.

-*Niccolo Machiavelli (1469 – 1527)*

I have a scheme for stopping war. It's this -- no nation is allowed to enter a war till they have paid for the last one.

-*Will Rogers (1879 – 1935)*

War is a game that is played with a smile. If you can't smile, grin. If you can't grin, keep out of the way till you can.

-*Winston Churchill (1874 – 1965)*

The war against hunger is truly mankind's war of liberation.

-*John Fitzgerald Kennedy (1917 – 63)*

If any man says he hates war more than I do, he better have a knife, that's all I have to say.

-*Jack Handy (1949 -)*

Thus, what is of supreme importance in war is to attack the enemy's strategy.

-*Sun Tzu (544 – 496 BC)*

History teaches that war begins when governments believe the price of aggression is cheap.

-*Ronald Reagan (1911 – 2004)*

We all remember how many religious wars were fought for a religion of love and gentleness; how many bodies were burned alive with the genuinely kind intention of saving souls from the eternal fire of hell.

-Karl Popper (1902 – 94)

CHAPTER 2 RELATIONSHIPS

MEN

When women are depressed, they eat or go shopping. Men invade another country. It's a whole different way of thinking.
-Elayne Boosler (1952 -)

Force always attracts men of low morality.
-Albert Einstein (1879-1925)

When a hundred men stand together, each of them loses his mind and gets another one.
-Friedrich Nietzsche (1844-1900)

Wise men speak because they have something to say; Fools because they have to say something.
-Plato (427 – 347 BC)

Women's Liberation is just a lot of foolishness. It's the men who are discriminated against. They can't bear children. And no one's likely to do anything about that.
-Golda Meir (1898 – 1978)

I see when men love women they give but a little of their lives, but women, when they love, give everything.
-Oscar Wilde (1854 – 1900)

I want a man whose kind and understanding. Is that too much to ask of a millionaire?
-Zsa Zsa Gabor (1917 -)

Men's minds are raised to the level of the women with whom they associate.
-*Alexander Dumas (1802 – 70)*

What would men be without women? Scarce, sir, mighty scarce.
-*Mark Twain (1835 – 1910)*

Part of the reason that men seem so much less loving than women is that men's behavior is measured with a feminine ruler.
-*Francesca M. Cancian*

Only one man in a thousand is a leader of men, the other 999 follow women.
-*Groucho Marx (1890 – 1977)*

When a man talks dirty to a woman, its sexual harassment. When a woman talks dirty to a man, it's $3.95 a minute.
-*Anon*

Man does not control his own fate. The women in his life do that for him.
-*Groucho Marx (1890 – 1977)*

Men want the same thing from their underwear that they want from women: a little bit of support, and a little bit of freedom.
-*Jerry Seinfeld (1954 -)*

Lonely men seek companionship. Lonely women sit at home and wait. They never meet.
-*Abraham Lincoln (1809 -65)*

A pessimist is a man who thinks all women are bad. An optimist is one who hopes they are.
-*Chancey Depew (1834 – 1928)*

Boys will be boys, and so will a lot of middle-aged men.
-*Kin Hubbard (1868 – 1930)*

Men play the game; women know the score.
-*Roger Woddis (1917 – 93)*

Men forget but never forgive. Women forgive but never forget.
-*Robert Jordan (1948 – 2007)*

On the one hand, we'll never experience childbirth. On the other hand, we can open all our own jars.
-*Bruce Willis (1955 -)*

Men are just as sensitive, and in some ways more sensitive, than women are.
-*Barbara De Angelis (1951 -)*

Few women care what a man looks like, and a good thing too.
-*Mignon McLaughlin (1913 – 83)*

A man's brain has a more difficult time shifting from thinking to feeling than a women's brain does.
-*Barbara De Angelis (1951 -)*

The analysis of man discloses three chemical elements — a job, a meal and a woman.
-*Martin H. Fischer (1879 – 1962)*

Men like war: they do not hold much sway over birth, so they make up for it with death. Unlike women, men menstruate by shedding other people's blood.
-*Lucy Ellman (1956 -)*

Here's all you have to know about men and women: women are crazy, men are stupid. And the main reason women are crazy is that men are stupid.
-*George Carlin (1937 – 2008)*

The only difference between men and boys is the cost of their toys.
-*Doris Rowland*

A retired husband is often a wife's full-time job.
-*Ella Harris*

Why are women so much more interesting to men than men are to women?
-*Virginia Woolf (1882 – 1941)*

Never trust a husband too far, nor a bachelor too near.
-*Helen Rowland (1875 – 1950)*

Any fool knows men and women think differently at times, but the biggest difference is this. Men forget, but never forgive; women forgive, but never forget.
-*Robert Jordan (1948 – 2007)*

See, the problem is that God gives men a brain and a penis, and only enough blood to run one at a time.
-*Robin Williams (1951 – 2014)*

I like men who have a future and women who have a past.
-*Oscar Wilde (1854 – 1900)*

Like a compass needle that points north, a man's accusing finger always finds a woman. Always.
-*Khaled Hosseini (1965-)*

Women may be able to fake orgasms, but men can fake whole relationships.
-James Shubert

The old theory was "Marry an older man, because they're more mature." But the new theory is: "Men don't mature. marry a younger one."
-Rita Rudner (1953 -)

Men can read maps better than women. 'Cause only the male mind could conceive of one inch equaling a hundred miles.
-Roseanne Barr (1952 -)

The more I see of men, the more I like dogs.
-Germaine de Staël (1766 – 1817)

Men want a woman whom they can turn on and off like a light switch.
-Ian Fleming (1908 – 64)

It's absolutely unfair for women to say that guys only want one thing: sex. We also want food.
-Jarod Kintz (1982 -)

When in a relationship, a real man doesn't make his woman jealous of others, he makes others jealous of his woman.
-Steve Maraboli (1975 -)

As long as she thinks of a man, nobody objects to a woman thinking.
-Virginia Woolf (1882 – 1941)

Sometimes a woman needs a man for company, no matter how useless he is.
-*Lisa Kleypas (1964 -)*

If a man hasn't what's necessary to make a woman love him, it's his fault, not hers.
-*W. Somerset Maugham (1874 – 1965)*

Telling lies is a fault in a boy, an art in a lover, an accomplishment in a bachelor, and second-nature in a married man.
-*Helen Rowland (1875 -1950)*

Men should think twice before making widowhood women's only path to power.
-*Gloria Steinem (1934 -)*

I require three things in a man: he must be handsome, ruthless, and stupid.
-*Dorothy Parker (1893 – 1967)*

A woman's flattery may inflate a man's head a little; but her criticism goes straight to his heart, and contracts it so that it can never again hold quite as much love for her.
-*Helen Rowland (1875 – 1950)*

It is a well-documented fact that guys will not ask for directions. This is a biological thing. This is why it takes several million sperm cells... to locate a female egg, despite the fact that the egg is, relative to them, the size of Wisconsin.
-*Dave Barry (1947 -)*

The history of men's opposition to women's emancipation is more interesting perhaps than the story of that emancipation itself.
-*Virginia Woolf (1882 – 1941)*

If I had a dollar for every time a random woman walked up to me and tried to seduce me, I'd have 50 cents. That's assuming drag queens are half price.
-*Jarod Kintz (1982 -)*

The follies which a man regrets most, in his life, are those he didn't commit when he had the opportunity.
-*Helen Rowland (1875 – 1950)*

A gentleman is simply a patient wolf.
-*Lana Turner (1921 – 55)*

Every man needs two women: a quiet home-maker, and a thrilling nymph.
-*Iris Murdoch (1919 – 99)*

Can you imagine a world without men? No crime and lots of happy fat women.
-*Nicole Hollander (1939 -)*

A man can become so accustomed to the thought of his own faults that he will begin to cherish them as charming little "personal characteristics".
-*Helen Rowland (1875 – 1950)*

When a man of forty falls in love with a girl of twenty, it isn't her youth he is seeking but his own.
-*Lenore Coffee (1896 – 1984)*

The first time you buy a house you see how pretty the paint is and buy it. The second time you look to see if the basement has termites. It's the same with men.
-*Lupe Velez (1908 – 44)*

Judge a man by his questions rather than his answers.

-Voltaire (1694 – 1778)

WOMEN

Well-behaved women rarely make history.
-Laurel Thatcher Ulrich (1938 -)

Ah, women. They make the highs higher and the lows more frequent.
-Friedrich Nietzsche (1844 – 1900)

According to a recent survey, men say the first thing they notice about a woman is their eyes, and women say the first thing they notice about men is they're a bunch of liars.
-Anon

Women have a wonderful instinct about things. They can discover everything except the obvious.
-Oscar Wilde (1854 – 1900)

Women, can't live with them, can't live without them.
-Desiderius Erasmus (1469 -1536)

A woman can defend her virtue from men much more easily than she can protect her reputation from women.
-Elbert Hubbard (1856 – 1915)

The bravest thing that men do is love women.
-Mort Sahl (1927 -)

We women talk too much, nevertheless we only say half of what we know.
-Nancy Astor (1879 -1964)

Men always want to be a woman's first love - women like to be a man's last romance.
-*Oscar Wilde (1854 – 1900)*

Women always worry about the things that men forget; men always worry about the things women remember.
-*Majorie Kinnan Rawlings (1896 – 1953)*

Women are like apples on trees, the best ones are on the top of the tree. The men don't want to reach for the good ones because they are afraid of falling and don't want to get hurt. Instead, they just get the rotten apples from the ground that aren't so good but easy. So, the apples at the top think something is wrong with them, when in reality they are amazing. They just have to wait for the right man to come along, the one who's brave enough to climb all the way to the top because they value quality.
-*Pete Wentz (1979 -)*

Most women have all other women as adversaries; most men have all other men as their allies.
-*Frank Gelett Burgess (1866 – 1951)*

Women and cats will do as they please, and men and dogs should relax and get used to the idea.
-*Robert A Heinlein (1907 -88)*

Women have hunger two-fold, shyness four-fold, daring six-fold, and lust eight-fold as compared to men.
-*Chanakya (371 – 283 BC)*

Women are considered deep - why? Because one can never discover any bottom to them. Women are not even shallow.
-*Friedrich Nietzsche (1844 – 1900)*

Most of us women like men, you know; it's just that we find them a constant disappointment.
-*Clare Short (1944 -)*

Women made us lose paradise, but how frequently we find it again in their arms.
-*Anon*

Even the wisest men make fools of themselves about women, and even the most foolish women are wise about men.
-*Theodor Reik (1888 – 1969)*

Why haven't women got labels on their foreheads saying, "Danger: Government Health Warning: Women can be dangerous to your brains, genitals, current account, confidence, razor blades and good standing among your friends".
-*Henry Louis Mencken (1880 – 1956)*

There are two kinds of women: those who want power in the world, and those who want power in bed.
-*Jacqueline Kennedy (1929 – 94)*

You see a lot of smart guys with dumb women, but you hardly ever see a smart woman with a dumb guy.
-*Erica Jong (1942 -)*

When women are depressed, they eat or go shopping. Men invade another country. It's a whole different way of thinking.
-*Elayne Boosler (1952 -)*

Whatever women do they must do twice as well as men to be thought half as good. Luckily, this is not difficult.
-*Charlotte Whitton*

Women should be obscene and not heard.
-*Groucho Marx (1890 – 1977)*

Clever and attractive women do not want to vote; they are willing to let men govern as long as they govern men.
-*George Bernard Shaw (1856 – 1950)*

On one issue, at least, men and women agree: they both distrust women.
-*Henry Louis Mencken (1880 – 1956)*

Women are like stars there are millions of them out there, but only one can make dreams come true.
-*Ritu Ghatourey*

I disregard the proportions, the measures, the tempo of the ordinary world. I refuse to live in the ordinary world as ordinary women. To enter ordinary relationships. I want ecstasy. I am a neurotic -- in the sense that I live in my world. I will not adjust myself to the world. I am adjusted to myself.
-*Anais Nin (1903 – 77)*

Women don't want to hear what you think. Women want to hear what they think -- in a deeper voice.
-*Bill Cosby (1937 -)*

Most books on witchcraft will tell you that witches work naked. This is because most books on witchcraft were written by men.
-*Neil Gaiman (1960 -)*

After all, Ginger Rogers did everything that Fred Astaire did. She just did it backwards and in high heels.
-*Ann Richards (1933 – 2006)*

Good girls go to heaven, bad girls go everywhere.
-*Mae West (1893 – 1980)*

Sometimes I wonder if men and women really suit each other. Perhaps they should live next door and just visit now and then.
-*Katharine Hepburn (1907 – 2003)*

Give a girl an education and introduce her properly into the world, and ten to one but she has the means of settling well, without further expense to anybody.
-*Jane Austen (1775 – 1817)*

Women have two weapons - cosmetics and tears. - Anon A man's face is his autobiography. A women's face is her work of fiction.
-*Oscar Wilde (1854 – 1900)*

Women are never disarmed by compliments. Men always are. That is the difference between the sexes.
-*Oscar Wilde (1854 – 1900)*

Why is it men are permitted to be obsessed about their work, but women are only permitted to be obsessed about men?
-*Barbara Streisand (1942 -)*

Women are superior to men. I don't even think we're equal.
-*Leonor Sullivan (1902 -88)*

A witty woman is a treasure' a witty beauty is a power.
-*George Meredith (1828 – 1909)*

No woman gets an orgasm from shining the kitchen floor.
- *Betty Friedan (1926 – 2006)*

Men are taught to apologize for their weaknesses, women for their strengths.
-Lois Wyse (1926 – 2007)

Women need real moments of solitude and self-reflection to balance out how much of ourselves we give away.
-Barbara De Angelis (1951 -)

Most women set out to try to change a man, and when they have changed him they don't like him.
-Marlene Dietrich (1901 – 92)

A man can be short and dumpy and getting bald but if he has fire, women will like him.
-Mae West (1892 – 1980)

Women with "pasts" interest men because men hope that history will repeat itself.
-Mae West (1892 – 1980)

And verily, a woman need know but one man well, in order to understand all men; whereas a man may know all women and understand not one of them.
-Helen Rowland (1875 – 1950)

The happiest women, like the happiest nations, have no history.
-George Elliot (1819 – 80)

What would women do if they could not cry? What poor, defenceless creatures they would be.
-Douglas Jerrold (1803 – 57)

There are only two types of women - goddesses and doormats.
-Pablo Picasso (1881 – 1973)

If women didn't exist, all the money in the world would have no meaning.
-Aristotle Onassis (1906 – 75)

All women should know how to take care of children. Most of them will have a husband someday.
-Franklin P Jones (1887 – 1929)

The only really happy folk are married women and single men.
-Henry Louis Mencken (1880 – 1956)

Women's Tongues are as sharp as two-edged Swords, and wound as much, when they are angered.
-Margaret Cavendish (1623 – 73)

I know enough to know that no woman should ever marry a man who hated his mother.
-Martha Gellhorn (1908 – 88)

She's the sort of woman who lives for others - you can tell the others by their hunted expression.
-C.S. Lewis (1898 – 1963)

If men swear that they want to harm you when you are asleep, you can go to sleep. If women say so, stay awake.
-African proverb

I asked a Burmese why women, after centuries of following their men, now walk ahead. He said there were many unexploded land mines since the war.
-Robert Mueller (1944-)

In less enlightened times, the best way to impress women was to own a hot car. But women wised up and realized it was better to buy their own hot cars so they wouldn't have to ride around with jerks.
-*Scott Adams (1957 -)*

Women are happier in the love they inspire than in that which they feel; men are just the contrary.
-*E. P. Beauchene (1874 – 1923)*

If I were a girl, I'd despair. The supply of good women far exceeds that of the men who deserve them.
-*Robert Graves (1895 – 1985)*

The difference between men and women is that, if given the choice between saving the life of an infant or catching a fly ball, a woman will automatically choose to save the infant, without even considering if there's a man on base.
-*Dave Barry (1947 -)*

Next to the wound, what women make best is the bandage.
-*Barbey d' Aureuilly (1808 – 89)*

Women are not going to be equal outside the home until men are equal in it.
-*Gloria Steinem (1934 -)*

When women go wrong, men go right after them.
-*Mae West (1892 – 1980)*

Women wish to be loved without a why or a wherefore; not because they are pretty, or good, or well-bred, or graceful, or intelligent, but because they are themselves.
-*Henri Frederic Amiel (1821 – 81)*

The word and works of God is quite clear, that women were made either to be wives or prostitutes.
-*Martin Luther (1483 – 1546)*

Women are wiser than men because they know less and understand more.
-*James Thurber (1894 – 1961)*

The more education a woman has, the wider the gap between men's and women's earnings for the same work.
-*Sandra Day (1930 -)*

Women are never stronger than when they arm themselves with their weaknesses.
-*Madame Marie du Deffand (1697 – 1780)*

I want women to be liberated and still be able to have a nice ass and shake it.
-*Shirley MacLaine (1934 -)*

If all men are born free, how is it that all women are born slaves?
-*Mary Astell (1666 – 1731)*

Plain women know more about men than beautiful ones do. But beautiful women don't need to know about men. It's the men who have to know about beautiful women.
-*Katherine Hepburn (1907 – 2003)*

Some women can be fooled all of the time, and all women can be fooled some of the time, but the same woman can't be fooled by the same man in the same way more than half of the time.
-*Helen Rowland (1876 – 1950)*

Men, their rights, and nothing more; women, their rights, and nothing less.
-*Susan B Anthony (1820 – 1906)*

If women ran the world we wouldn't have wars, just intense negotiations every 28 days.
-*Robin Willliams (1951 – 2014)*

You know that look women get when they want sex? Me neither.
-*Drew Carey (1958 -)*

Guys are simple... women are not simple and they always assume that men must be just as complicated as they are, only way more mysterious. The whole point is guys are not thinking much. They are just what they appear to be. Tragically.
-*Dave Barry (1947 -)*

Men reach their sexual peak at eighteen. Women reach theirs at thirty-five. Do you get the feeling that God is playing a practical joke?
-*Rita Rudner (1953 -)*

There are a number of mechanical devices which increase sexual arousal, particularly in women. Chief among these is the Mercedes-Benz 380SL convertible.
-*PJ O'Rourke (1947 -)*

Among men, sex sometimes results in intimacy; among women, intimacy sometimes results in sex.
-*Barbara Cartland (1901 – 2000)*

Beauty is the wisdom of women. Wisdom is the beauty of men.
-*Chinese proverb*

Women complain about sex more often than men. Their gripes fall into two major categories: (1) Not enough. (2) Too much.
-Ann Landers (1918 – 2002)

Women speak two languages - one of which is verbal.
-William Shakespeare (1564 – 1616)

Beware of the man who denounces women writers; his penis is tiny and he cannot spell.
-Erica Jong (1942 -)

They say women talk too much. If you have worked in Congress you know that the filibuster was invented by men.
-Clare Boothe Luce (1903 – 87)

I'm not denying the women are foolish: God almighty made 'em to match the men.
-George Elliot (1819 – 80)

Instead of warning pregnant women not to drink, I think female alcoholics should be told not to fuck.
-George Carlin (1937 -)

After about 20 years of marriage, I'm finally starting to scratch the surface of what women want. And I think the answer lies somewhere between conversation and chocolate.
-Mel Gibson (1956 -)

Money and women are the most sought after and the least known about of any two things we have.
-Will Rogers (1879 – 1935)

Feminism is the radical notion that women are people.
-Marie Shear

Anyone who says he can see through women is missing a lot.
-Groucho Marx (1890 -77)

Anyone who believes that men are the equal of women has never seen a man trying to wrap a Christmas present.
-Anon

Women still remember the first kiss after men have forgotten the last.
-Remy de Gourmont (1858 – 1915)

Women are nothing but machines for producing children.
-Napoleon Bonaparte (1769 – 1821)

Women are like elephants. I like to look at 'em, but I wouldn't want to own one.
-WC Fields (1880 – 1946)

After an acquaintance of ten minutes many women will exchange confidences that a man would not reveal to a lifelong friend.
-Page Smith (1917 – 95)

Women are like teabags. We don't know our true strength until we are in hot water!
-Eleanor Roosevelt (1884 – 1962)

If women want any rights more than they's got, why don't they just take them, and not be talking about it.
-Sojourner Truth (1797 -83)

Misogynist: A man who hates women as much as women hate one another.
-Henry Louis Mencken (1880 – 1956)

I always play women I would date.
-Angelina Jolie (1975 -)

Many women long for what eludes them, and like not what is offered them.
-Ovid (43 BC – 17 AD)

A woman never forgets the men she could have had; a man, the women he couldn't.
-Marjorie Kinnan Rawlings (1896 – 1955)

Whether they give or refuse, it delights women just the same to have been asked.
-Ovid (43 BC – 17 AD)

One can find women who have never had one love affair, but it is rare indeed to find any who have had only one.
-François de la Rochefoucauld (1613 – 80)

Only men who are not interested in women are interested in women's clothes. Men who like women never notice what they wear.
-Anatole France (1844 – 1924)

Women will forgive anything. Otherwise, the race would have died out long ago.
-Robert A Heinlein (1907 – 88)

The trouble with some women is that they get all excited about nothing - and then marry him.
-Cher (1946 -)

Women prefer emotions to reasoning.
-Stendhal (1783 – 1842)

I haven't trusted polls since I read that 62% of women had affairs during their lunch hour. I've never met a woman in my life who would give up lunch for sex.
-Erma Bombeck (1927 – 96)

Women like silent men. They think they're listening.
-Marcel Achard (1899 – 1974)

God made man stronger but not necessarily more intelligent. He gave women intuition and femininity. And, used properly, that combination easily jumbles the brain of any man I've ever met.
-Farrah Fawcett (1947 – 2009)

As usual there is a great woman behind every idiot.
-John Lennon (1940 -80)

A women who doesn't wear perfume has no future.
-Coco Chanel (1883 – 1971)

For most of history, Anonymous was a woman.
-Virginia Woolf (1882 – 1941)

A lady's imagination is very rapid; it jumps from admiration to love, from love to matrimony in a moment.
-Jane Austen (1775 – 1817)

Being a woman is a terribly difficult task, since it consists principally in dealing with men.
-Joseph Conrad (1857 – 1924)

Women need a reason to have sex. Men just need a place.
Billy Crystal (1947 -)

There are no good girls gone wrong - just bad girls found out.
-Mae West (1893 – 1980)

I would always rather be happy than dignified.
-Charlotte Brontë (1816 – 1855)

You educate a man; you educate a man. You educate a woman; you educate a generation.
-Brigham Young (1801 -77)

When a man gives his opinion, he's a man. When a woman gives her opinion, she's a bitch.
-Bette Davis (1908 – 89)

In politics, if you want anything said, ask a man. If you want anything done, ask a woman.
-Margaret Thatcher (1925 – 2013)

There is more to sex appeal than just measurements. I don't need a bedroom to prove my womanliness. I can convey just as much sex appeal, picking apples off a tree or standing in the rain.
-Audrey Hepburn (1929 – 1993)

Every man I meet wants to protect me. I can't figure out what from.
-Mae West (1893 – 1980)

It is a woman's business to get married as soon as possible, and a man's to keep unmarried as long as possible.
-George Bernard Shaw (1856 – 1950)

No woman really wants a man to carry her off; she only wants him to want to do it.
-Barbara Mertz (1927 – 2013)

The only time a woman really succeeds in changing a man is when he is a baby.

-Natalie Wood (1938 – 81)

MARRIAGE

Women marry men hoping they will change. Men marry women hoping they will not. So each is inevitably disappointed.
-*Albert Einstein (1879 – 1955)*

In the sex war, thoughtlessness is the weapon of the male, vindictiveness of the female.
-*Cyril Connolly (1903 – 74)*

Bachelors know more about women than married men; if they didn't they'd be married too.
-*Henry Louis Mencken (1880 – 1956)*

Marriage is for women the commonest mode of livelihood, and the total amount of undesired sex endured by women is probably greater in marriage than in prostitution.
-*Bertrand Russell (1872 – 1970)*

God's great cosmic joke on the human race was requiring that men and women live together in marriage.
-*Mark Twain (1835 – 1910)*

To keep your marriage brimming with love in the loving cup; whenever you're wrong, admit it, whenever you're right, shut up.
-*Ogden Nash (1902 -71)*

A successful marriage requires falling in love many times, always with the same person.
-*Mignon McLaughlin (1913 -83)*

The proper basis for marriage is mutual misunderstanding.
-*Oscar Wilde (1854 – 1900)*

The trouble with many married people is that they are trying to get more out of marriage than there is in it.
-*Elbert Hubbard (1856 – 1915)*

Remember that a successful marriage depends on two things: (1) finding the right person and (2) being the right person.
-*Carrie P Snow*

How marriage ruins a man! It is as demoralizing as cigarettes, and far more expensive.
-*Oscar Wilde (1854 – 1900)*

Marriage has no guarantees. If that's what you're looking for, go live with a car battery.
-*Erma Bombeck (1927 -96)*

A happy marriage is a long conversation which always seems too short.
-*Andre Maurois (1885 – 1967)*

Marriage is neither heaven nor hell, it is simply purgatory.
-*Abraham Lincoln (1809 – 65)*

There is no perfect marriage, for there are no perfect men.
-*French proverb*

Marriage is give and take. You'd better give it to her or she'll take it anyway.
-*Marvin Gaye (1939 – 84)*

The formula for a happy marriage? It's the same as the one for living in California: when you find a fault, don't dwell on it.
-*Jay Trachman (1939 – 2009)*

Marriage is when a man and woman become as one; the trouble starts when they try to decide which one.
-*Mae West (1893 – 1980)*

Marriage is a great institution, but I'm not ready for an institution.
-*Mae West (1892 – 1980)*

Let us now set forth one of the fundamental truths about marriage: the wife is in charge.
-*Bill Cosby (1937 -)*

The husband who wants a happy marriage should learn to keep his mouth shut and his check book open.
-*Groucho Marks (1890 -1977)*

Sensual pleasures have the fleeting brilliance of a comet; a happy marriage has the tranquility of a lovely sunset.
-*Ann Landers (1918 -2002)*

Before marriage, a man will go home and lie awake all night thinking about something you said; after marriage, he'll go to sleep before you finish saying it.
-*Helen Rowland (1876 – 1950)*

A liberated woman is one who has sex before marriage and a job after.
-*Gloria Steinem (1935 -)*

Marriage is three parts love and seven parts forgiveness of sins.
-*Lao Tzu (600 – 531 BC)*

Marriage is an adventure, like going to war.
-*GK Chesterton (1874 – 1936)*

Love is the dawn of marriage, and marriage is the sunset of love.
-*French proverb*

Marriage is the process of finding out what kind of man your wife would have preferred.
-*Jay Trachman (1939 – 2009)*

Marriage is the one subject on which all women agree and all men disagree.
-*Oscar Wilde (1854 – 1900)*

One advantage of marriage is that, when you fall out of love with him or he falls out of love with you, it keeps you together until you fall in again.
-*Judith Viorst (1931 -)*

Marriage is the only war in which you sleep with the enemy.
-*French proverb*

Politics doesn't make strange bedfellows, marriage does.
-*Groucho Marx (1890 – 1977)*

Only choose in marriage a woman whom you would choose as a friend if she were a man.
-*Joseph Joubert (1754 – 1824)*

Pleasure for one hour, a bottle of wine. Pleasure for one year a marriage; but pleasure for a lifetime, a garden.
-*Erica Jong (1942 -)*

Women are the only exploited group in history to have been idealized into powerlessness.
-*Erica Jong (1942 -)*

Show me a woman who doesn't feel guilty and I'll show you a man.
-Erica Jong (1942 -)

There's a way of transferring funds that is even faster than electronic banking. It's called marriage.
-Oscar Wilde (1854 – 1900)

Marriage is popular because it combines the maximum of temptation with the maximum of opportunity.
-George Bernard Shaw (1856 – 1950)

Marriage is nature's way of keeping us from fighting with strangers.
-Alan King (1927 – 2004)

You could talk about same-sex marriage, but people who have been married (say) 'It's the same sex all the time.'
-Robin Williams (1951 – 2014)

After a few years of marriage a man can look right at a woman without seeing her and a woman can see right through a man without looking at him.
-Helen Rowland (1876 – 1950)

All men should freely use those seven words which have the power to make any marriage run smoothly: You know dear, you may be right.
-Anon

In every marriage more than a week old, there are grounds for divorce. The trick is to find, and continue to find, grounds for marriage.
-Robert Anderson (1861 – 1939)

I have yet to hear a man ask for advice on how to combine marriage and a career.
-*Gloria Steinem (1935 -)*

Marriage is like putting your hand into a bag of snakes in the hope of pulling out an eel.
-*Leonardo da Vinci (1452 – 1519)*

Marriage is the miracle that transforms a kiss from a pleasure into a duty.
-*Helen Rowland (1876 – 1950)*

Marriage resembles a pair of shears, so joined that they cannot be separated, often moving in opposite directions, yet always punishing anyone who comes in between them.
-*Sydney Smith (1771 – 1845)*

The heart of marriage is memories; and if the two of you happen to have the same ones and can savor your reruns, then your marriage is a gift from the gods.
-*Bill Cosby (1937 -)*

The one charm about marriage is that it makes a life of deception absolutely necessary for both parties.
-*Oscar Wilde (1854 – 1900)*

I think men who have a pierced ear are better prepared for marriage. They've experienced pain and bought jewelry.
-*Rita Rudner (1955 -)*

Marriage is like a coffin and each kid is like another nail.
-*Dan Castellaneta/Homer Simpson (1958-)*

In marriage, as in war, it is permitted to take every advantage of the enemy.
-*Oscar Wilde (1854 – 1900)*

It was a perfect marriage. She didn't want to and he couldn't.
-*Spike Milligan (1918 – 2002)*

Before marriage a man yearns for a woman. Afterward the y is silent.
-*WA Clarke*

If there is such a thing as a good marriage, it is because it resembles friendship rather than love.
-*Michel de Montaigne (1533 -92)*

Marriage is like a beleaguered fortress: those who are outside want to get in, and those inside want to get out.
-*French proverb*

Twenty years of romance makes a woman look like a ruin; but twenty years of marriage make her something like a public building.
-*Oscar Wilde (1854 – 1900)*

It is always incomprehensible to a man that a woman should refuse an offer of marriage.
-*Jane Austen (1775 – 1817)*

Love may be blind, but marriage is a real eye-opener.
-*Pauline Thomason*

Any woman who still thinks marriage is a fifty-fifty proposition is only proving that she doesn't understand either men or percentages.

-Rose Kennedy (1890 – 1995)

Insanity: grounds for divorce in some states, grounds for marriage in all.

-Anon

Marriage is the operation by which a woman's vanity and a man's egotism are extracted without an anesthetic.

-Helen Rowland (1876 – 1950)

Marriage is a very good thing, but I think it's a mistake to make a habit out of it.

-William Somerset Maugham (1874 – 1965)

Take care of him. And make him feel important. And if you can do that, you'll have a happy and wonderful marriage. Like two out of every ten couples.

-Neil Simon (1927 -)

Love the quest; marriage the conquest; divorce the inquest.

-Helen Rowland (1876 – 1950)

A good marriage would be between a blind wife and a deaf husband.

-Balzac (1799 – 1850)

A marriage certificate is just another word for a work permit.

-Helen Rowland (1876 – 1950)

All tragedies are finished by a death, all comedies are ended by a marriage.
-*Lord Byron (1788 – 1824)*

If you lose your job, your marriage and your mind all in one week, try to lose your mind first, because then the other stuff won't matter that much.
-*Jack Handy (1949 -)*

Love is an ideal thing, marriage a real thing; a confusion of the real with the ideal never goes unpunished.
-*Johann Wolfgang von Goethe (1749 – 1832)*

Happiness in marriage is entirely a matter of chance.
-*Jane Austen (1775 – 1817)*

Chains do not hold a marriage together. It is threads, hundreds of tiny threads which sew people together through the years. That is what makes a marriage last, more than passion or even sex!
-*Simone Signoret (1921 - 85)*

Marriage is a bribe to make a housekeeper think she's a householder.
-*Thornton Wilder (1897 – 1975)*

Marriage is a matter of give and take, but so far I haven't been able to find anybody who'll take what I have to give.
-*Cass Daley*

Marriage - a book of which the first chapter is written in poetry and the remaining chapters in prose.
-*Beverley Nichols*

Before marriage, a man declares that he would lay down his life to serve you; after marriage, he won't even lay down his newspaper to talk to you.

-Helen Rowland (1876 – 1950)

They asked her (Ruth Graham) did she ever think about divorce and she said, 'No, I've never thought of divorce in all these 35 years of marriage, but,' she said, 'I did think of murder a few times'.

-Billy Graham (1918 -)

Love is often the fruit of marriage.

-Moliere (1622 – 1673)

My wife and I tried to breakfast together, but we had to stop or our marriage would have been wrecked.

-Winston Churchill (1874 – 1965)

Marriage is about love. Divorce is about money.

-Anon

Marriage is like a cage; one sees the birds outside desperate to get in, and those inside equally desperate to get out.

-Michel de Montaigne (1533 – 92)

What counts in making a happy marriage is not so much how compatible you are, but how you deal with incompatibility.

-Leo Tolstoy (1828 – 1910)

Marriage is the only adventure open to the cowardly.

-Voltaire (1694 – 1778)

It is a truth universally acknowledged, that a single man in possession of a good fortune, must be in want of a wife.
-Jane Austen (1775 – 1817)

The trouble is not that I am single and likely to stay single, but that I am lonely and likely to stay lonely.
-Charlotte Brontë (1816 – 55)

And she's got brains enough for two, which is the exact quantity the girl who marries you will need.
-P.G. Wodehouse (1881 – 1975)

To say that one waits a lifetime for his soulmate to come around is a paradox. People eventually get sick of waiting, take a chance on someone, and by the art of commitment become soulmates, which takes a lifetime to perfect.
-Criss Jami (1986 -)

Some people claim that marriage interferes with romance. There's no doubt about it. Anytime you have a romance, your wife is bound to interfere.
-Groucho Marx (1890 -1977)

Do you know what it means to come home at night to a woman who'll give you a little love, a little affection, a little tenderness? It means you're in the wrong house, that's what it means.
-Henny Youngman (1906 – 98)

A great marriage is not when the 'perfect couple' comes together. It is when an imperfect couple learns to enjoy their differences.
-Dave Meurer (1958 -)

An object in possession seldom retains the same charm that it had in pursuit.
-Pliny the Younger (61 – 112)

My wife and I were happy for twenty years. Then we met.
-Rodney Dangerfield (1921 – 2004)

Matrimony is a process by which a grocer acquired an account the florist had.
-Frances Rodman

Never feel remorse for what you have thought about your wife; she has thought much worse things about you.
-Jean Rostand (1894 – 1977)

Bigamy is having one husband or wife too many. Monogamy is the same.
-Oscar Wilde (1854 – 1900)

Marriage means commitment. Of course, so does insanity.
-Anon

By all means marry; if you get a good wife you'll become happy; if you get a bad one you'll become a philosopher.

-Socrates (439 – 399BC)

I never knew what real happiness was until I got married. And by then it was too late.
-Max Kauffman

Marriage is not a word — it is a sentence.
-Oscar Wilde (1854 – 1900)

I still miss my ex-wife, but my aim is getting better.
-Rodney Dangerfield (1921 – 2004)

Getting married is very much like going to a restaurant with friends. In both marriage and a restaurant you order what you want, then when you see what the other folks get, you wish you had ordered that.

-Anon

A man likes his wife to be just clever enough to appreciate his cleverness, and just stupid enough to admire it.

-Israel Zangwill (1864 – 1926)

Marriage is nature's way of ensuring that a woman picks up some mothering experience before she has her first child.

-Robert Brault (1963 -)

I have learned that only two things are necessary to keep one's wife happy. First, let her think she's having her own way. And second, let her have it.

-Lyndon B. Johnson (1908 -73)

Marriage is a lottery, but you can't tear up your ticket if you lose.

-Jerry Lewis (1926 -)

It is not a lack of love, but a lack of friendship that makes unhappy marriages.

-Friedrich Nietzsche (1844 – 1900)

To be happy with a man you must understand him a lot and love him a little. To be happy with a woman you must love her a lot and not try to understand her at all.

-Helen Rowland (1875 – 1950)

Marriage is like the army. Everybody complains, but you'd be surprised how many re-enlist.

-James Garner (1928 – 2014)

There's only one way to have a happy marriage and as soon as I learn what it is I'll get married again.

-Clint Eastwood (1930 -)

LOVE

Falling in love consists merely in uncorking the imagination and bottling the common sense.
-Helen Rowland (1875 – 1950)

Life has taught us that love does not consist in gazing at each other, but in looking outward together in the same direction.
-Antoine de Saint-Exupery (1900-44)

Keep love in your heart. A life without it is like a sunless garden when the flowers are dead.
-Oscar Wilde (1854-1900)

I'm selfish, impatient and a little insecure. I make mistakes, I am out of control and at times hard to handle. But if you can't handle me at my worst, then you sure as hell don't deserve me at my best.
-Marilyn Monroe (1926 – 62)

Somewhere there is someone that dreams of your smile, and finds in your presence that life is worthwhile, so when you are lonely remember its true, someone somewhere is thinking of you.
-Atul Purohit (1957 -)

What most people need to learn in life is how to love people and use things instead of using people and loving things.
-Zelda Fitzgerald (1900 – 48)

You know you're in love when you can't fall asleep because reality is finally better than your dreams.
-Dr. Seuss (1904 – 91)

Loving can cost a lot but not loving always costs more, and those who fear to love often find that want of love is an emptiness that robs the joy from life.
-*Merle Shain (1935 – 89)*

Love is the Fire of Life; it either consumes or purifies.
-*Swedish proverb*

A friend is someone who knows all about you and still loves you.
-*Elbert Hubbard (1856 – 1915)*

A woman has got to love a bad man once or twice in her life, to be thankful for a good one.
-*Marjorie Kinnan Rawlings (1896 – 1953)*

To fall in love is to create a religion that has a fallible god.
-*Jorge Luis Borges (1899 – 1986)*

Don't come crawlin' to a man for love--he likes to get a run for his money.
-*Mae West (1892-1980)*

We accept the love we think we deserve.
-*Stephen Chbosky (1970 -)*

It is better to be hated for what you are than to be loved for what you are not.
-*André Gide (1869 – 1951)*

The big difference between sex for money and sex for free is that sex for money usually costs a lot less.
-*Brendan Behan (1923 – 64)*

The opposite of love is not hate, its indifference.
-Elie Wiesel (1928 -)

Sex is like money; only too much is enough.
-John Updike (1932 – 2009)

I love you without knowing how, or when, or from where. I love you simply, without problems or pride: I love you in this way because I do not know any other way of loving but this, in which there is no I or you, so intimate that your hand upon my chest is my hand, so intimate that when I fall asleep your eyes close.
-Pablo Neruda (1904 – 73)

I can live without money, but I cannot live without love.
-Judy Garland (1922 – 69)

Have you ever been in love? Horrible isn't it? It makes you so vulnerable. It opens your chest and it opens up your heart and it means that someone can get inside you and mess you up.
-Neil Gaiman (1960 -)

For every beauty there is an eye somewhere to see it. For every truth there is an ear somewhere to hear it. For every love there is a heart somewhere to receive it.
-Ivan Panin (1855 – 1942)

The law of love could be best understood and learned through little children.
-Mahatma Gandhi (1869 – 1948)

Love all, trust a few, do wrong to none.
-William Shakespeare (1564 – 1616)

There is never a time or place for true love. It happens accidentally, in a heartbeat, in a single flashing, throbbing moment.

-Sarah Dessen (1970 -)

Love is the flower of life, and blossoms unexpectedly and without law, and must be plucked where it is found, and enjoyed for the brief hour of its duration.

-DH Lawrence (1885 – 1930)

I see when men love women they give but a little of their lives, but women, when they love, give everything.

-Oscar Wilde (1854 – 1900)

Being deeply loved by someone gives you strength, while loving someone deeply gives you courage.

-Lao Tzu (604 – 531 BC)

In love, women are professionals, men are amateurs.

-Francois Truffaut (1932 – 84)

I am nothing special, of this I am sure. I am a common man with common thoughts and I've led a common life. There are no monuments dedicated to me and my name will soon be forgotten, but I've loved another with all my heart and soul, and to me, this has always been enough.

-Nicholas Sparks (1965 -)

Love is something far more than desire for sexual intercourse; it is the principal means of escape from the loneliness which afflicts most men and women throughout the greater part of their lives.

-Bertrand Russell (1872 – 1970)

Many men kill themselves for love, but many more women die of it.
-Helen Rowland (1875 – 1950)

Love is like the wind, you can't see it but you can feel it.
-Nicholas Sparks (1965 -)

When men and women are able to respect and accept their differences then love has a chance to blossom.
-John Gray (1948 -)

If you can make a woman laugh, you can make her do anything.
-Marilyn Monroe (1926 – 62)

Love is like a friendship caught on fire. In the beginning a flame, very pretty, often hot and fierce, but still only light and flickering. As love grows older, our hearts mature and our love becomes as coals, deep-burning and unquenchable.
-Bruce Lee (1940 – 73)

We're all a little weird. And life is a little weird. And when we find someone whose weirdness is compatible with ours, we join up with them and fall into mutually satisfying weirdness—and call it love—true love.
-Robert Fulghum (1937 -)

The real lover is the man who can thrill you by kissing your forehead or smiling into your eyes or just staring into space.
-Marilyn Monroe (1926 – 62)

A rose without thorns is like love without heartbreak; it doesn't make sense.
-Anatole France (1844 – 1924)

Love doesn't make the world go 'round. Love is what makes the ride worthwhile.
-*Franklin P Jones (1887 – 1929)*

Love never dies a natural death. It dies because we don't know how to replenish its source. It dies of blindness and errors and betrayals. It dies of illness and wounds; it dies of weariness, of witherings, of tarnishings.
-*Anaïs Nin (1903 – 77)*

In the arithmetic of love, one plus one equals everything, and two minus one equals nothing.
-*Mignon McLaughlin (1913 – 83)*

Love is like pi - natural, irrational, and very important.
-*Lisa Hoffman (1954-)*

If I had a flower for every time I thought of you...I could walk through my garden forever.
-*Alfred Lord Tennyson (1809 – 92)*

Love is like a Rubik Cube, there are countless numbers of wrong twists and turns, but when you get it right, it looks
-*Brian Cramer (1978 -)*

There is nothing I would not do for those who are really my friends. I have no notion of loving people by halves, it is not my nature.
-*Jane Austen (1775 – 1817)*

In true love the smallest distance is too great, and the greatest distance can be bridged.
-*Hans Nouwens (1932 – 96)*

When someone loves you, the way they talk about you is different. You feel safe and comfortable.
-Jess C. Scott

Love comes unseen; we only see it go.
-Austin Dobson (1840 -1921)

Tis better to have loved and lost
Than never to have loved at all.
-Alfred Tennyson (1809 – 92)

Love is missing someone whenever you're apart, but somehow feeling warm inside because you're close in heart.
-Kay Knudsen (1903 – 77)

A lady's imagination is very rapid; it jumps from admiration to love, from love to matrimony in a moment.
-Jane Austen (1775 – 1817)

We come to love not by finding a perfect person, but by learning to see an imperfect person perfectly.
-Sam Keen (1931 -)

I love you as certain dark things are to be loved,
in secret, between the shadow and the soul.
-Pablo Neruda (1904 – 73)

Love is like an hourglass, with the heart filling up as the brain empties.
-Jules Renard (1864 – 1910)

Love wasn't put in your heart to stay. Love isn't love until you give it away.
-Michael W. Smith (1957 -)

I no longer believed in the idea of soul mates, or love at first sight. But I was beginning to believe that a very few times in your life, if you were lucky, you might meet someone who was exactly right for you. Not because he was perfect, or because you were, but because your combined flaws were arranged in a way that allowed two separate beings to hinge together.
-Lisa Kleypas (1964 -)

Most people have a harder time letting themselves love than finding someone to love them.
-Bill Russell (1934 -)

Real love is more than a physical feeling. If there's even the slightest doubt in your head about a guy, then forget about it. It's not real.
-Ethan Embry (1978 -)

We love the things we love for what they are.
-Robert Frost (1874 – 1963)

Love me when I least deserve it, because that's when I really need it.
-Swedish proverb

Love is shown in your deeds, not in your words.
-Fr. Jerome Cummings

I would die for you. But I won't live for you.
-Stephen Chbosky (1970 -)

You know that when I hate you, it is because I love you to a point of passion that unhinges my soul.
-Julie de Lespinasse (1732 – 76)

People love others not for who they are but for how they make them feel.
-*Irwin Federman (1936 -)*

The greater your capacity to love, the greater your capacity to feel the pain.
-*Jennifer Anniston (1969 -)*

Nobody has ever measured, not even poets, how much the heart can hold.
-*Zelda Fitzgerald (1900 – 48)*

The beginning of love is to let those we love be perfectly themselves, and not to twist them to fit our own image. Otherwise we love only the reflection of ourselves we find in them.
-*Thomas Merton (1915 -68)*

So, I love you because the entire universe conspired to help me find you.
-*Paulo Coelho (1947 -)*

You have to walk carefully in the beginning of love; the running across fields into your lover's arms can only come later when you're sure they won't laugh if you trip.
-*Jonathan Carroll (1949 -)*

Love is much like a wild rose, beautiful and calm, but willing to draw blood in its defense.
-*Mark Overby*

Once upon a time there was a boy who loved a girl, and her laughter was a question he wanted to spend his whole life answering.
-*Nicole Krauss (1970-)*

Love is as much of an object as an obsession, everybody wants it everybody seeks it, but few ever achieve it, those who do, will cherish it, be lost in it, and among all, will never...never forget it.
-Curtis Judalet

Some women choose to follow men, and some women choose to follow their dreams. If you're wondering which way to go, remember that your career will never wake up and tell you that it doesn't love you anymore.
-Lady Gaga (1986 -)

Gravitation cannot be held responsible for people falling in love.
-Albert Einstein (1879 – 1955)

Love is the condition in which the happiness of another person is essential to your own.
-Robert Heinlein (1907 -88)

I heard what you said. I'm not the silly romantic you think. I don't want the heavens or the shooting stars. I don't want gemstones or gold. I have those things already. I want...a steady hand. A kind soul. I want to fall asleep, and wake, knowing my heart is safe. I want to love, and be loved.
-Shana Abe

You know its love when all you want is that person to be happy, even if you're not part of their happiness.
-Julia Roberts (1967 -)

Eventually you will come to understand that love heals everything, and love is all there is.
-Gary Zukav (1942 -)

This is a good sign, having a broken heart. It means we have tried for something.
-Elizabeth Gilbert (1969 -)

Love is being stupid together.
-Paul Valery (1871 – 1945)

I don't want to live. I want to love first, and live incidentally.
-Zelda Fitzgerald (1900 – 48)

The more I know of the world, the more I am convinced that I shall never see a man whom I can really love. I require so much!
-Jane Austen (1775 – 1817)

We waste time looking for the perfect lover, instead of creating the perfect love.
-Tom Robbins (1936 -)

Your task is not to seek for love, but merely to seek and find all the barriers within yourself that you have built against it.
-Rumi (1207 -73)

Every heart sings a song, incomplete, until another heart whispers back. Those who wish to sing always find a song. At the touch of a lover, everyone becomes a poet.
-Plato (427 – 347 BC)

Love is like seaweed; even if you have pushed it away, you will not prevent it from coming back.
-Nigerian proverb

What's meant to be will always find a way.
-Trisha Yearwood (1964 -)

Love is the ultimate outlaw. It just won't adhere to any rules. The most any of us can do is sign on as its accomplice.
-Tom Watson (1949 -)

Love is the harmony of two souls singing together.
-Gregory J. P. Godek

Never love anyone who treats you like you're ordinary.
-Oscar Wilde (1854 – 1900)

Pure love produces pure nonsense.- Jonathan Klinger
Two people in love, alone, isolated from the world, that's beautiful.
-Milan Kundera (1929 -)

There is always some madness in love. But there is also always some reason in madness.
-Friedrich Nietzsche (1844 -1900)

When a love comes to an end, weaklings cry, efficient ones instantly find another love, and the wise already have one in reserve.
-Oscar Wilde (1854 – 1900)

The heart was made to be broken.
-Oscar Wilde (1854 – 1900)

Perhaps love is the process of my leading you gently back to yourself.
-Antoine de Saint-Exupery (1900 - 44)

True Love burns the brightest, but the brightest flames leave the deepest scars.
-Brandi Snyder

Any man who can drive safely while kissing a pretty girl is simply not giving the kiss the attention it deserves.
-Albert Einstein (1874 – 1955)

You don't love someone for their looks, or their clothes, or for their fancy car, but because they sing a song only you can hear.
-Oscar Wilde (1854 – 1900)

If I never met you, I wouldn't like you. If I didn't like you, I wouldn't love you. If I didn't love you, I wouldn't miss you. But I did, I do, and I will.
-Anon

There is no feeling more comforting and consoling than knowing you are right next to the one you love.
-Kay Knudsen (1903 – 77)

Love is a fire. But whether it is going to warm your hearth or burn down your house, you can never tell.
-Joan Crawford (1905 – 77)

My daddy said, that the first time you fall in love, it changes you forever and no matter how hard you try, that feeling just never goes away.
-Nicholas Sparks (1965 -)

Love is what makes two people sit in the middle of a bench when there is plenty of room at both ends.
-Barbara Johnson (1947 – 2009)

To love someone is nothing, to be loved by someone is something, but to be loved by the one you love is everything.
-Bill Russell (1934 -)

I am not sure exactly what heaven will be like, but I know that when we die and it comes time for God to judge us, he will not ask, 'How many good things have you done in your life?' rather he will ask, 'How much love did you put into what you did?
-*Mother Teresa (1910 – 97)*

He's more myself than I am. Whatever our souls are made of, his and mine are the same.
-*Emily Brontë (1818 -1948)*

Never frown, because you never know when someone is falling in love with your smile.
-*Christina Phan (1989 -)*

Love is saying 'I feel differently' instead of 'You're wrong'.
-*Brandi Synder*

The very essence of romance is uncertainty.
-*Oscar Wilde (1854 – 1900)*

I love you not because of who you are, but because of who I am when I am with you.
-*Roy Croft*

If you love something let it go free. If it doesn't come back, you never had it. If it comes back, love it forever.
-*Doug Horton (1891 – 1968)*

For the two of us, home isn't a place. It is a person. And we are finally home.
-*Stephanie Perkins*

Love doesn't just sit there, like a stone, it has to be made, like bread; remade all the time, made new.
-*Ursula K. Le Guin (1929 -)*

I love you more than there are stars in the sky and fish in the sea.
-*Nicholas Sparks (1965 -)*

I love you, and because I love you, I would sooner have you hate me for telling you the truth than adore me for telling you lies.
-*Pietro Aretino (1492 – 1556)*

Man may have discovered fire, but women discovered how to play with it.
-*Candace Bushnell (1958 -)*

A woman's heart should be so hidden in God that a man has to seek Him just to find her.
-*Max Lucado (1955 -)*

Hatred is blind, as well as love.
-*Oscar Wilde (1854 – 1900)*

There is nothing in the world so wonderful as to love and be loved; there is nothing so devastating as love lost.
-*Larry Latta*

Love does not begin and end the way we seem to think it does. Love is a battle, love is a war; love is a growing up.
-*James Baldwin (1924 -87)*

I have decided to stick to love...Hate is too great a burden to bear.
-*Martin Luther King Jr (1929 – 68)*

Meeting you was fate, becoming your friend was a choice, but falling in love with you I had no control over.
-Anon

When love is not madness it is not love.
-Pedro Calderón de la Barca (1600 – 81)

Love is an irresistible desire to be irresistibly desired.
-Robert Frost (1874 – 1963)

Immature love says: 'I love you because I need you'. Mature love says: 'I need you because I love you'.
-Erich Fromm (1900 – 80)

When you fish for love, bait with your heart, not your brain.
-Mark Twain (1835 – 1910)

Love means to commit oneself without guarantee, to give oneself completely in the hope that our love will produce love in the loved person. Love is an act of faith, and whoever is of little faith is also of little love.
-Eric Fromm (1900 – 80)

Love is of all passions the strongest, for it attacks simultaneously the head, the heart and the senses.
-Lao Tzu (600 – 531 BC)

Love is more afraid of change than destruction.
-Friedrich Nietzsche (1844 – 1900)

To keep your marriage brimming, with love in the loving cup, whenever you're wrong, admit it; Whenever you're right, shut up.
-Ogden Nash (1902 – 71)

Love is one of the hardest words to say and one of the easiest to hear.
-Johnny Depp (1963 -)

When one is in love, one always begins by deceiving one's self, and one always ends by deceiving others. That is what world calls a romance.
-Oscar Wilde (1854 – 1900)

To a woman in love, loving too much is not loving enough.
-Anon

One of the hardest things in life is watching the person you love, love someone else.
-Anon

If you have to think about whether you love someone or not then the answer is no. When you love someone you just know.
-Janice Markowitz

Love begins with a smile, grows with a kiss, and ends with a teardrop.
Augustine of Hippo (354 – 430 AD)

The perfect love affair is one which is conducted entirely by post.
-George Bernard Shaw (1856 – 1950)

In dreams and in love there are no impossibilities.
-Janos Arnay (1817 – 82)

The more I give to thee, the more I have, for both are infinite.
-William Shakespeare (1564 – 1616)

Love is as much of an object as an obsession, everybody wants it, everybody seeks it, but few ever achieve it, those who do will cherish it, be lost in it, and among all, never... never forget it.
-*Curtis Judalet*

Pleasure of love lasts but a moment, Pain of love lasts a lifetime.
-*Bette Davis (1908 – 89)*

Divorce

My wife Mary and I have been married for forty-seven years and not once have we had an argument serious enough to consider divorce; murder, yes, but divorce, never.
-Jack Benny (1894 – 74)

Nice people don't necessarily fall in love with nice people.
-Jonathan Franzen (1959 -)

So many persons think divorce a panacea for every ill, who find out, when they try it, that the remedy is worse than the disease.
-Dorothy Dix (1870 -1951)

Divorce isn't such a tragedy. A tragedy's staying in an unhappy marriage, teaching your children the wrong things about love. Nobody ever died of divorce.
-Jennifer Weiner (1970 -)

Divorce begins with too many unspoken words and things at the end of the day.
-Anon

Such silence has an actual sound, the sound of disappearance.
-Suzanne Finnamore

In every marriage more than a week old, there are grounds for divorce. The trick is to find, and continue to find, grounds for marriage.
-Robert Anderson (1861 – 1939)

If you spend your time hoping someone will suffer the consequences for what they did to your heart, then you're allowing them to hurt you a second time in your mind.
-Shannon L. Alder

I maintain that it should cost as much to get married as to get divorced. Make it look like marriage is worth as much as divorce, even if it ain't.
-Will Rogers (1879 – 1935)

Your relationship may be "Breaking Up," but you won't be "Breaking Down." If anything you're correcting a mistake that was hurting four people, you and the person you're with, not to mention the two people who you were destined to meet.
-D. Ivan Young

There are two sides to every divorce: Yours and shithead's.
-Anon

Hollywood brides keep the bouquets and throw away the grooms.
-Groucho Marx (1890 – 1977)

Ah, yes, divorce ... from the Latin word meaning to rip out a man's genitals through his wallet.
-Robin Williams (1951 – 2014)

Paying alimony is like feeding hay to a dead horse.
-Groucho Marx (1890 – 1977)

My divorce came to me as a complete surprise. That's what happens when you haven't been home in eighteen years.
-Lee Trevino (1939 -)

Delusion detests focus and romance provides the veil.
-*Suzanne Finnamore*

Insanity: grounds for divorce in some states, grounds for marriage in all.
-*Anon*

Grief is the emotional contract of divorce.
-*Cheryl Nielsen*

Love the quest; marriage the conquest; divorce the inquest.
-*Helen Rowland (1876 – 1950)*

Many married couples separate because they quarrel incessantly, but just as many separate because they were never honest enough or courageous enough to quarrel when they should have.
-*Sydney J. Harris (1917 – 86)*

Love is grand; divorce is a hundred grand.
-*Anon*

Divorce is a fire exit. When a house is burning, it doesn't matter who set the fire. If there is no fire exit, everyone in the house will be burned!
-*Mehmet Murat Ildan (1965 -)*

When two people decide to get a divorce, it isn't a sign that they "don't understand" one another, but a sign that they have, at last, begun to.
-*Helen Rowland (1876 – 1950)*

Losing a mate to death is devastating but it's not a personal attack like divorce. When somebody you love stops loving you and walks away, it's an insult beyond comparison.
-*Sue Merrell*

Marriage is about love; divorce is about money.
-*Anon*

An unresolved issue will be like a cancer with the potential to spread into other areas of your relationship, eroding the joy, lightness, love and beauty.
-*Joyce Vissell*

I'm an excellent housekeeper. Every time I get a divorce, I keep the house.
-*Zsa Zsa Gabor (1917 – 2014)*

I don't miss him, I miss who I thought he was.
-*Anon*

The happiest time in any man's life is just after the first divorce.
-*John Kenneth Galbraith (1908 – 2006)*

She cried—and the judge wiped her tears with my checkbook.
-*Tommy Manville (1894 – 1967)*

Divorced men are more likely to meet their car payments than their child support obligations.
-*Susan Faludi (1959 -)*

My mother always said don't marry for money, divorce for money.
-*Wendy Liebman (1961 -)*

Friendship

Love is blind; friendship closes its eyes.
-Friedrich Nietzsche (1844 – 1900)

To the world you may be just one person, but to one person you may be the world.
-Brandi Snyder

Friendship is born at that moment when one man says to another: "What! You too? I thought that no one but myself . . ."
-CS Lewis (1898 – 1963)

Even though we've changed and we're all finding our own place in the world, we all know that when the tears fall or the smile spreads across our face, we'll come to each other because no matter where this crazy world takes us, nothing will ever change so much to the point where we're not all still friends.
-Anon

Good friends, good books, and a sleepy conscience: this is the ideal life.
-Mark Twain (1835 – 1910)

If you live to be 100, I hope I live to be 100 minus 1 day, so I never have to live without you.
-AA Milne (1882 – 1956)

The truth is, everyone is going to hurt you. You just got to find the ones worth suffering for.
-Bob Marley (1945 – 81)

What is uttered from the heart alone, Will win the hearts of others to your own.

-Johann Wolfgang von Goethe (1749 – 1832)

Truly great friends are hard to find, difficult to leave, and impossible to forget.

-Anon

Piglet sidled up to Pooh from behind. "Pooh?" he whispered. "Yes, Piglet?"
"Nothing," said Piglet, taking Pooh's hand. "I just wanted to be sure of you."

-AA Milne (1882 – 1956)

If I had a flower for every time I thought of you...I could walk through my garden forever.

–Alfred Lord Tennyson (1809 – 92)

Love is when two people know everything about each other and are still friends.

-Mary Oliver (1935 -)

Keep away from those who try to belittle your ambitions. Small people always do that, but the really great make you believe that you too can become great.

-Mark Twain (1835 -1910)

There is nothing I would not do for those who are really my friends. I have no notion of loving people by halves, it is not my nature.

-Jane Austen (1775 – 1817)

There is nothing better than a friend, unless it is a friend with chocolate.

-Linda Grayson

One kiss breaches the distance between friendship and love.
-Josh Hartnett (1978 -)

True friends stab you in the front.
-Oscar Wilde (1854 – 1900)

It's the friends you can call up at 4 a.m. that matter.
-Marlene Dietrich (1901 - 92)

A true friend is someone who thinks that you are a good egg even though he knows that you are slightly cracked.
-Bernard Meltzer (1916- 98)

Life is an awful, ugly place to not have a best friend.
-Sarah Dessen (1970 -)

Life is partly what we make it, and partly what it is made by the friends we choose.
-Tennessee Williams (1911 – 83)

I would rather walk with a friend in the dark, than alone in the light.
-Helen Keller (1880 – 1968)

Friendship is unnecessary, like philosophy, like art.... It has no survival value; rather it is one of those things which give value to survival.
-CS Lewis (1898 – 63)

Friendship is the hardest thing in the world to explain. It's not something you learn in school. But if you haven't learned the meaning of friendship, you really haven't learned anything.
-Muhammad Ali (1942-)

True friendship comes when the silence between two people is comfortable.
-David Tyson Gentry

Only a true best friend can protect you from your immortal enemies.
-Richelle Mead (1976 -)

The friend who can be silent with us in a moment of despair or confusion, who can stay with us in an hour of grief and bereavement, who can tolerate not knowing... not healing, not curing... that is a friend who cares.
-Henri Nouwen (1932 – 96)

There are no faster or firmer friendships than those formed between people who love the same books.
-Irving Stone (1903 – 89)

The difference between friendship and love is how much you can hurt each other.
-Ashleigh Brilliant (1933 -)

Men kick friendship around like a football but it doesn't seem to break. Women treat it like glass and it goes to pieces.
-Anne Morrow Lindbergh (1906 – 2001)

Do I not destroy my enemies when I make them my friends?

-Abraham Lincoln (1809 – 65)

In the End, we will remember not the words of our enemies, but the silence of our friends.
-Martin Luther King (1929 – 68)

Words are easy, like the wind; Faithful friends are hard to find.
- *William Shakespeare (1564 – 1616)*

Friendship is always a sweet responsibility, never an opportunity.
-*Khalil Gibran (1883 – 1931)*

Silence make the real conversations between friends. Not the saying, but the never needing to say that counts.
-*Margaret Lee Runbeck (1905 – 56)*

We all take different paths in life, but no matter where we go, we take a little of each other everywhere.
-*Tim McGraw (1967 -)*

Growing apart doesn't change the fact that for a long time we grew side by side; our roots will always be tangled. I'm glad for that.
-*Ally Condie*

Friendship is like a glass ornament, once it is broken it can rarely be put back together exactly the same way.
-*Charles Kingsley (1819 – 75)*

Tis the privilege of friendship to talk nonsense, and to have her nonsense respected.
-*Charles Lamb (1775 – 1834)*

The capacity for friendship is God's way of apologizing for our families.
-*Jay McInerney (1955 -)*

In prosperity, our friends know us; in adversity, we know our friends.

-*John Churton Collins (1848 – 1908)*

The worst part of success is trying to find someone who is happy for you.

-*Bette Midler (1945 -)*

The most beautiful discovery true friends make is that they can grow separately without growing apart.

-*Elisabeth Foley (1965 -)*

The man of knowledge must be able not only to love his enemies but also to hate his friends.

-*Friedrich Nietzsche (1844 – 1900)*

But what is the good of friendship if one cannot say exactly what one means? Anybody can say charming things and try to please and to flatter, but a true friend always says unpleasant things, and does not mind giving pain. Indeed, if he is a really true friend he prefers it, for he knows that then he is doing good.

-*Oscar Wilde (1854 – 1900)*

If you have good friends, no matter how much life is sucking, they can make you laugh.

-*P.C. Cast (1960 -)*

Friends are God's way of taking care of us.

-*Anon*

Friendship marks a life even more deeply than love. Love risks degenerating into obsession, friendship is never anything but sharing.

-*Elie Wiesel (1928 -)*

Friends are God's way of apologizing to us for our families.
Tennessee Williams (1911 – 83)

I cannot even imagine where I would be today were it not for that handful of friends who have given me a heart full of joy. Let's face it, friends make life a lot more fun.
-Charles R Swindoll (1934 -)

Friends show their love in times of trouble, not in happiness.
-Euripides (480 – 406BC)

A snowball in the face is surely the perfect beginning to a lasting friendship.
-Markus Zusak (1975 -)

Friendship- my definition- is built on two things. Respect and trust. Both elements have to be there. And it has to be mutual. You can have respect for someone, but if you don't have trust, the friendship will crumble.
-Stieg Larsson (1954 – 2004)

I don't need a friend who changes when I change and who nods when I nod; my shadow does that much better.
-Plutarch (46 -119AD)

You can go through life and make new friends every year - every month practically - but there was never any substitute for those friendships of childhood that survive into adult years. Those are the ones in which we are bound to one another with hoops of steel.
-Alexander McCall Smith (1948 -)

You find out who your real friends are when you're involved in a scandal.
-Elizabeth Taylor (1932 – 2011)

I am always saying "Glad to've met you" to somebody I'm not at all glad I met. If you want to stay alive, you have to say that stuff, though.

-J.D. Salinger (1919 – 2010)

A true friend is one who knows all about you and likes you anyway.

-Christi Mary Warner

Anybody can sympathise with the sufferings of a friend, but it requires a very fine nature to sympathise with a friend's success.

-Oscar Wilde (1894 – 1900)

The best mirror is an old friend.

-George Herbert (1593 – 1633)

When someone tells you the truth, lets you think for yourself, experience your own emotions, he is treating you as a true equal. As a friend.

-Whitney Otto

Why are old lovers able to become friends? Two reasons. They never truly loved each other, or they love each other still.

-Whitney Otto

A friend is someone who helps you up when you're down, and if they can't, they lay down beside you and listen.

-Anon

And if your friend does evil to you, say to him, "I forgive you for what you did to me, but how can I forgive you for what you did to yourself?"

-Friedrich Nietzsche (1844 – 1900)

The only way to have a friend is to be one.
-*Ralph Waldo Emmerson (1803 – 82)*

The language of friendship is not words but meanings.
-*Henry David Thoreau (1817 – 62)*

The proper office of a friend is to side with you when you are wrong. Nearly anybody will side with you when you are right.
-*Mark Twain (1835 – 1910)*

Are you upset little friend? Have you been lying awake worrying? Well, don't worry...I'm here. The flood waters will recede, the famine will end, the sun will shine tomorrow, and I will always be here to take care of you.
-*Charles M Schulz (1922 – 2000)*

Friendship is the only cement that will ever hold the world together.
-*Woodrow T. Wilson (1856 – 1924)*

A good friend will pick you back up when you fall but your best friend will laugh and trip you again.
-*Anon*

Friends are the sunshine of life.
-*John Hay (1838 – 1905)*

Friends are like good bras: supportive, hard to find, and close to your heart.
-*Anon*

Don't walk in front of me; I may not follow. Don't walk behind me; I may not lead. Just walk beside me and be my friend.
-*Albert Camus (1913 – 60)*

Friendship consists in forgetting what one gives and remembering what one receives.
-Alexander Dumas (1802 – 70)

The best kind of friend is the kind you can sit on a porch swing with, never say a word, then walk away feeling like it was the best conversation that you ever had.
-Anon

Be slow to fall into friendship; but when thou art in, continue firm & constant.
-Socrates (469 – 399 BC)

Friendship is like money, easier made than kept.
-Samuel Butler (1835 – 1902)

A friend is someone who knows the song in your heart and can sing it back to you when you have forgotten the words.
-CS Lewis (1898 – 63)

A friend is one that knows you as you are, understands where you have been, accepts what you have become, and still, gently allows you to grow.
-William Shakespeare (1564 – 1616)

Friendship is like vitamins, we supplement each other's minimum daily requirements.
-Anon

Eros will have naked bodies; Friendship naked personalities.
-CS Lewis (1898 – 1963)

A good friend can tell you what is the matter with you in a minute. He may not seem such a good friend after telling.
-*Arthur Brisbane (1864 – 1936)*

My best friend is the one who brings out the best in me.
-*Henry Ford (1863 – 1947)*

Woman reaches love through friendship; man reaches friendship through love.
-*Mohammed Hejazi (1900 – 74)*

I value the friend who for me finds time on his calendar, but I cherish the friend who for me does not consult his calendar.
-*Robert Brault (1963 -)*

One measure of friendship consists not in the number of things friends can discuss, but in the number of things they need no longer mention.
-*Clifton Fadiman (1904 – 99)*

A friendship that can end never really began.
-*Publilius Syrus (46 BC – 29 AD)*

Eventually soulmates meet, for they have the same hiding place.
-*Robert Brault (1963 -)*

Time or distance cannot touch the friendship of the heart.
-*Anon*

No person is your friend who demands your silence, or denies your right to grow.
-*Alice Walker (1944 -)*

Friendship without self-interest is one of the rare and beautiful things of life.
-James F Byrne (1882 – 1972)

In the end there doesn't have to be anyone who understands you. There just has to be someone who wants to.
-Robert Brault (1963 -)

Where you find true friendship, you find true love.
-Anon

For the friendship of two, the patience of one is required.
-Indian proverb

You can tell a real friend: when you've made a fool of yourself he doesn't feel as though you've done a permanent job.
-Laurence I. Peter (1919 – 90)

You can make more friends in two months by becoming interested in other people than you can in two years by trying to get other people interested in you.
-Dale Carnegie

One kiss breaches the distance between friendship and love.
-Josh Hartnett (1978 -)

Some people go to priests, others to poetry, I to my friends.
-Virginia Woolf (1882 – 1941)

Truth and tears clear the way to a deep and lasting friendship. –
Anon

The essence of true friendship is to make allowance for another's little lapses.
-*David Storey (1933 –)*

We're born alone, we live alone, we die alone. Only through our love and friendship can we create the illusion for the moment that we're not alone.
-*Orson Welles (1915 – 85)*

Friendship is love with understanding.
-*Proverb*

Friendship improves happiness, and abates misery, by doubling our joys, and dividing our grief.
-*Marcus Tullius Cicero (106 – 43 BC)*

Friendship always benefits; love sometimes injures.
-*Seneca (4 BC – 65 AD)*

True friendship is seen through the heart, not through the eyes.
-*Friedrich Nietzche (1844 – 1900)*

Do not save your loving speeches
For your friends till they are dead;
Do not write them on their tombstones,
Speak them rather now instead.
-*Anna Cummins*

Friendship is a horizon – which expands whenever we approach it.
-*ER Hazlip (1938 – 2003)*

No man is a failure who has friends.
-*Philip Van Doren Stern (1900 – 84)*

Chapter 3 Spiritual

Religion

When fascism comes to America it will be wrapped in the flag and carrying a cross.
-*Sinclair Lewis (1885-1951)*

We have just enough religion to make us hate, but not enough to make us love one another.
-*Jonathan Swift (1667- 1745)*

Fundamentalists are to Christianity what paint-by-numbers is to art.
-*Robin Tyler*

If there were no God, it would have been necessary to invent him.
-*Voltaire (1694 – 1778)*

I fear one day I'll meet God, he'll sneeze and I won't know what to say.
-*Ronnie Shakes (1947 -)*

Eskimo: If I did not know about God and sin, would I go to hell?
Priest: No, not if you did not know.
Eskimo: Then why did you tell me?
-*Annie Dillard (1945 -)*

God has no religion.
-*Mahatma Gandhi (1869 – 1948)*

No man ever believes that the Bible means what it says: He is always convinced that it says what he means.

-George Bernard Shaw (1856 – 1950)

The church is always trying to get other people to reform; it might not be a bad idea to reform itself a little, by way of example.
-Mark Twain (1835 – 1910)

When we blindly adopt a religion, a political system, a literary dogma, we become automatons. We cease to grow.
-Anais Nin (1903-77)

Those who say religion has nothing to do with politics do not know what religion is.
-Mahatma Gandhi (1869 – 1948)

I am against religion because it teaches us to be satisfied with not understanding the world.
-Richard Dawkins (1941 -)

All religions are founded on the fear of the many and the cleverness of the few.
-Stendhal (1783 – 1842)

Religion consists of a set of things which the average man thinks he believes and wishes he was certain.
-Mark Twain (1835 – 1910)

Religion has caused more harm than any other idea since the beginning of time. There's nothing good I can say about it. People use it as a crutch.
-Larry Flynt (1942 -)

If there is a God, atheism must seem to Him as less of an insult than religion.
-Edmond de Goncourt (1822 – 96)

The problem with writing about religion is that you run the risk of offending sincerely religious people, and then they come after you with machetes.

-Dave Barry (1947 -)

Religion is regarded by the common people as true, by the wise as false, and by the rulers as useful.

-Seneca (4BC – 65AD)

Religion is something left over from the infancy of our intelligence, it will fade away as we adopt reason and science as our guidelines.

-Bertrand Russell (1872 – 1970)

Of all religions, Christianity is without a doubt the one that should inspire tolerance most, although, up to now, the Christians have been the most intolerant of all men.

-Voltaire (1694 – 1778)

Many have quarreled about religion that never practiced it.

-Benjamin Franklin (1706 - 90)

When the missionaries came to Africa they had the Bible and we had the land. They said, 'Let us pray.' We closed our eyes. When we opened them we had the Bible and they had the land.

-Bishop Desmond Tutu (1931 -)

People who want to share their religious views with you almost never want you to share yours with them.

-Henry Louis Mencken (1880 – 1956)

The religion of the future will be a cosmic religion. The religion which based on experience, which refuses dogmatic. If there's any religion that would cope the scientific needs it will be Buddhism.
-Albert Einstein (1879 – 1955)

This is my simple religion. There is no need for temples; no need for complicated philosophy. Our own brain, our own heart is our temple; the philosophy is kindness.
-Dalai Lama (1935 -)

When one is in trouble, one remembers God.
-Proverb

I have ... a terrible need ... shall I say the word? ... of religion. Then I go out at night and paint the stars.
-Vincent van Gogh (1853 – 1890)

Religion is what keeps the poor man from murdering the rich.
-Napoleon Bonaparte (1769 – 1821)

A thorough reading and understanding of the Bible is the surest path to atheism.
-Donald Morgan

If you have a particular faith or religion that is good. But you can survive without it.
-Dalai Lama (1935 -)

It is an interesting and demonstrable fact, that all children are atheists and were religion not inculcated into their minds, they would remain so.
-Ernestine Rose (1810 – 92)

God's wounds cure, sin's kisses kill.
-William Gurnall (1617 – 79)

It is possible that mankind is on the threshold of a golden age; but, if so, it will be necessary first to slay the dragon that guards the door, and this dragon is religion.
-Bertrand Russell (1872-1970)

More people have been slaughtered in the name of religion than for any other single reason. That, my friends, is true perversion.
-Harvey Milk (1930 -78)

In some awful, strange, paradoxical way, atheists tend to take religion more seriously than the practitioners.
-Jonathan Miller (1934 -)

We all remember how many religious wars were fought for a religion of love and gentleness; how many bodies were burned alive with the genuinely kind intention of saving souls from the eternal fire of hell.
-Karl Popper (1902 – 94)

Religion is just mind control.
-George Carlin (1937 -)

The only good thing ever to come out of religion was the music.
-George Carlin (1937 -)

Happiness is a mystery like religion, and it should never be rationalized.
-GK Chesterton (1874 -1936)

Whether one believes in a religion or not, and whether one believes in rebirth or not, there isn't anyone who doesn't appreciate kindness and compassion.
-Robert Green Ingersoll (1833-89)

Religion is an illusion and it derives its strength from the fact that it falls in with our instinctual desires.
-Sigmund Freud (1856 – 1939)

He who possesses art and science has religion; he who does not possess them, needs religion.
-Johann Wolfgang von Goethe (1749 – 1832)

Every religion is true one way or another. It is true when understood metaphorically. But when it gets stuck in its own metaphors, interpreting them as facts, then you are in trouble.
-Joseph Campbell (1904-87)

If I had to choose a religion, the sun as the universal giver of life would be my god.
-Napoleon Bonaparte – (1769-1821)

I consider that the chief dangers which confront the coming century will be religion without the Holy Ghost, Christianity without Christ, forgiveness without repentance, salvation without regeneration, politics without God, and heaven without hell.
-William Booth (1829-1916)

The government of the United States is not in any sense founded on the Christian Religion.
-George Washington (1732-1799)

The more powerful and original a mind, the more it will incline towards the religion of solitude.
-Aldous Huxley – (1894-1963)

There is no higher religion than human service. To work for the common good is the greatest creed.
-*Woodrow T Wilson (1856-1924)*

I do not believe in revealed religion - I will have nothing to do with your immortality; we are miserable enough in this life, without speculating on another.
-*Lord Byron (1788-1824)*

I love you when you bow in your mosque, kneel in your temple, pray in your church. For you and I are sons of one religion, and it is the spirit.
-*Kahlil Gibran (1883 – 1931)*

A little philosophy inclineth man's mind to atheism, but depth in philosophy bringeth men's minds about to religion.
-*Francis Bacon (1561 – 1626)*

Organized religion is a sham and a crutch for weak-minded people who need strength in numbers.
-*Jesse Ventura (1952 -)*

Being unable to reason is not a positive character trait outside religion.
-*Dewey Henize*

Religion is love; in no case is it logic.
-*Beatrice Potter (1858 – 1943)*

The greatest religion is to be true to your own nature. Have faith in yourselves.
-*Swami Vivekananda (1863 – 19002)*

If atheism is a religion, then bald is a hair colour.
-*Mark Schnitzius*

The first requisite for the happiness of the people is the abolition of religion.
-*Karl Marx (1818-1883)*

Science is a differential equation. Religion is a boundary condition.
-*Alan Turing (1912 – 1954)*

The Americans combine the notions of religion and liberty so intimately in their minds that it is impossible to make them conceive of one without the other.
-*Alexis de Tocqueville (1805 – 95)*

The greatest tragedy in mankind's entire history may be the hijacking of morality by religion.
-*Arthur C Clarke (1917 – 2008)*

Of all the tyrannies that affect mankind, tyranny in religion is the worst.
-*Thomas Paine (1737 – 1809)*

The real religion of the world comes from women much more than from men - from mothers most of all, who carry the key of our souls in their bosoms.
-*Oliver Wendell (1809 – 94)*

I believe in a religion that believes in freedom. Any time I have to accept a religion that won't let me fight a battle for my people, I say to hell with that religion.
-*Malcolm X (1925 -65)*

A man devoid of religion is like a horse without a bridle.
-*Latin proverb*

Nothing defines humans better than their willingness to do irrational things in the pursuit of phenomenally unlikely payoffs. This is the principle behind lotteries, dating, and religion.
-*Scott Adams (1957 -)*

Businesses may come and go, but religion will last forever, for in no other endeavor does the consumer blame himself for product failure.
-*Anon*

In the course of history many more people have died for their drink and their dope than have died for their religion or their country.
-*Aldous Huxley (1894 – 1963)*

Marge, there's an empty spot I've always had inside me. I tried to fill it with family, religion, community service, but those were dead ends! I think this chair is the answer.
-*Dan Castellaneta/Homer Simpson (1957 -)*

Formerly, when religion was strong and science weak, men mistook magic for medicine; now, when science is strong and religion weak, men mistake medicine for magic.
-*Thomas S Szasz (1920 - 2012)*

We may not understand how the spirit works; but the effect of the spirit on the lives of men is there for all to see; and the only unanswerable argument for Christianity is a Christian life. No man can disregard a religion and a faith and a power which is able to make bad men good.
-*William Barclay (1907 -78)*

Religion is fundamentally opposed to everything I hold in veneration - courage, clear thinking, honesty, fairness, and above all, love of the truth.
-*Henry Louis Mencken (1880 – 1956)*

Humanity without religion is like a serial killer without a chainsaw.
-*Anon*

In morals what begins in fear usually ends in wickedness; in religion what begins in fear usually ends in fanaticism. Fear, either as a principle or a motive, is the beginning of all evil.
-*Anna Jameson (1794 – 1860)*

Any system of religion that has anything in it that shocks the mind of a child, cannot be true.
-*Thomas Paine (1737 – 1809)*

Persecution is not an original feature in any religion; but it is always the strongly marked feature of all religions established by law.
-*Thomas Paine (1737 – 1809)*

Religion is induced insanity.
-*Madalyn Murray (1919-95)*

Nothing is so fatal to religion as indifference.
-*Edmund Burke (1729 – 1797)*

I believe that religion, generally speaking, has been a curse to mankind - that its modest and greatly overestimated services on the ethical side have been more than overcome by the damage it has done to clear and honest thinking.
-*Henry Louis Mencken (1880 – 1956)*

Religion is no more the parent of morality than an incubator is the mother of a chicken.
-Lemuel K Washburn

A one sentence definition of mythology? "Mythology" is what we call someone else's religion.
-Joseph Campbell (1904 – 87)

Sceptical scrutiny is the means, in both science and religion, by which deep insights can be winnowed from deep nonsense.
-Dr. Carl Sagan (1934 – 96)

Religion is the last refuge of human savagery.
-Alfred North Whitehead (1861 – 1947)

The only difference between a cult and a religion is the amount of real estate they own.
-Frank Zappa (1940 -93)

Men despise religion. They hate it and are afraid it may be true.
-Blaise Pascal (1623 – 1662)

Each of us in our own way can try to spread compassion into people's hearts. Western civilizations these days place great importance on filling the human 'brain' with knowledge, but no one seems to care about filling the human 'heart' with compassion. This is what the real role of religion is.
-Dalai Lama (1935 -)

Religion is the opium of the masses.
-Karl Marx (1818 -93)

There is no surer sign of decay in a country than to see the rites of religion held in contempt.
-*Niccolo Machiavelli (1469 -1527)*

Man is the religious animal. He is the only religious animal. He is the only animal that has the True Religion -- several of them. He is the only animal that loves his neighbor as himself and cuts his throat, if his theology isn't straight.
-*Mark Twain (1835 – 1910)*

Religion to me is a bureaucracy between man and God that I don't need.
-*Bill Maher (1956 -)*

My principal objections to orthodox religion are two - slavery here and hell hereafter.
-*Robert Green Ingersoll (1833-99)*

God has no place within these walls, just as facts have no place within organized religion.
Dan Castellaneta/ Homer Simpson (1957 -)

Religion can never reform mankind because religion is slavery.
-*Robert Green Ingersoll (1833 – 99)*

Just in terms of allocation of time resources, religion is not very efficient. There's a lot more I could be doing on a Sunday morning.
-*Bill Gates (1955 -)*

When superstition goes, religion remains.
-*Cicero (106 – 43 BC)*

Whenever a taboo is broken, something good happens, something vitalizing. Taboos after all are only hangovers, the product of diseased minds, you might say, of fearsome people who hadn't the courage to live and who under the guise of morality and religion have imposed these things upon us.
-Henry Miller (1891 – 1980)

I am quite sure now that often, very often, in matters concerning religion and politics a man's reasoning powers are not above the monkey's.
-Mark Twain (1835 – 1910)

Religion is the masterpiece of the art of animal training, for it trains people as to how they shall think.
-Arthur Schopenhauer (1788 – 1860)

It is easy enough to be friendly to one's friends. But to befriend the one who regards himself as your enemy is the quintessence of true religion. The other is mere business.
-Mahatma Gandhi (1869 – 1948)

Men wearing pants so tight that you can tell what religion they are.
-Robin Williams (1951 – 2014)

When politics and religion are intermingled, a people is suffused with a sense of invulnerability, and gathering speed in their forward charge, they fail to see the cliff ahead of them.
-Frank Herbert (1920 – 86)

The idea of a good society is something you do not need a religion and eternal punishment to buttress; you need a religion if you are terrified of death.
-Gore Vidal (1925 – 12)

Religion is not merely the opium of the masses, it's the cyanide.
-*Tom Robbins (1936 -)*

Religion is the possibility of the removal of every ground of confidence except confidence in God alone.
-*Karl Barth (1886 – 1968)*

A tyrant must put on the appearance of uncommon devotion to religion. Subjects are less apprehensive of illegal treatment from a ruler whom they consider god-fearing and pious. On the other hand, they do less easily move against him, believing that he has the gods on his side.
-*Aristotle (384 – 322BC)*

I do not know how to teach philosophy without becoming a disturber of established religion.
-*Baruch Spinoza (1632 – 77)*

Science can purify religion from error and superstition. Religion can purify science from idolatry and false absolutes.
-*Pope John Paul II (1920 – 2005)*

A religion without a goddess is halfway to atheism.
-*Don Fortune*

To die for a religion is easier than to live it absolutely.
-*Jose Luis Borges (1899 – 1986)*

Religion is probably, after sex, the second oldest resource which human beings have available to them for blowing their minds.
-*Susan Sontag (1933 – 2004)*

Religion is the impotence of the human mind to deal with occurrences it cannot understand.
-*Karl Marx (1818 – 83)*

The main object of religion is not to get a man into heaven, but to get heaven into him.
-*Thomas Hardy (1840 – 1928)*

Where knowledge ends, religion begins.
-*Benjamin Disraeli (1804 – 1881)*

Religion is not a popular error; it is a great instinctive truth, sensed by the people, expressed by the people.
-*Ernest Renan (1823 – 1892)*

Doubt is part of all religion. All the religious thinkers were doubters.
-*Isaac Bashevis Singer (1904 – 91)*

Priests are no more necessary to religion than politicians to patriotism.
-*John Haynes Holmes (1879 – 1964)*

Freedom prospers when religion is vibrant and the rule of law under God is acknowledged.
-*Ronald Reagan (1911 – 2004)*

A cult is a religion with no political power.
-*Thomas Wolfe (1900 – 38)*

The framers of our Constitution meant we were to have freedom of religion, not freedom from religion.
-*Billy Graham (1918 – 2007)*

To devote your life to the good of all and to the happiness of all is religion. Whatever you do for your own sake is not religion.
-*Swami Vivekananda (1863 – 1902)*

Religions die when they are proved to be true. Science is the record of dead religions.
-*Oscar Wilde (1854 – 1900)*

Theology is never any help; it is searching in a dark cellar at midnight for a black cat that isn't there. Theologians can persuade themselves of anything.
-*Robert A Heinlein (1907 – 88)*

One can't prove that God doesn't exist, but science makes God unnecessary.
-*Stephen Hawking (1942 -)*

Everyone who is seriously involved in the pursuit of science becomes convinced that a spirit is manifest in the laws of the Universe – a spirit vastly superior to that of man...
-*Albert Einstein (1879 – 1955)*

Life without God is like an unsharpened pencil - it has no point.
-*Anon*

In Christianity neither morality nor religion come into contact with reality at any point.
-*Friedrich Nietzsche (1844 – 1900)*

If you have abandoned one faith, do not abandon all faith. There is always an alternative to the faith we lose. Or is it the same faith under another name?
-*Graham Greene (1904 – 91)*

LIFE

When I was young, I thought that money was the most important thing in life; now that I am old, I know it is.
-Oscar Wilde (1854-1900)

Looking good and dressing well is a necessity. Having a purpose in life is not.
-Oscar Wilde (1854-1900)

There are many things in life that will catch your eye, but only a few will catch your heart...pursue those.
-Michael Nolan

Life would be infinitely happier if we could only be born at the age of eighty and gradually approach eighteen.
-Mark Twain (1835 – 1910)

If you want to live a happy life, tie it to a goal, not to people or things.
-Albert Einstein (1879-1955)

How strange is the lot of us mortals! Each of us is here for a brief sojourn; for what purpose he knows not, though he senses it. But without deeper reflection one knows from daily life that one exists for other people.
-Albert Einstein (1879-1955)

Live your own life, for you will die your own death.
-Latin proverb

He who experiences the unity of life sees his own Self in all beings, and all beings in his own Self, and looks on everything with an impartial eye.
-*Shri Purohit Swami (1882-1941)*

What a wee little part of a person's life are his acts and his words! His real life is led in his head, and is known to none but himself.
-*Mark Twain (1835-1910)*

Thousands of candles can be lit from a single candle, and the life of the candle will not be shortened. Happiness never decreases by being shared.
-*Gautama Buddha*

What if a demon were to creep after you one night, in your loneliest loneliness, and say, 'This life which you live must be lived by you once again and innumerable times more; and every pain and joy and thought and sigh must come again to you, all in the same sequence. The eternal hourglass will again and again be turned and you with it, dust of the dust!' Would you throw yourself down and gnash your teeth and curse that demon? Or would you answer, 'Never have I heard anything more divine'?
-*Friedrich Nietzsche (1844-1900)*

We can have in life but one great experience at best, and the secret of life is to reproduce that experience as often as possible.
-*Oscar Wilde (1854-1900)*

One of the hardest things in life is watching the person you love, love someone else.
-*Anon*

What we are today comes from our thoughts of yesterday, and our present thoughts build our life of tomorrow: Our life is the creation of our mind.
-*Gautama Buddha*

What is human life? The first third a good time; the rest remembering about it.
-*Mark Twain (1835-1910)*

To laugh often and much; to win the respect of intelligent people and the affection of children...to leave the world a better place...to know even one life has breathed easier because you have lived. This is to have succeeded.
-*Ralph Waldo Emerson (1803-82)*

Never mistake knowledge for wisdom. One helps you make a living; the other helps you make a life.
-*Eleanor Roosevelt (1884 – 1962)*

There are two primary choices in life: to accept conditions as they exist, or accept the responsibility for changing them.
-*Denis Waitley (1933-)*

Let us not underestimate the privileges of the mediocre. As one climbs higher, life becomes ever harder; the coldness increases, responsibility increases.
-*Friedrich Nietzsche (1844-1900)*

It is not length of life, but depth of life.
-*Ralph Waldo Emerson (1803-82)*

Life is the art of drawing without an eraser.
-*John W. Gardner (1912-2002)*

Life wastes itself while we are preparing to live.
-*Ralph Waldo Emerson (1803-82)*

Believe me! The secret of reaping the greatest fruitfulness and the greatest enjoyment from life is to live dangerously!

-*Friedrich Nietzsche (1844-1900)*

Life is like riding a bicycle. To keep your balance you must keep moving.
-*Albert Einstein (1879-1955)*

There is only one happiness in this life, to love and be loved.
-*George Sand (1804-76)*

Execute every act of thy life as though it were thy last.
-*Marcus Aurelius (121-180 AD)*

If I had my life to live over again, I'd be a plumber.
-*Albert Einstein (1879-1955)*

Live life so completely that when death comes to you like a thief in the night, there will be nothing left for him to steal.
-*Anon*

When I hear somebody sigh, "Life is hard," I am always tempted to ask, "Compared to what?"
-*Sydney J Harris (1917-86)*

This life is yours. Take the power to choose what you want to do and do it well. Take the power to love what you want in life and love it honestly. Take the power to walk in the forest and be a part of nature. Take the power to control your own life. No one else can do it for you. Take the power to make your life happy.
-*Susan Polis Schutz (1944 -)*

Of course life is bizarre, the more bizarre it gets, the more interesting it is. The only way to approach it is to make yourself some popcorn and enjoy the show.
David Gerrold (1944 -)

Life isn't weird: it's just the people in it.
-*Anon*

Look at life through the windshield, not the rear-view mirror.
-*Byrd Baggett (1949-)*

If you believed more in life you would fling yourself less to the moment.
-*Friedrich Nietzsche (1844-1900)*

Life is 10% what happens to you and 90% how you react to it.
-*Charles R Swindoll (1934-)*

When we remember we are all mad, the mysteries disappear and life stands explained.
-*Mark Twain (1835-1910)*

Life is really simple, but we insist on making it complicated.
-*Confucius (551-479 BC)*

Life is too important to be taken seriously.
-*Oscar Wilde (1854-1900)*

When I look back on all these worries, I remember the story of the old man who said on his deathbed that he had had a lot of trouble in his life, most of which had never happened.
-*Winston Churchill (1874-1965)*

To live in this world, you must be able to do three things: to love what is mortal; to hold it against your bones knowing your own life depends on it; and, when the time comes to let it go, to let it go.
-*Mary Oliver (1935 -)*

I believe you should live each day as if it is your last, which is why I don't have any clean laundry, because, come on, who wants to wash clothes on the last day of their life?
-*Albert Einstein (1879 – 1955)*

Pain makes man think. Thought makes man wise. Wisdom makes life endurable.
-*John Patrick (1905 – 95)*

To be idle is a short road to death and to be diligent is a way of life; foolish people are idle, wise people are diligent.
-*Dwight Goddard (1861 – 1939)*

Life is like a piano... what you get out of it depends on how you play it.
-*Tom Lehrer (1928 -)*

One of the hardest things in life is having words in your heart that you can't utter.
-*James Earl Jones (1931 -)*

Your life does not get better by chance, it gets better by change.
-*Jim Rohn (1930 – 2009)*

Don't worry about life, you're not going to survive it anyway.
-Anon

The soul is born old but grows young. That is the comedy of life. And the body is born young and grows old. That is life's tragedy.
-Oscar Wilde (1854-1900)

The greatest happiness of life is the conviction that we are loved - loved for ourselves, or rather, loved in spite of ourselves.
-Victor Hugo (1802-85)

I think of life as a good book. The further you get into it, the more it begins to make sense.
-Harold Kushner (1935 -)

I really don't think life is about the I-could-have-beens. Life is only about the I-tried-to-do. I don't mind the failure but I can't imagine that I'd forgive myself if I didn't try.
-Nikki Giovanni (1943-)

The tragedy of life is not that it ends so soon, but that we wait so long to begin it.
-W.M. Lewis (1878 – 1945)

Life's challenges are not supposed to paralyze you, they're supposed to help you discover who you are.
-Bernice Johnson Reagon (1942-)

The hardest thing in life is to know which bridge to cross and which to burn.
-David Russell (1942-)

Life is all about timing... the unreachable becomes reachable, the unavailable become available, the unattainable... attainable. Have the patience, wait it out. It's all about timing.
-*Stacey Charter (1970 -)*

If I had to live my life again, I'd make the same mistakes, only sooner.
-*Tallulah Bankhead (1903-68)*

How much of human life is lost in waiting.
-*Ralph Waldo Emerson (1803-82)*

Only a life lived for others is worth living.
-*Albert Einstein (1879-1955)*

Life is a great big canvas, and you should throw all the paint you can on it.
-*Danny Kaye (1913-87)*

Death is not the greatest loss in life. The greatest loss is what dies inside us while we live.
-*Norman Cousins (1912-90)*

What a wonderful life I've had! I only wish I'd realized it sooner.
-*Sidonie-Gabrielle Collette (1873 – 1954)*

The man who regards his own life and that of his fellow creatures as meaningless is not merely unfortunate but almost disqualified for life.
-*Albert Einstein (1879-1955)*

Life has no rehearsals, only performances.
-*Anon*

The major value in life is not what you get. The major value in life is what you become.
-*Jim Rohn (1930 – 2009)*

Life is dull only to dull people.
-*Brian Zilinek*

Do you believe in immortality? No, and one life is enough for me.
-*Albert Einstein (1879-1955)*

Life is just one damned thing after another.
-*Elbert Hubbard (1856-1915)*

Life is like an onion: you peel it off one layer at a time, and sometimes you weep.
-*Carl Sandburg (1878-1967)*

Life, like a mirror, never gives back more than we put into it.
-*Anon*

It's easy to let life deteriorate into making a living instead of making a life.
-*Jim Rohn (1930 – 2009)*

The paradox of courage is that a man must be a little careless of his life even in order to keep it.
-*GK Chesterton (1874-1936)*

Life is the greatest bargain - we get it for nothing.
-*Yiddish proverb*

Sometimes the answer to prayer is not that it changes life, but that it changes you.
-*James Dillet Freeman (1912 – 2003)*

The true object of all human life is play.
-GK Chesterton (1874-1936)

A good friend is a connection to life- a tie to the past, a road to the future, the key to sanity in a totally insane world.
-Lois Wyse (1926 – 2007)

Wealth is the ability to fully experience life.
-Henry David Thoreau (1817-62)

You have enemies? Good. That means you've stood up for something, sometime in your life.
-Winston Churchill (1874-1965)

The best years of your life are the ones in which you decide your problems are your own. You do not blame them on your mother, the ecology, or the president. You realize that you control your own destiny.
-Albert Ellis (1913-)

Today, you have 100% of your life left.
-Tom Landry (1924 – 2000)

Life is suffering.
-Prince Gautama Siddharta (563-483 BC)

The only thing that stands between a man and what he wants from life is often merely the will to try it and the faith to believe that it is possible.
-David Viscott (1938 – 1996)

You will never change your life until you change something you do daily.
-John C Maxwell (1947 -)

Life is partly what we make it, and partly what it is made by the friends we choose.
-*Tennessee Williams (1911-83)*

It is always the simple things that change our lives. And these things never happen when you are looking for them to happen. Life will reveal answers at the pace life wishes to do so. You feel like running, but life is on a stroll. This is how God does things.
-*Donald Miller (1971 -)*

One of the secrets of a long and fruitful life is to forgive everybody everything before you go to bed.
-*Ann Landers (1918 – 2002)*

Our choices in life are made according to our sense of our own worth.
-*Kaylan Pickford (1930 - 2004)*

You leave old habits behind by starting out with the thought, 'I release the need for this in my life'.
-*Wayne Dyer (1940-)*

Change is the essence of life. Be willing to surrender what you are for what you could become.
-*Reinhold Niebuhr (1892 – 1971)*

Life's real failure is when you do not realize how close you were to success when you gave up.
-*Anon*

You see, in life, lots of people know what to do, but few people actually do what they know. Knowing is not enough! You must take action.
-*Anthony Robbins (1960 -)*

Life has no meaning the moment you lose the illusion of being eternal.
-*Jean Paul Sartre (1905-1980)*

The secret of success is learning how to use pain and pleasure instead of having pain and pleasure use you. If you do that, you're in control of your life. If you don't, life controls you.
-*Anthony Robbins (1960 -)*

God allows us to experience the low points of life in order to teach us lessons we could not learn in any other way. The way we learn those lessons is not to deny the feelings but to find the meanings underlying them.
-*Stanley Lindquist*

Life is mostly froth and bubble. Two things stand like stone, kindness in another's trouble, courage in your own.
-*Adam Lindsay Gordon (1833 – 1870)*

Friends are helpful not only because they will listen to us, but because they will laugh at us; through them we learn a little objectivity, a little modesty, a little courtesy; We learn the rules of life and become better players of the game.
-*Will Durant (1885 – 1981)*

Reality continues to ruin my life.
-*Bill Watterson (1958 -)*

Think of the long view of life, not just what's going to happen today or tomorrow. Don't give up what you most want in life for something you think you want now.
-*Elder Richard G Scott (1928 -)*

Life gives us brief moments with another...but sometimes in those brief moment we get memories that last a life time...
-*Anon*

Unless a life is lived for others, it is not worthwhile.
-*Mother Theresa (1910-97)*

The life of every man is a diary in which he means to write one story, and writes another.
-*James Matthew Barrie (1860-1937)*

Dreams do come true, if we only wish hard enough. You can have anything in life if you will sacrifice everything else for it.
-*James Matthew Barrie (1860-1937)*

Life is never fair, and perhaps it is a good thing for most of us that it is not.
-*Oscar Wilde (1854-1900)*

The biggest adventure you can take is to live the life of your dreams.
-*Oprah Winfrey (1954 -)*

I find my life is a lot easier the lower I keep everyone's expectations.
-*Bill Watterson (1958 -)*

Life is never easy for those who dream.
-*Robert James Waller (1939 -)*

Life is thickly sown with thorns, and I know no other remedy than to pass quickly through them. The longer we dwell on our misfortunes, the greater is their power to harm us.
-*Voltaire (1694-1778)*

I am more and more convinced that our happiness or our unhappiness depends far more on the way we meet the events of life than on the nature of those events themselves.
-*Karl Wilhelm Humboldt (1767 – 1835)*

Each player must accept the cards life deals him or her: but once they are in hand, he or she alone must decide how to play the cards in order to win the game.
-*Voltaire (1694 - 1778)*

The price of anything is the amount of life you exchange for it.
-*Henry David Thoreau (1817-62)*

We make a living by what we get, but we make a life by what we give.
-*Winston Churchill (1874-1965)*

Most people fail in life because they major in minor things.
-*Anthony Robbins (1960 -)*

In life as in dance: Grace glides on blistered feet.
-*Alice Abrams*

Life is inherently risky. There is only one big risk you should avoid at all costs, and that is the risk of doing nothing.
-*Denis Waitley (1933 -)*

The more you praise and celebrate your life, the more there is in life to celebrate.
-*Oprah Winfrey (1954 -)*

Life is not a spectator sport.
-*Jackie Robinson (1919 – 72)*

He can who thinks he can, and he can't who thinks he can't. This is an inexorable, indisputable law.
-Pablo Picasso (1881 – 1973)

I don't know if mama was right, that we each have a destiny, or if it was Lt Dan, that we are all just floating around, accidental, like on a breeze, but I think... I think... maybe... it's both happening at the same time.
-Winston Groom (1943 -), Forrest Gump

I don't want to get to the end of my life and find that I lived just the length of it. I want to have lived the width of it as well.
-Diane Ackerman (1948 -)

Logic will get you from A to B. Imagination will take you everywhere.
-Albert Einstein (1879 – 1955)

Such is life.
-Ned Kelly (1854 – 80)

It may be that your sole purpose in life is to serve as a warning to others.
-Anon

Some mistakes are too much fun to only make once
-Anon

Prejudices are what fools use for reason.
-Voltaire (1694 – 1778)

Contraceptives should be used on every conceivable occasion.
-Spike Milligan (1918 – 2002

Imagination is everything. It is the preview of life's coming attractions.
-Albert Einstein (1879-1955)

Life doesn't imitate art, it imitates bad television.
-Woody Allen (1935 -)

The difference between school and life? In school, you're taught a lesson and then given a test. In life, you're given a test that teaches you a lesson.
-Tom Bodett (1955-)

Imagination is the one weapon in the war against reality.
-Jules de Gaultier (1858 – 1942)

Life does not consist mainly, or even largely, of facts and happenings. It consists mainly of the storm of thought that is forever flowing through one's head.
-Mark Twain (1835-1910)

A hundred years from now it will not matter what my bank account was, the sort of house I lived in, or the kind of car I drove...but the world may be different because I was important in the life of a child.
-Forest E Witcraft (1894-1967)

Don't go through life, grow through life.
-Eric Butterworth (1916-)

There are only two tragedies in life: one is not getting what one wants, and the other is getting it.
-Oscar Wilde (1854-1900)

DEATH

Death must be so beautiful. To lie in the soft brown earth, with the grasses waving above one's head, and listen to silence. To have no yesterday, and no to-morrow. To forget time, to forgive life, to be at peace.
-Oscar Wilde (1854-1900)

Live life so completely that when death comes to you like a thief in the night, there will be nothing left for him to steal.
-Anon

Courage is the art of being the only one who knows you're scared to death.
-Earl Wilson (1907-87)

Life is the illusion Death is the ultimate truth.
-Anon

The only difference between death and taxes is that death doesn't get worse every time Congress meets.
-Will Rogers (1879-35)

Death is nothing, but to live defeated and inglorious is to die daily.
-Napoleon Bonaparte (1769-1821)

Death takes no bribes.
-Benjamin Franklin (1706-90)

Death is one moment, and life is so many of them.
-Tennessee Williams (1911-83)

Death does not concern us, because as long as we exist, death is not here. And when it does come, we no longer exist.
-*Epicurus (341 BC – 270 BC)*

It is necessary to have wished for death in order to know how good it is to live.
-*Alexandre Dumas (1802-70)*

Life and death are one thread, the same line viewed from different sides.
-*Lao Tzu (604 BC – 531 BC)*

I am not afraid of death, I just don't want to be there when it happens.
-*Woody Allen (1935-)*

In gardens, beauty is a by-product. The main business is sex and death.
-*Sam Llewelyn (1948-)*

Death is nature's way of telling you to slow down.
-*Anon*

Men like war: they do not hold much sway over birth, so they make up for it with death. Unlike women, men menstruate by shedding other people's blood.
-*Lucy Ellmann (1956-)*

Who knows what death is? Maybe life is nothing more than a beam of light passing slowly over our changing faces.
-*Anon*

Absence and death are the same - only that in death there is no suffering.
-*Theodore Roosevelt (1858-1919)*

Art is the tree of life. Science is the tree of death. God is Jesus.
-*William Blake (1757-1827)*

Death may be the greatest of all human blessings.
-*Socrates (470/469 BC – 399 BC)*

Leisure without literature is death and burial alive.
-*Seneca (4 BC – 65 AD)*

Poverty is death in another form.
-*Latin proverb*

People fear death even more than pain. It's strange that they fear death. Life hurts a lot more than death. At the point of death, the pain is over. Yeah, I guess it is a friend...
-*Jim Morrison (1943-71)*

There's no tragedy in life like the death of a child. Things never get back to the way they were.
-*Dwight David Eisenhower (1890-1969)*

Fear of death has been the greatest ally of tyranny past and present.
-*Sidney Hook (1902- 89)*

No one ever choked to death swallowing his pride.
-*Anon*

Cowards die many times before their deaths; the valiant never taste of death but once.
-*William Shakespeare (1564-1616)*

Our death is not an end if we can live on in our children and the younger generation. For they are us, our bodies are only wilted leaves on the tree of life.
-*Albert Einstein (1879-1955)*

What you possess in the world will be found at the day of your death to belong to someone else. But what you are will be yours forever.
-*Henry Van Dyke (1852-1933)*

I am become death, the destroyer of worlds.
-*J. Robert Oppenheimer (1904-67)*

A person starts dying when they stop dreaming.
-*William Blake (1757-1827)*

No poor bastard ever won a war by dying for his country. He won it by making other bastards die for their country.
-*General George S. Patton (1885-1945)*

I don't want to achieve immortality through my work. I want to achieve it through not dying.
-*Woody Allen (1935-)*

Dying is a very dull, dreary affair. And my advice to you is to have nothing whatever to do with it.
-*William Somerset Maugham (1874-1965)*

Anyone who has ever looked into the glazed eyes of a soldier dying on the battlefield will think hard before starting a war.
-*Otto von Bismarck (1815-98)*

There are many things worth living for, a few things worth dying for, and nothing worth killing for.
-*Tom Robbins (1932-)*

Life is not lost by dying; life is lost minute by minute, day by dragging day, in all the thousand small uncaring ways.
-*Stephen Vincent Benet (1898-1943)*

The fear of death is the most unjustified of all fears, for there's no risk of accident for someone who's dead.
-*Albert Einstein (1879-1955)*

Dying is easy. Comedy is difficult.
-*Edmund Gwenn (1877-1959)*

To die would be an awfully big adventure.
-*J.M. Barrie (1860 – 1937)*

All men are cremated equal.
-*Spike Milligan (1918 – 2002)*

MORALITY

Morality is a venereal disease. Its primary stage is called virtue; its secondary stage, boredom; its tertiary stage, syphilis.
-*Karl Kraus (1874 – 1936)*

Morality is herd instinct in the individual.
-*Friedrich Nietzsche (1844 - 1900)*

'Wrong' is one of those concepts that depends on witnesses.
-*Scott Adams (1957 -)*

Do you know why I have credibility? Because I don't exude morality.
-*Bob Hawke (1929 -)*

The media loved him. Why? Because he was a great exemplar of the new morality - in which you are judged not by your own sins, but by how savagely you damn those of others.
-*Andrew Bolt (1959 -)*

It is long accepted by the missionaries that morality is inversely proportional to the amount of clothing people wore.
-*Alex Carey (1922 – 88)*

A wowser is...a person who is more shocked at seeing two inches of underskirt than a mountain of misery.
-*John Scaddan (1876 – 1934)*

It is amazing how complete is the delusion that beauty is goodness.
-*Leo Tolstoy (1828 – 1910)*

Force always attracts men of low morality.
-*Albert Einstein (1879 – 1955)*

The most important human endeavor is the striving for morality in our actions. Our inner balance and even our very existence depend on it. Only morality in our actions can give beauty and dignity to life.
-*Albert Einstein (1879 – 1955)*

A man that has lost moral sense is like a man in battle with both of his legs shot off: he has nothing to stand on.
-*Henry Ward Beecher (1813 – 87)*

Fear is the mother of morality.
-*Friedrich Nietzsche (1844 – 1900)*

If one should desire to know whether a kingdom is well governed, if its morals are good or bad, the quality of its music will furnish the answer.
-*Confucius (551 – 479 BC)*

Morality consists in suspecting other people of not being legally married.
-*George Bernard Shaw (1856 – 1950)*

Morality is the custom of one's country and the current feeling of one's peers. Cannibalism is moral in a cannibal country.
-*Samuel Butler (1835 - 1902)*

I have to live for others and not for myself; that's middle class morality.
-*George Bernard Shaw (1856 – 1950)*

The purpose of morality is to teach you, not to suffer and die, but to enjoy yourself and live.
-Ayn Rand (1905 - 82)

Morality is the weakness of the brain.
-Arthur Rimbaud (1854 – 91)

It's easy enough to preach morality on a full belly.
-Erwin Sylvanus (1917 - 85)

Money, not morality, is the principle of commerce and commercial nations.
-Thomas Jefferson (1762 – 1826)

Too cheerful a morality is a loose morality; it is appropriate only to decadent peoples and is found only among them.
-Emile Durkheim (1858 – 1917)

A man does what he must-in spite of personal consequences, in spite of obstacles and dangers and pressures-and that is the basis of all human morality.
-John Fitzgerald Kennedy (1917 – 63)

I say that a man must be certain of his morality for the simple reason that he has to suffer for it.
-G. K. Chesterton (1874 - 1936)

An Englishman thinks he is moral when he is only uncomfortable.
-George Bernard Shaw (1856 - 1950)

The people who are regarded as moral luminaries are those who forego ordinary pleasures themselves and find compensation in interfering with the pleasures of others.
-Bertrand Russell (1872 - 1970)

Force and mind are opposites; morality ends where a gun begins.
-Ayn Rand (1905 - 82)

To set up as a standard of public morality a notion which can neither be defined nor conceived is to open the door to every kind of tyranny.
-Simone Weil (1909 – 43)

Let us with caution indulge the supposition that morality can be maintained without religion. Reason and experience both forbid us to expect that national morality can prevail in exclusion of religious principle.
-George Washington (1732 - 99)

Learn to distinguish the difference between errors of knowledge and breaches of morality.
-Ayn Rand (1905 - 82)

Respect for the truth comes close to being the basis for all morality.
-Frank Herbert (1920 -86)

The books that the world calls immoral are books that show the world its own shame.
-Oscar Wilde (1854 – 1900)

It's discouraging to think how many people are shocked by honesty and how few by deceit.
-Noël Coward (1899 – 1973)

It is forbidden to kill; therefore all murderers are punished unless they kill in large numbers and to the sound of trumpets.
-Voltaire (1694 – 1778)

The higher the buildings, the lower the morals.
-*Noel Coward (1899 - 1973)*

Morality, like art, means drawing a line someplace.
-*Oscar Wilde (1854 - 1900)*

Scandal is gossip made tedious by morality.
-*Oscar Wilde (1854 - 1900)*

Compassion is the basis of morality.
-*Arthur Schopenhauer (1788 – 1860)*

Always do what is right. It will gratify half of mankind and astound the other.
-*Mark Twain (1835 – 1910)*

Moral indignation is jealousy with a halo.
-*H.G. Wells (1866 – 1946)*

Do not be too moral. You may cheat yourself out of much life so. Aim above morality. Be not simply good, be good for something.
-*Henry David Thoreau (1817 -62)*

If your morals make you dreary, depend on it, they are wrong.
-*Robert Louis Stevenson (1850 - 1894)*

The greatness of a nation and its moral progress can be judged by the way its animals are treated.
-*Mahatma Gandhi (1869 – 1948)*

The hottest places in hell are reserved for those who, in times of great moral crisis, maintain their neutrality.
-*John F. Kennedy (1917 -65)*

The spread of evil is the symptom of a vacuum. Whenever evil wins, it is only by default: by the moral failure of those who evade the fact that there can be no compromise on basic principles.
-*Ayn Rand (1905 -82)*

The pendulum of the mind oscillates between sense and nonsense, not between right and wrong.
-*C.G. Jung (1875 – 1961)*

Those who are easily shocked should be shocked more often.
-*Mae West (1893 – 1980)*

Do not be deceived: bad company corrupts good morals.
-*Anon*

Modern morality and manners suppress all natural instincts, keep people ignorant of the facts of nature and make them fighting drunk on bogey tales.
-*Aleister Crowley (1875 – 1947)*

Real integrity is doing the right thing, knowing that nobody's going to know whether you did it or not.
-*Oprah Winfrey (1954 -)*

In a word, I was too cowardly to do what I knew to be right, as I had been too cowardly to avoid doing what I knew to be wrong.
-*Charles Dickens (1812 -70)*

Without freedom there can be no morality.
-*Carl Jung (1875 – 1961)*

There is no such thing as a moral or an immoral book. Books are well written, or badly written. That is all.
-*Oscar Wilde (1854 – 1900)*

So far, about morals, I know only that what is moral is what you feel good after and what is immoral is what you feel bad after.
-*Ernest Hemingway (1899 – 1961)*

I learned from him that often contradiction is the clearest way to truth.
-*Patti Smith (1946 -)*

The essence of immorality is the tendency to make an exception of myself.
-*Jane Addams (1860 – 1935)*

To educate a person in the mind but not in morals is to educate a menace to society.
-*Theodore Roosevelt (1858 – 1919)*

Most of the evil in this world is done by people with good intentions.
-*T.S. Eliot (1888 – 1965)*

The assumption that animals are without rights and the illusion that our treatment of them has no moral significance is a positively outrageous example of Western crudity and barbarity. Universal compassion is the only guarantee of morality.
-*Arthur Schopenhauer (1788 – 1860)*

I am a humanist, which means, in part, that I have tried to behave decently without expectations of rewards or punishments after I am dead.
-*Kurt Vonnegut (1922 – 2007)*

If no set of moral ideas were truer or better than any other, there would be no sense in preferring civilized morality to savage morality.
-*C.S. Lewis (1898 – 1963)*

Right is right even if no one is doing it; wrong is wrong even if everyone is doing it.
-Augustine of Hippo (354 – 430 AD)

War does not decide who is right but who is left.
-George Bernard Shaw (1856 – 1950)

A quiet conscience makes one strong!
-Anne Frank (1929 -45)

Conventionality is not morality. Self-righteousness is not religion. To attack the first is not to assail the last.
-Charlotte Brontë (1816 – 55)

Never let your sense of morals prevent you from doing what is right!
-Isaac Asimov (1920 -92)

No moral system can rest solely on authority.
-A. J. Ayer (1910 - 1989)

CHAPTER 4 FACT AND FICTION

KNOWLEDGE

A man's errors are his portals of discovery.
-*James Joyce (1882 – 1941)*

A fool can throw a stone in a pond that a 100 wise men can't get out.
-*Saul Bellow*

Sometimes I'm confused by what I think is really obvious. But what I think is really obvious obviously isn't obvious.
-*Michael Stipe (1960 -)*

We are not so much as disillusioned but illusion free.
-*Miranda Devine (1960 -)*

Nothing that is worth knowing can be taught.
-*Oscar Wilde (1854 – 1900)*

I love talking about nothing. It is the only thing I know anything about.
-*Oscar Wilde (1854 – 1900)*

Knowing is not enough; we must apply. Willing is not enough; we must do.
-*Johann Wolfgang von Goethe (1749 – 1832)*

Information is not knowledge.
-*Albert Einstein (1879 – 1955)*

Knowledge is of no value unless you put it into practice.
-*Anton Chekov (1860 -1904)*

Thinking is more interesting than knowing, but less interesting than looking.
-*Johann Wolfgang von Goethe (1749 – 1832)*

You know more than you think you know, just as you know less than you want to know.
-*Oscar Wilde (1854 – 1910)*

Knowing others is wisdom, knowing yourself is enlightenment.
-*Lao Tzu (600 – 531 BC)*

We can understand almost anything, but we can't understand how we understand.
-*Albert Einstein (1879 – 1955)*

The only source of knowledge is experience.
-*Albert Einstein (1879 – 1955)*

I am not young enough to know everything.
-*Oscar Wilde (1854 – 1910)*

Imagination is more important than knowledge. Knowledge is limited. Imagination encircles the world.
-*Albert Einstein (1879 – 1955)*

To know that we know what we know, and that we do not know what we do not know, that is true knowledge.
-*Henry David Thoreau (1817 – 62)*

Beware of false knowledge; it is more dangerous than ignorance.
-*George Bernard Shaw (1856 – 1950)*

I believe that imagination is stronger than knowledge - myth is more potent than history - dreams are more powerful than facts - hope always triumphs over experience - laughter is the cure for grief - love is stronger than death.
-Robert Fulghum (1837 -)

Knowledge is a process of piling up facts; wisdom lies in their simplification.
-Martin H Fischer (1879 – 62)

To know and not to do is not to know.
-Proverb

Better know nothing than half-know many things.
-Friedrich Nietzsche (1844 – 1900)

All wish to possess knowledge, but few, comparatively speaking, are willing to pay the price.
-Juvenal (55 – 139 AD)

Those that know, do. Those that understand, teach.
-Aristotle (384 – 322 BC)

To appreciate the beauty of a snowflake, it is necessary to stand out in the cold.
-Aristotle (384 – 322 BC)

A conclusion is the place where you got tired thinking.
-Martin H Fischer (1879 – 62)

Real knowledge is to know the extent of one's ignorance.
- Confucius (551 – 479BC)

Those who have knowledge, don't predict. Those who predict, don't have knowledge.
-Lao Tzu (600 – 531 BC)

Those who know nothing of foreign languages know nothing of their own.
-Johann Wolfgang von Goethe (1749 – 1832)

I'm not young enough to know everything.
-James Matthew Barrie (1860 – 1937)

There is a great difference between knowing and understanding: you can know a lot about something and not really understand it.
-Charles F Kettering (1876 – 1958)

Perplexity is the beginning of knowledge.
-Kahlil Gibran (1883 – 1931)

Discussion is an exchange of knowledge; an argument an exchange of ignorance.
-Robert Quillen (1887 – 1948)

The art and science of asking questions is the source of all knowledge.
-Thomas Berger (1924 – 2014)

The more you know, the less you understand.
-Proverb

This I know - that I know nothing.
-Plato (428 – 348 BC)

The possession of knowledge does not kill the sense of wonder and mystery. There is always more mystery.
-Anais Nin (1903 – 77)

There is no knowledge that is not power.
-Ralph Waldo Emmerson (1803 -82)

The learning and knowledge that we have, is, at the most, but little compared with that of which we are ignorant.
-Plato (428 – 348 BC)

Someday, in the distant future, our grandchildren's grandchildren will develop a new equivalent of our classrooms. They will spend many hours in front of boxes with fires glowing within. May they have the wisdom to know the difference between light and knowledge.
-Plato (428 – 348 BC)

All our knowledge has its origins in our perceptions.
-Leonardo da Vinci (1452 – 1519)

Learning is finding out what you already know.
-Richard Bach (1936 -)

All men are born with a nose and ten fingers, but no one was born with a knowledge of God.
-Voltaire (1694 – 1778)

Every person I work with knows something better than me. My job is to listen long enough to find it and use it.
-Jack Nichols (1938 – 2005)

Not to know is bad, not to wish to know is worse.
-Proverb

Where knowledge ends, religion begins.
-Benjamin Disraeli (1804 -81)

Never reveal all of yourself to other people; hold back something in reserve so that people are never quite sure if they really know you.
-Michael Korda (1933 -)

Knowledge exists to be imparted.
-Ralph Waldo Emmerson (1803 – 82)

There is much pleasure to be gained from useless knowledge.
-Bertrand Russell (1872 – 1970)

Whenever we're afraid, it's because we don't know enough. If we understood enough, we would never be afraid.
-Earl Nightingale (1921 -89)

Knowledge is power and enthusiasm pulls the switch.
-Steve Droke

The knowledge of God is very far from the love of Him.
-Blaise Pascal (1623 – 62)

The beginning of knowledge is the discovery of something we do not understand.
-Frank Herbert (1920 -86)

Wisdom is the right use of knowledge. To know is not to be wise. Many men know a great deal, and are all the greater fools for it. There is no fool so great a fool as a knowing fool. But to know how to use knowledge is to have wisdom.
-Charles H Spurgeon (1834 – 92)

If what Proust says is true, that happiness is the absence of fever, then I will never know happiness. For I am possessed by a fever for knowledge, experience, and creation.
-Anais Nin (1903 – 77)

Knowledge is a polite word for dead but not buried imagination.
-EE Cummings (1894 – 1962)

One thing they never tell you about child raising is that for the rest of your life, at the drop of a hat, you are expected to know your child's name and how old he or she is.
-Erma Bombeck (1927 – 96)

Wisdom sets bounds even to knowledge.
-Friedrich Nietzsche (1844 – 1900)

The more extensive a man's knowledge of what has been done, the greater will be his power of knowing what to do.
-Benjamin Disraeli (1804 – 91)

Play is the beginning of knowledge.
-George Dorsey (1868 – 1931)

When I examine myself and my methods of thought, I come to the conclusion that the gift of fantasy has meant more to me than any talent for abstract, positive thinking.
-Albert Einstein (1879 – 1955)

An investment in knowledge always pays the best interest.
-Benjamin Franklin (1706 -90)

Those people who develop the ability to continuously acquire new and better forms of knowledge that they can apply to their work and to their lives will be the movers and shakers in our society for the indefinite future.
-Brian Tracy (1944-)

Love takes up where knowledge leaves off.
-St Aquinas (1225 – 1274)

Suppose that we are wise enough to learn and know - and yet not wise enough to control our learning and knowledge, so that we use it to destroy ourselves? Even if that is so, knowledge remains better than ignorance.
-Isaac Asimov (1920 -92)

Knowledge comes, but wisdom lingers.
Alfred Lord Tennyson (1809 – 92)
I prefer tongue-tied knowledge to ignorant loquacity.
-Cicero (106 – 43 BC)

The one exclusive sign of thorough knowledge is the power of teaching.
-Aristotle (384 – 322 BC)

There can be no knowledge without emotion. We may be aware of a truth, yet until we have felt its force, it is not ours. To the cognition of the brain must be added the experience of the soul.
-Arnold Bennett (1867 – 1931)

Knowledge is being aware that fire can burn; wisdom is remembering the blister.
-Leo Tolstoy (1828 – 1910)

There is no substitute for accurate knowledge. Know yourself, know your business, know your men.
-Lee Iacocca (1924 -)

We can be knowledgeable with other men's knowledge but we cannot be wise with other men's wisdom.
-Michel de Montaigne (1533 – 1592)

Since we cannot know all that there is to be known about anything, we ought to know a little about everything.
-Blaise Pascal (1623 – 62)

The difference between risk and uncertainty is that you can attach a probability to risk but not to uncertainty.
-Frank Knight (1885 – 1972)

I wash my hands of those who imagine chattering to be knowledge, silence to be ignorance, and affection to be art.
-Kahlil Gibran (1883 – 1931)

Wonder rather than doubt is the root of knowledge.
-Abraham Joshua Heschel (1907 – 72)

It is the province of knowledge to speak, and it is the privilege of wisdom to listen.
-Oliver Wendell Holmes (1809 -94)

Knowledge slowly builds up what Ignorance in an hour pulls down.
-George Elliot (1819 -90)

Necessity is the mother of invention, it is true, but its father is creativity, and knowledge is the midwife.
-Jonathan Schattke (1966 -)

Knowledge is like money: the more one gets, the more one craves.
-Josh Billings (1818 – 85)

The greatest enemy of knowledge is not ignorance, it is the illusion of knowledge.
-Stephen Hawking (1942 -)

It is astounding to realize that perhaps half of all human knowledge has been discovered or created in the past century. But then again, so has half the bullshit.
-D. H. Futterman

A good decision is based on knowledge and not numbers.
-Plato (428 – 348 BC)

To acquire knowledge one must study; but to acquire wisdom one must observe.
-Marilyn vos Savant (1946 -)

Opinion is the medium between knowledge and ignorance.
-Plato (428 -348 BC)

No man's knowledge here can go beyond his experience.
-John Locke (1632 – 1704)

Confidence is ignorance. If you're feeling cocky, it's because there's something you don't know.
-Eoin Colfer (1965 -)

It is the absence of facts that frightens people: the gap you open, into which they pour their fears, fantasies, desires.
-Hilary Mantel (1952 -)

Write what you know. That should leave you with a lot of free time.
-*Howard Nemerov (1920 – 91)*

People don't care how much you know until they know how much you care.
-*Theodore Roosevelt (1858 – 1919)*

A woman, especially if she have the misfortune of knowing anything, should conceal it as well as she can.
-*Jane Austen (1775 – 1817)*

The knowledge of all things is possible.
-*Leonardo da Vinci (1452 – 1529)*

Your assumptions are your windows on the world. Scrub them off every once in a while, or the light won't come in.
-*Isaac Asimov (1920 – 92)*

I can calculate the motion of heavenly bodies but not the madness of people.
-*Isaac Newton (1643 – 1727)*

Small minds have always lashed out at what they don't understand.
-*Dan Brown (1964 -)*

The advancement and diffusion of knowledge is the only guardian of true liberty.
-*James Madison (1751 – 1836)*

There are known knowns; there are things we know we know. We also know there are known unknowns; that is to say we know there are some things we do not know. But there are also unknown unknowns -- the ones we don't know we don't know. And if one looks throughout the history of our country and other free countries, it is the latter category that tend to be the difficult ones.
-Donald Rumsfeld (1832 -)

The public have an insatiable curiosity to know everything, except what is worth knowing.
-Oscar Wilde (1854 – 1900)

The greatest obstacle to discovery is not ignorance—it is the illusion of knowledge.
-Daniel J Boorstin (1914 – 2004)

Blessed is the man who, having nothing to stay, abstains from giving us worthy evidence of the fact.
-George Eliot (1819 -80)

To be ignorant of one's ignorance is the malady of the ignorant.
-Amos Bronson Alcott (1799 – 1888)

Knowledge makes a man unfit to be a slave.
-Frederick Douglass (1818 – 1895)

That men do not learn very much from the lessons of history is the most important of all the lessons that History has to teach.
-Aldous Huxley (1894 – 1963)

An ignorant person is one who doesn't know what you have just found out."
-Will Rogers (1879 – 1935)

Logic will get you from A to B. Imagination will take you everywhere.
-Albert Einstein (1879 – 1955)

TRUTH

A thing is not necessarily true because a man dies for it.
-Oscar Wilde (1854 – 1900)

You can bend it and twist it... You can misuse and abuse it... But even God cannot change the Truth.
-Michael Levy (1944 -)

All truths are easy to understand once they are discovered; the point is to discover them.
-Galileo Galilei (1564 -1642)

The truth is rarely pure and never simple.
-Oscar Wilde (1854 – 1900)

If you tell the truth you don't have to remember anything.
-Mark Twain (1835 – 1910)

You never find yourself until you face the truth.
-Pearl Bailey (1918 – 1990)

Whoever is careless with the truth in small matters cannot be trusted with important matters.
-Albert Einstein (1879 – 1955)

When you are sorrowful look again in your heart, and you shall see that in truth you are weeping for that which has been your delight.
-Kahlil Gibran   (1883 – 1931)

The truth is incontrovertible, malice may attack it, ignorance may deride it, but in the end; there it is.

What you perceive, your observations, feelings, interpretations, are all your truth. Your truth is important. Yet it is not The Truth.
-Linda Ellinor

Unthinking respect for authority is the greatest enemy of truth.
-Albert Einstein (1879 -1955)

If you want your dreams to come true, don't sleep.
-Yiddish proverb

Never assume the obvious is true.
-William Safire (1929 – 2005)

The first reaction to truth is hatred.
-Tertullian (160-220AD)

Whenever you have truth it must be given with love, or the message and the messenger will be rejected.
-Mahatma Gandhi (1969 – 1948)

The search for truth is more precious than its possession.
-Albert Einstein (1879 – 1955)

Truth is like the sun. You can shut it out for a time, but it ain't goin' away.
-Elvis Presley (1935 -77)

The truth is not for all men, but only for those who seek it.
-Ayn Rand (1905 – 82)

It's no wonder that truth is stranger than fiction. Fiction has to make sense.

-Mark Twain (1835 – 1910)

It ain't what you don't know that's the problem. The problem is what you think you know which ain't true.
-Proverb

A lie gets halfway around the world before the truth has a chance to get its pants on.
-Winston Churchill (1874 – 1965)

Truth, in matters of religion, is simply the opinion that has survived.
-Oscar Wilde (1854 – 1900)

True holiness consists in doing God's will with a smile.
-Mother Theresa (1910 -77)

The love of truth has its reward in heaven and even on earth.
-Friedrich Nietzsche (1844 – 1900)

If you look for truth, you may find comfort in the end; if you look for comfort you will not get either comfort or truth only soft soap and wishful thinking to begin, and in the end, despair.
-CS Lewis (1898 – 1963)

The truth, of course, is that a billion falsehoods told a billion times by a billion people are still false.
-Travis Walton (1953 -)

Truth is beautiful, without doubt; but so are lies.
-Ralph Waldo Emmerson (1803 – 82)

The belief that there is only one truth, and that oneself is in possession of it, is the root of all evil in the world.

-Max Born (1882 – 1970)

There are very few human beings who receive the truth, complete and staggering, by instant illumination. Most of them acquire it fragment by fragment, on a small scale, by successive developments, cellularly, like a laborious mosaic.
-Anais Nin (1903 – 77)

Speak your truth quietly and clearly; and listen to others, even to the dull and the ignorant, they too have their story.
-Max Ehrman (1872 – 1945)

Truth is the property of no individual but is the treasure of all men.
-Ralph Waldo Emmerson (1803 -82)

Even if you are a minority of one, the truth is the truth.
-Mahatma Gandhi (1869 – 1948)

False face must hide what the false heart doth know.
-William Shakespeare (1564 – 1616)

Falsehood is cowardice, the truth courage.
-Hosea Ballou (1771 – 1852)

We seek the truth and will endure the consequences.
-Charles Seymour (1885 – 1963)

Truth is generally the best vindication against slander.
-Abraham Lincoln (1809 – 65)

In a controversy, the instant we feel anger, we have already ceased striving for truth and have begun striving for ourselves.
-Abraham J Herschel (1907 – 72)

Truth is by nature self-evident. As soon as you remove the cobwebs of ignorance that surround it, it shines clear.
-*Mahatma Gandhi (1869 – 1948)*

Half a truth is often a great lie.
-*Benjamin Franklin (1706 – 90)*

It is man that makes truth great, not truth that makes man great.
-*Confucius (551 – 449 BC)*

Truth is something which can't be told in a few words. Those who simplify the universe only reduce the expansion of its meaning.
-*Anais Nin (1903 -77)*

In seeking truth you have to get both sides of a story.
-*Walter Cronkite (1916 – 2009)*

The object of the superior man is truth.
-*Confucius (551 – 449 BC)*

Truth is the most valuable thing we have. Let us economize it.
-*Mark Twain (1835 – 1910)*

Every truth has four corners: as a teacher I give you one corner, and it is for you to find the other three.
-*Confucius (551 – 449 BC)*

Time discovers truth.
-*Seneca (4 BC – 65 AD)*

Today I bent the truth to be kind, and I have no regret, for I am far surer of what is kind than I am of what is true.
Robert Breault (1963 -)

Nothing hurts a new truth more than an old error.
-*Johann Wolfgang von Goethe (1749 – 1832)*

All truth is simple... is that not doubly a lie.
-*Friedrich Nietzsche (1844 – 1900)*

Remember that all through history the way of truth and love has always won. There have been tyrants and murderers and for a time they seem invincible but in the end, they always fall -- think of it, always.
-*Mahatma Gandhi (1869 – 1948)*

Truth exists, only falsehood has to be invented.
-*Georges Braque (1882 – 1963)*

Truth will always be truth, regardless of lack of understanding, disbelief or ignorance.
-*W Clement Stone (1902 – 2002)*

It takes two to speak truth, one to speak and another to hear.
-*Henry David Thoreau (1817 – 62)*

If you're going to tell people the truth, be funny or they'll kill you.
-*Billy Wilder (1906 – 2002)*

Tell your friend a lie. If he keeps it secret, then tell him the truth.
-*Proverb*

The naked truth is always better than the best dressed lie.
-*Ann Landers (1918 – 2002)*

He who sees the truth, let him proclaim it, without asking who is for it or who is against it.
-*Henry George*

Speak the truth, but leave immediately after.
-*Proverb*

Man will occasionally stumble over the truth, but most times he will pick himself up and carry on.
-*Winston Churchill (1874 – 1965)*

There's a world of difference between truth and facts. Facts can obscure the truth.
-*Maya Angelou (1914 – 2008)*

The greatest homage we can pay to truth is to use it.
-*Ralph Waldo Emmerson (1803 – 82)*

Truth is always strange.
-*Lord Byron (1788 – 1824)*

Death cancels everything but truth.
-*Proverb*

First and last, what is demanded of genius is love of truth.
-*Johann Wolfgang von Goethe (1749 – 1832)*

Truth, though it has many disadvantages, is at least changeless. You can always find it where you left it.
-*Phyllis Bottome (1884 – 1963)*

Facts are many, but the truth is one.
-*Rabindranath Tagore (1861 – 1941)*

Truth is not only violated by falsehood; it may be equally outraged by silence.
-*Henri Frederic Amiel (1821 – 81)*

Every truth has two sides; it is as well to look at both, before we commit ourselves to either.
-*Aesop (620 – 560 BC)*

It is perfectly monstrous the way people go about nowadays saying things against one, behind one's back, that are absolutely and entirely true.
-*Oscar Wilde (1854 – 1900)*

A vocabulary of truth and simplicity will be of service throughout your life.
-*Winston Churchill (1874 – 1965)*

No man, for any considerable period, can wear one face to himself and another to the multitude, without finally getting bewildered as to which one is true.
-*Nathaniel Hawthorne (1804 – 1864)*

Truth, when not sought after, rarely comes to light.
-*Oliver Wendell Holmes (1809 – 94)*

Peace if possible, truth at all costs.
-*Martin Luther (1483 – 1546)*

I speak the truth not so much as I would, but as much as I dare, and I dare a little more as I grow older.
-*Michel de Montaigne (1533 – 1592)*

Truth is a gem that is found at a great depth; whilst on the surface of this world, all things are weighed by the false scale of custom.
-*Lord Byron (1788 -1824)*

The color of truth is gray.
-*Andre Gide (1869 – 1951)*

Men have always detested women's gossip because they suspect the truth: their measurements are being taken and compared.
-*Erica Jong (1942 -)*

Truth is often eclipsed but never extinguished.
-*Titus Livy (59 BC – 17 AD)*

When in doubt, tell the truth.
-*Mark Twain (1835 – 1910)*

I think a man's duty is to find out where the truth is, or if he cannot, at least to take the best possible human doctrine and the hardest to disprove, and to ride on this like a raft over the waters of life.
-*Plato (428 – 348 BC)*

A lie stands on one leg, truth on two.
-*Benjamin Franklin (1706 – 90)*

Beyond a doubt truth bears the same relation to falsehood as light to darkness.
-*Leonardo da Vinci (1452 – 1519)*

Truth is so obscure in these times, and falsehood so established, that, uless we love the truth, we cannot know it.
-*Blaise Pascal (1623 – 62)*

He that takes truth for his guide, and duty for his end, may safely trust to God's providence to lead him alright.
-*Blaise Pascal (1623 – 62)*

The truth is a snare: you cannot have it, without being caught. You cannot have the truth in such a way that you catch it, but only in such a way that it catches you.
-*Soren Kirkegaard (1813 – 55)*

Of life's two chief prizes, beauty and truth, I found the first in a loving heart and the second in a labourer's hand.
-*Kahlil Gibran (1883 – 1931)*

Truth, like gold, is to be obtained not by its growth, but by washing away from it all that is not gold.
-*Leo Tolstoy (1828 – 1910)*

We should not pretend to understand the world only by the intellect. The judgement of the intellect is only part of the truth.
-*Carl Jung (1875 – 1961)*

Only enemies speak the truth; friends and lovers lie endlessly, caught in the web of duty.
-*Stephen King (1947 -)*

Truth is mighty and will prevail. There is nothing wrong with this, except that it ain't so.
-*Mark Twain (1835 – 1910)*

Every truth passes through three stages before it is recognized. In the first it is ridiculed, in the second it is opposed, in the third it is regarded as self-evident.
-*Arthur Schopenhauer (1788 – 1860)*

I never give them hell. I just tell the truth and they think its hell.
-*Harry S Truman (1884 – 1972)*

Truth alone wounds.
-*Napoleon Bonaparte (1769 – 1821)*

The pursuit of truth and beauty is a sphere of activity in which we are permitted to remain children all our lives.
-*Albert Einstein (1879 – 1955)*

All the truth in the world adds up to one big lie.
-*Bob Dylan (1941 -)*

The great enemy of the truth is very often not the lie - deliberate, contrived and dishonest - but the myth - persistent, persuasive and unrealistic.
-*John Fitzgerald Kennedy (1917 – 63)*

Poetry is nearer to vital truth than history.
-*Plato (428 – 348 BC)*

People say they love truth, but in reality they want to believe that which they love is true.
-*Robert J Ringer (1938 -)*

Those who know the truth are not equal to those who love it.
-*Confucius (551 – 479 BC)*

It is a truth universally acknowledged, that a single man in possession of a good fortune, must be in want of a wife.
-*Jane Austen (1775 – 1817)*

This above all; to thine own self be true.
-*William Shakespeare (1564 – 1616)*

In wine there is truth.
-*Roman proverb*

Man discovers truth by reason only, not by faith.
-Leo Tolstoy (1828 – 1910)

Truth, and goodness, and beauty, are but different faces of the same All.
-Ralph Waldo Emmerson (1803 – 82)

It is not because the truth is too difficult to see that we make mistakes... we make mistakes because the easiest and most comfortable course for us is to seek insight where it accords with our emotions - especially selfish ones.
-Alexander Solzhenitsyn (1918 – 2008)

It is in our idleness, in our dreams, that the submerged truth sometimes comes to the top.
-Virginia Wolfe (1882 – 1941)

How dreadful knowledge of the truth can be when there's no help in the truth.
-Sophocles (496 – 405 BC)

Learning is always rebellion... Every bit of new truth discovered is revolutionary to what was believed before. *-Margaret Lee Runbeck (1905 -56)*

Truth is not only stranger than fiction, it is more interesting.
-William Randolph (1650 – 1711)

The pursuit of truth shall set you free - even if you never catch up with it.
-Clarence Darrow (1857 – 1938)

How much truth can a spirit bear, how much truth can a spirit dare? ... that became for me more and more the real measure of value.
-Friedrich Nietzsche (1844 – 1900)

The opposite of a fact is falsehood, but the opposite of one profound truth may very well be another profound truth.
-Niels Bohr (1885 – 1962)

Advice is seldom welcome, and those who need it the most, like it the least.
-Lord Chesterfield (1694 – 1773)

During times of universal deceit, telling the truth becomes a revolutionary act.
-George Orwell (1903 -50)

Of course it's the same old story. Truth usually is the same old story.
-Margaret Thatcher (1925 – 2013)

Pain reaches the heart with electrical speed, but truth moves to the heart as slowly as a glacier.
-Barbara Kingsolver (1955 -)

The best ammunition against lies is the truth, there is no ammunition against gossip. It is like a fog and the clear wind blows it away and the sun burns it off.
-Ernest Hemmingway (1899 – 1961)

Truth has nothing to do with the number of people it convinces.
-Paul Claudel (1868 – 1955)

Fraud and falsehood only dread examination. Truth invites it.
-Samuel Johnson (1709 – 84)

When you shoot an arrow of truth, dip its point in honey.
-Arab proverb

Philosophy is the science which considers truth.
-Aristotle (384 – 322 BC)

By doubting we come at truth.
-Cicero (106 – 43 BC)

It is easier to find a score of men wise enough to discover the truth than to find one intrepid enough, in the face of opposition, to stand up for it.
-AA Hodge (1823 – 86)

Beware: some liars tell the truth.
-Arab proverb

When my information changes, I alter my conclusions. What do you do, sir?
-John Maynard Keynes (1883 – 1946)

LIES

I'm not upset that you lied to me, I'm upset that from now on I can't believe you.
-*Friedrich Nietzsche (1844 – 1900)*

Politeness is the art of choosing among one's real thoughts.
-*Abel Stevens (1815 – 97)*

I love you, and because I love you, I would sooner have you hate me for telling you the truth than adore me for telling you lies.
-*Pietro Aretino*

Sometimes I lie awake at night, and ask, 'Where have I gone wrong?' Then a voice says to me, 'This is going to take more than one night'.
-*Charles M Schulz/Charlie Brown (1922 – 2000)*

Tell your friend a lie. If he keeps it secret, then tell him the truth.
-*Proverb*

The naked truth is always better than the best dressed lie.
-*Ann Landers (1918 -2002)*

Make the lie big, make it simple, keep saying it, and eventually they will believe it.
-*Adolf Hitler (1889 – 1945)*

A half-truth is a whole lie.
-*Yiddish proverb*

The most common lie is that which one lies to himself; lying to others is relatively an exception.

-Friedrich Nietzsche (1844 – 1900)

Lying is done with words and also with silence.
-Adrienne Rich (1929 – 2012)

People do not believe lies because they have to, but because they want to.
-Malcolm Muggeridge (1903 -90)

It is easier to believe a lie that one has heard a thousand times than to believe a fact that no one has heard before.
-Robert D Ballard (1942 -)

The liar's punishment is not in the least that he is not believed, but that he cannot believe anyone else.
-George Bernard Shaw (1856 – 1950)

There are lies, damned lies and statistics.
-Mark Twain (1835 – 1910)

That God cannot lie, is no advantage to your argument, because it is no proof that priests cannot, or that the Bible does not.
-Thomas Paine (1737 – 1809)

I'm not smart enough to lie.
-Ronald Reagan (1911 – 2004)

Men hate those to whom they have to lie.
-Victor Hugo (1802 -85)

A half-truth is the worst of all lies, because it can be defended in partiality.
-Solon (638 - 558 BC)

When a well-packaged web of lies has been sold gradually to the masses over generations, the truth will seem utterly preposterous and its speaker a raving lunatic.
-Donald James Wheal (1931-2008)

To pretend to know when you do not know is a disease.
-Lao-Tzu (570-490 BC)

A truth that's told with bad intent, beats all the lies you can invent.
-William Blake (1757-1827)

Through clever and constant application of propaganda, people can be made to see paradise as hell, and also the other way round, to consider the most wretched sort of life as paradise.
-Adolf Hitler (1889 – 1945)

It's not a matter of what is true that counts but a matter of what is perceived to be true.
-Henry Kissinger (1923 -)

As scarce as truth is, the supply has always been in excess of the demand.
-Josh Billings (1818 – 1885)

The trust of the innocent is the liar's most useful tool.
-Stephen King (1947-)

The history of the race, and each individual's experience, are thick with evidence that a truth is not hard to kill and that a lie told well is immortal.
-Mark Twain (1835 – 1910)

Most of the greatest evils that man has inflicted upon man have come through people feeling quite certain about something which, in fact, was false.
-*Bertrand Russell (1872 – 1970)*

It is better to be defeated on principle than to win on lies.
-*Arthur Calwell (1896 – 1973)*

The longer the explanation, the bigger the lie.
-*Chinese Proverb*

PHYSICS

Now he has departed from this strange world a little ahead of me. That means nothing. People like us, who believe in physics, know that the distinction between past, present, and future is only a stubbornly persistent illusion.
-*Albert Einstein (1879 – 1955)*

The observer, when he seems to himself to be observing a stone, is really, if physics is to be believed, observing the effects of the stone upon himself.
-*Bertrand Russell (1872 – 1970)*

Relativity applies to physics, not ethics.
-*Albert Einstein (1879 – 1955)*

All science is either physics or stamp collecting.
-*Ernest Rutherford (1871 – 1937)*

Politics is far more complicated than physics.
-*Albert Einstein (1879 – 1955)*

If anybody says he can think about quantum physics without getting giddy, that only shows he has not understood the first thing about them.
-*Niels Bohr (1885 – 1962)*

In physics, you don't have to go around making trouble for yourself - nature does it for you.
-*Frank Wilczek (1951 -)*

Nothing is accidental in the universe -- this is one of my Laws of Physics -- except the entire universe itself, which is Pure Accident, pure divinity.
-*Joyce Carol Oates (1938 -)*

I am now convinced that theoretical physics is actually philosophy.
-*Max Born (1882 – 1970)*

In the beginning there was nothing, which exploded.
-*Terry Pratchett (1948-)*

Nothing happens until something moves.
-*Albert Einstein (1879 – 1955)*

Photons have mass? I didn't even know they were Catholic.
-*Woody Allen (1935 -)*

It is my task to convince you not to turn away because you don't understand it. You see my physics students don't understand it... That is because I don't understand it. Nobody does.
-*Richard P. Feynman (1918 – 88)*

Not only is the Universe stranger than we think, it is stranger than we can think.
-*Werner Heisenberg (1901 -76)*

It is often stated that of all the theories proposed in this century, the silliest is quantum theory. In fact, some say that the only thing that quantum theory has going for it is that it is unquestionably correct.
-*Michio Kaku (1947 -)*

Nonsense is that which does not fit into the prearranged patterns which we have superimposed on reality...Nonsense is nonsense only when we have not yet found that point of view from which it makes sense.
-Gary Zukav (1942 -)

A physicist learns more and more about less and less, until he knows everything about nothing; whereas a philosopher learns less and less about more and more, until he knows nothing about everything.
-Anon

The more the universe seems comprehensible the more it seems pointless.
-Steven Weinberg (1933 -)

The more success the quantum theory has, the sillier it looks.
-Albert Einstein (1879 – 1955)

God does not play dice.
-Albert Einstein (1879 – 1955)

Now he has departed from this strange world a little ahead of me. That means nothing. People like us, who believe in physics, know that the distinction between past, present, and future is only a stubbornly persistent illusion.
-Albert Einstein (1879 – 1955)

The observer, when he seems to himself to be observing a stone, is really, if physics is to be believed, observing the effects of the stone upon himself.
-Bertrand Russell (1872 – 1970)

Relativity applies to physics, not ethics.
-Albert Einstein (1879 – 1955)

All science is either physics or stamp collecting.
-Ernest Rutherford (1871 – 1937)

Politics is far more complicated than physics.
-Albert Einstein (1879 – 1955)

If anybody says he can think about quantum physics without getting giddy, that only shows he has not understood the first thing about them.
-Niels Bohr (1885 – 1962)

In physics, you don't have to go around making trouble for yourself - nature does it for you.
-Frank Wilczek (1951 -)

Nothing is accidental in the universe -- this is one of my Laws of Physics -- except the entire universe itself, which is Pure Accident, pure divinity.
-Joyce Carol Oates (1938 -)

I am now convinced that theoretical physics is actually philosophy.
-Max Born (1882 – 1970)

In the beginning there was nothing, which exploded.
-Terry Pratchett (1948 -)

Nothing happens until something moves.
-Albert Einstein (1879 – 1955)

Photons have mass? I didn't even know they were Catholic.
-Woody Allen (1935 -)

It is my task to convince you not to turn away because you don't understand it. You see my physics students don't understand it... That is because I don't understand it. Nobody does.
-Richard P. Feynman (1918 – 88)

Not only is the Universe stranger than we think, it is stranger than we can think.
-Werner Heisenberg (1901 -76)

It is often stated that of all the theories proposed in this century, the silliest is quantum theory. In fact, some say that the only thing that quantum theory has going for it is that it is unquestionably correct.
-Michio Kaku (1947 -)

Nonsense is that which does not fit into the prearranged patterns which we have superimposed on reality...Nonsense is nonsense only when we have not yet found that point of view from which it makes sense.
-Gary Zukav (1942 -)

A physicist learns more and more about less and less, until he knows everything about nothing; whereas a philosopher learns less and less about more and more, until he knows nothing about everything.
-Anon

The more the universe seems comprehensible the more it seems pointless.
-Steven Weinberg (1933 -)

The more success the quantum theory has, the sillier it looks.
-Albert Einstein (1879 – 1955)

God does not play dice with nature.
-Albert Einstein (1879 – 1955)

CHAPTER 5 INTELLIGENCE

WISDOM

Knowing others is intelligence; knowing yourself is true wisdom. Mastering others is strength; mastering yourself is true power.
-Lao Tzu (604 – 531 BC)

Be happy. It's one way of being wise.
-Sidonie Gabrielle Collette (1873 – 1954)

Wise men speak because they have something to say; Fools because they have to say something.
-Plato (428 – 348 BC)

In examinations, the foolish ask questions the wise cannot answer.
-Oscar Wilde (1854 – 1900)

Wisdom is not a product of schooling but of the lifelong attempt to acquire it.
-Albert Einstein (1979 – 1954)

Never mistake knowledge for wisdom. One helps you make a living; the other helps you make a life.
-Sandra Carey

God, grant me the serenity to accept the things I cannot change, the courage to change the things I can, and the wisdom to know the difference.
-Reinhold Niebuhr (1892 – 1971)

I know what I have given you. I do not know what you have received.
-*Antonio Porchia (1886 – 1968)*

Sometimes I lie awake at night, and ask, 'Where have I gone wrong?' Then a voice says to me, 'This is going to take more than one night'.
-*Charles M Schulz (1922 – 2000)*

The key to wisdom is knowing all the right questions.
-*John A Simone (1912 – 2000)*

Wisdom is knowing what to do next, skill is knowing how to do it, and virtue is doing it.
-*David Starr Jordan (1851 – 1931)*

A man only becomes wise when he begins to calculate the approximate depth of his ignorance.
-*Gian Carlo Menotti (1911 – 2007)*

Wisdom ceases to be wisdom when it becomes too proud to weep, too grave to laugh, and too selfish to seek other than itself.
-*Kahlil Gibran (1883 – 1931)*

The invariable mark of wisdom is to see the miraculous in the common.
-*Ralph Waldo Emmerson (1803 – 82)*

When an argument flares up, the wise man quenches it with silence.
-*Anon*

I do not think much of a man who is not wiser today than he was yesterday.
-Abraham Lincoln (1809 – 65)

When it is obvious that the goals cannot be reached, don't adjust the goals, adjust the action steps.
-Confucius (551 – 479 BC)

Knowing others is wisdom, knowing yourself is enlightenment.
-Lao Tzu (600 -531 BC)

Courageous, untroubled, mocking and violent-that is what Wisdom wants us to be. Wisdom is a woman, and loves only a warrior.
-Friedrich Nietzsche (1844 – 1900)

It is strange how often a heart must be broken before the years can make it wise.
-Sara Teasdale (1884 – 1933)

By three methods we may learn wisdom: first, by reflection, which is noblest; second, by imitation, which is easiest; and third, by experience, which is the most bitter.
-Confucius (551 – 479 BC)

Of all the things which wisdom provides to make life entirely happy, much the greatest is the possession of friendship.
-Epicurus (341 – 270 BC)

A wise man fights to win, but he is twice a fool who has no plan for possible defeat.
-Louis L'Amour (1908 – 88)

A wise man makes his own decisions, an ignorant man follows public opinion.
-*Chinese proverb*

No one can make you feel inferior without your consent.
-*Eleanor Roosevelt (1884 – 1962)*

The fool doth think he is wise, but the wise man knows himself to be a fool.
-*William Shakespeare (1564 – 1616)*

Knowing yourself is the beginning of all wisdom.
-*Aristotle (384 – 322 BC)*

The only true wisdom is in knowing you know nothing.
-*Socrates (469 – 399 BC)*

The saddest aspect of life right now is that science gathers knowledge faster than society gathers wisdom.
-*Isaac Asimov (1920 – 72)*

It is the mark of an educated mind to be able to entertain a thought without accepting it.
-*Aristotle (384 – 322 BC)*

Think before you speak. Read before you think.
-*Fran Lebowitz (1950)*

Turn your wounds into wisdom.
-*Oprah Winfrey (1986 -)*

The unexamined life is not worth living.
-*Socrates (469 – 399 BC)*

The simple things are also the most extraordinary things, and only the wise can see them.

-*Paulo Coelho (1947 -)*

God will not look you over for medals, degrees or diplomas but for scars.

-*Elbert Hubbard (1856 – 1915)*

Angry people are not always wise.

-*Jane Austen (1775 – 1817)*

Any fool can know. The point is to understand.

-*Albert Einstein (1879 – 1955)*

I'm not young enough to know everything.

-*J.M. Barrie (1860- 1937)*

Knowing others is intelligence; knowing yourself is true wisdom. Mastering others is strength; mastering yourself is true power. If you realize that you have enough, you are truly rich.

-*Lao Tzu (604 – 531)*

Knowledge speaks, but wisdom listens.

-*Jimi Hendrix (1942 – 70)*

Don't gain the world & lose your soul, wisdom is better than silver or gold.

-*Bob Marley (1945 – 81)*

There are three things all wise men fear: the sea in storm, a night with no moon, and the anger of a gentle man.

-*Patrick Rothfuss (1971 -)*

The man of knowledge must be able not only to love his enemies but also to hate his friends.
-*Friedrich Nietzsche (1844 – 1900)*

It is not that I'm so smart. But I stay with the questions much longer.
-*Albert Einstein (1879 – 1955)*

The measure of intelligence is the ability to change.
-*Albert Einstein (1879 – 1955)*

If you have nothing, then you have everything, because you have the freedom to do anything, without the fear of losing something.
-*Jarod Kintz (1982 -)*

Don't waste your time with explanations: people only hear what they want to hear.
-*Abraham Maslow (1908 -70)*

Even strength must bow to wisdom sometimes.
-*Rick Riordan (1964 -)*

He who knows all the answers has not been asked all the questions.
-*Confucius (551 – 479 BC)*

The older I grow, the more I distrust the familiar doctrine that age brings wisdom.
-*Henry Louis Mencken (1880 – 1956)*

I'm not waiting until my hair turns white to become patient and wise. Nope, I'm dying my hair tonight.
-*Jarod Kintz (1982 -)*

Common sense in an uncommon degree is what the world calls wisdom.

-Samuel Taylor Coleridge (1772 – 1834)

Sometimes one likes foolish people for their folly, better than wise people for their wisdom.

-Elizabeth Gaskell (1810 – 65)

Yesterday I was clever, so I wanted to change the world. Today I am wise, so I am changing myself.

-Rumi (1207 – 73)

Honesty is the first chapter of the book wisdom.

-Thomas Jefferson (1743 – 1826)

A wise man will make more opportunities than he finds.

-Francis Bacon (1561 – 1626)

Wonder is the beginning of wisdom.

-Socrates (469 – 399 BC)

It (1948 -) is one thing to be clever and another to be wise.

-George RR Martin

Wise? No, I simply learned to think.

-Christopher Paolini (1983 -)

Half of seeming clever is keeping your mouth shut at the right times.

-Patrick Rothfuss (1973 -)

Wisdom waits.

-Gary Amirault

I hope our wisdom will grow with our power, and teach us, that the less we use our power the greater it will be.
-Thomas Jefferson (1743 – 1826)

Wisdom is not wordy.
-Gary Amirault

Make men wise, and by that very operation you make them free. Civil liberty follows as a consequence of this; no usurped power can stand against the artillery of opinion.
-William Godwin (1756-1836)

The doorstep to the temple of wisdom is a knowledge of our own ignorance.
-Benjamin Franklin (1706 -90)

A person who won't read has no advantage over one who can't read.
-Mark Twain (1835 – 1910)

Nothing in the world is more dangerous than sincere ignorance and conscientious stupidity.
-Martin Luther King (1929 – 68)

There are many gates to the house of wisdom.
-Edward Counsel (1849 – 1939)

Memory is the mother of all wisdom.
-Aeschylus (525 – 456 BC)

Second thoughts are ever wiser.
-Euripides (480 -406 BC)

Wisdom is not communicable. The wisdom which a wise man tries to communicate always sounds foolish... Knowledge can be communicated, but not wisdom. One can find it, live it, do wonders through it, but one cannot communicate and teach it.
-Hermann Hesse (1877 – 1962)

Wisdom is the never-failing granary of thought.
-Edward Counsel (1849 – 1939)

Wisdom and folly are equal before the face of Infinity, for Infinity knows them not.
-Leonid Andreyev (1871 – 1919)

Knowledge is proud that he has learn'd so much; Wisdom is humble that he knows no more.
-William Cowper (1731 – 1800)

Never, no, never did Nature say one thing and Wisdom say another.
-Edmund Burke (1929 – 97)

Of all the forms of wisdom, hindsight is by general consent the least merciful, the most unforgiving.
-John Fletcher (1579 – 1625)

What wisdom can you find that is greater than kindness?
-Jean-Jacques Rousseau (1712 -78)

A wise man ... proportions his belief to the evidence.
-David Hume (1711 -76)

Knowledge is flour, but wisdom is bread.
-Austin O'Malley (1858 – 1932)

You may not have very much sense. But if you have enough to keep your mouth shut and look wise, it will not be long before you acquire a wide reputation as a fountain of Wisdom.
-*Robert Elliot Gonzales (1857 – 1926)*

Justice without wisdom is impossible.
-*James Anthony Froude (1818 – 94)*

The wealth of mankind is the wisdom they leave.
-*John Boyle O'Reilly (1844 - 90)*

The wise may find in trifles light as atoms in the air, some useful lesson to enrich the mind.
-*John Godfrey Saxe (1816 -87)*

The wise man hath his thoughts in his head; the fool, on his tongue.
-*Ivan Panin (1855 – 1942)*

When wisdom leaves the house folly enters it.
-*Edward Counsel (1849 – 1939)*

Wisdom comes to us when it can no longer do any good.
-*Gabriel Garcia Marquez (1927 – 2014)*

It requires wisdom to understand wisdom: The music is nothing if the audience is deaf.
-*Walter Lippmann (1889 – 1974)*

A man remains ignorant because he loves ignorance, and chooses ignorant thoughts; a man becomes wise because he loves wisdom and chooses wise thoughts.
-*James Allen (1864 – 1912)*

Folly is like the growth of weeds, always luxurious and spontaneous; wisdom, like flowers, requires cultivation.
-Hosea Ballou (1771 – 1852)

No man has all the wisdom in the world; everyone has some.
-Edgar Watson Howe (1853 – 1937)

Some would be sages if they did not believe they were so already.
-Baltasar Gracian (1601 – 58)

Where ignorance is bliss, 'Tis folly to be wise.
-Thomas Gray (1716 – 71)

The cleverest of all, in my opinion, is the man who calls himself a fool at least once a month.
-Fyodor Dostoevsky (1821 – 81)

The most exquisite Folly is made of Wisdom spun too fine.
-Benjamin Franklin (1706 – 90)

The next best thing to being wise oneself is to live in a circle of those who are.
-CS Lewis (1898 – 63)

In seeking wisdom thou art wise; in imagining that thou hast attained it -- thou art a fool.
-Lord Chesterfield (1694 – 1773)

Just because nobody complains doesn't mean all parachutes are perfect.
-Benny Hill (1924 – 92)

GENIUS

Ridicule is the tribute paid to the genius by the mediocrities.
-Oscar Wilde (1854 – 1900)

If confusion is the first step to knowledge, I must be a genius.
-Larry Leissner

Any fool can make things bigger, more complex, and more violent. It takes a touch of genius-and a lot of courage-to move in the opposite direction.
-Albert Einstein (1879 – 1955)

To see things in the seed, that is genius.
-Lao Tzu (600 – 531 BC)

The man of genius inspires us with a boundless confidence in our own powers.
-Ralph Waldo Emmerson (1803 – 82)

Do not train a child to learn by force or harshness; but direct them to it by what amuses their minds, so that you may be better able to discover with accuracy the peculiar bent of the genius of each.
-Plato (420 – 348 BC)

When Nature has work to be done, she creates a genius to do it.
-Ralph Waldo Emmerson (1803 -82)

Whatever you do, or dream you can, begin it. Boldness has genius and power and magic in it.
-Johann Wolfgang van Goethe (1749 – 1832)

No great genius has ever existed without some touch of madness.
-Aristotle (384 -322 BC)

The true genius shudders at incompleteness - and usually prefers silence to saying something which is not everything it should be.
-Edgar Allan Poe (1809 – 49)

The public is wonderfully tolerant. It forgives everything except genius.
-Oscar Wilde (1854 – 1900)

Alexander, Caesar, Charlemagne, and myself founded empires; but what foundation did we rest the creations of our genius? Upon force. Jesus Christ founded an empire upon love; and at this hour millions of men would die for Him.
-Napoleon Bonaparte (1769 – 1821)

Genius has limitations; stupidity is boundless.
-Albert Einstein (1879 – 1955)

Common sense is genius dressed in its working clothes.
-Ralph Waldo Emmerson (1803 – 82)

Men of lofty genius when they are doing the least work are most active.
-Leonardo da Vinci (1452 – 1519)

I don't want to be a genius - I have enough problems just trying to be a man.
-Albert Camus (1913 – 60)

Silence is the genius of fools and one of the virtues of the wise.

-Bernard de Bonnard (1744 – 1784)

Genius - the ability to produce fantastic amounts of equally fantastic bullshit that all makes perfect sense.
-Jason Zebehazy

There's a Genius in all of us.
-Albert Einstein (1879 – 1955)

Genius is never understood in its own time.
-Bill Watterson (1958 -)

Genius is perseverance in disguise.
-Mike Newlin (1949 -)

Improvement makes straight roads; but the crooked roads without improvement are roads of genius.
-William Blake (1757 – 1827)

I have nothing to declare but my genius.
-Oscar Wilde (1854 – 1900)

Genius ... means little more than the faculty of perceiving in an unhabitual way.
-William James (1842 – 1910)

There is a fine line between genius and insanity. I have erased this line.
-Oscar Levant (1906 – 72)

Genius is the ability to reduce the complicated to the simple.
-CW Ceram (1915 – 72)

Enthusiasm is that secret and harmonious spirit which hovers over the production of genius.
-*Benjamin Disraeli (1804 – 81)*

Common sense is as rare as genius, - is the basis of genius.
-*Ralph Waldo Emmerson (1803 – 82)*

People of humor are always in some degree people of genius.
-*Samuel Taylor Coleridge (1772 – 1834)*

The function of genius is not to give new answers, but to pose new questions - which time and mediocrity can solve.
-*Hugh Trevor-Roper (1914 – 2003)*

Men of genius are meteors intended to burn to light their century.
-*Napoleon Bonaparte (1769 – 1821)*

Talent may be in time forgiven, but genius never.
-*Lord Byron (1788 – 1824)*

Genius is always allowed some leeway, once the hammer has been pried from its hands and the blood has been cleaned up.
-*Terry Pratchett (1948 -)*

True genius resides in the capacity for evaluation of uncertain, hazardous, and conflicting information.
-*Winston Churchill (1874 – 1965)*

True genius sees with the eyes of a child and thinks with the brain of a genie.
-*Puzant Kevork Thomajan*

The world is always ready to receive talent with open arms. Very often it does not know what to do with genius.

-Oliver Wendell Holmes (1809 -94)

Genius is the capacity for seeing relationships where lesser men see none.
-William James (1842 – 1910)

The most tragic thing in the world is a man of genius who is not a man of honor.
-George Bernard Shaw (1856 – 1950)

The essence of genius is to know what to overlook.
-William James (1842 – 1910)

The leader of genius must have the ability to make different opponents appear as if they belonged to one category.
-Adolf Hitler (1889 – 1945)

Skill is fine, and genius is splendid, but the right contacts are more valuable than either.
-Arthur Conan Doyle (1859 – 1930)

Neither genius, fame, nor love show the greatness of the soul. Only kindness can do that.
-Jean Baptiste Lacordaire (1802 -61)

Force always attracts men of low morality, and I believe it to be an invariable rule that tyrants of genius are succeeded by scoundrels.
-Albert Einstein (1879 – 1955)

Every man of genius sees the world at a different angle from his fellows, and there is his tragedy.

-Havelock Ellis (1859 – 1939)

The principle mark of genius is not perfection but originality, the opening of new frontiers.
-Arthur Koestler (1905 – 38)

Genius - To know without having learned; to draw just conclusions from unknown premises; to discern the soul of things.
-Ambrose Bierce (1842 – 1914)

Genius develops in quiet places, character out in the full current of human life.
-Johann Wolfgang von Goethe (1749 – 1832)

For 37 years I've practiced 14 hours a day, and now they call me a genius.
-Pablo de Sarasate (1844 – 1908)

The guy who invented the first wheel was an idiot. The guy who invented the other three, HE was a genius.
-Sid Caesar (1922 – 2014)

Genius is talent set on fire by courage.
-Henry Van Dyke (1852 – 1933)

Jealousy is the tribute mediocrity pays to genius.
-Fulton J Sheen (1895 – 1975)

Neither a lofty degree of intelligence nor imagination nor both together go to the making of genius. Love, love, love, that is the soul of genius.

-Wolfgang Amadeus Mozart (1756 -91)

Men of genius are often dull and inert in society; as the blazing meteor, when it descends to earth, is only a stone.
-Henry Longfellow (1807 – 82)

Genius begins great works; labor alone finishes them.
-Joseph Joubert (1754 – 1824)

To know everything everyone else knows is clever. To know one thing no one else knows is genius .
-David Osmond (1956 -)

When a true genius appears in this world, you may know him by this sign that the dunces are all in confederacy against him.
-Jonathan Swift (1667 – 1745)

Talent does what it can, and genius does what it must.
-Edward G. Bulwer-Lytton (1803 -73)

Adversity reveals genius, prosperity conceals it.
-Horace (65 – 8 BC)

A science is any discipline in which the fool of this generation can go beyond the point reached by the genius of the last generation.
-Max Gluckman (1911 -75)

"I'm a misunderstood genius."
"What's misunderstood?"
"Nobody thinks I'm a genius."
-Bill Watterson (1958 -)

Mediocrity knows nothing higher than itself; but talent instantly recognizes genius.
-*Arthur Conan Doyle (1859 – 1930)*

To forgive is wisdom, to forget is genius.
-*Joyce Cary (1888 – 1957)*

We mustn't forget how quickly the visions of genius become the canned goods of intellectuals.
-*Saul Bellow (1915 – 2005)*

Almost everyone is born a genius and buried an idiot.
-*Charles Bukowski (1920 – 94)*

Great minds discuss ideas; average minds discuss events; small minds discuss people.
-*Eleanor Roosevelt (1884 – 1962)*

The distance between insanity and genius is measured only by success.
-*Bruce Feirstein (1956 -)*

Genius is 1% inspiration, and 99% perspiration.
-*Thomas Edison (1847 – 1931)*

ABILITY

Ability is what you're capable of doing. Motivation determines what you do. Attitude determines how well you do it.
-Lou Holtz (1937-80)

There is something that is much more scarce, something finer far, something rarer than ability. It is the ability to recognize ability.
-Ethel Hubbard (1856-1915)

Men often become what they believe themselves to be. If I believe I cannot do something, it makes me incapable of doing it. But when I believe I can, then I acquire the ability to do it even if I didn't have it in the beginning.
-Mahatma Gandhi (1869-1948)

Our duty, as men and women, is to proceed as if limits to our ability did not exist. We are collaborators in creation.
-Teilhard de Chardin (1881 – 1955)

The Creator has not given you a longing to do that which you have no ability to do.
-Orison Swett Marden (1850 -1924)

Your greatest asset is your earning ability. Your greatest resource is your time.
-Brian Tracy (1944 -)

Excellence is the unlimited ability to improve the quality of what you have to offer.
-Rick Pitino (1952 -)

No amount of ability is of the slightest avail without honor.

-Andrew Carnegie (1835-1919)

The ability to accept responsibility is the measure of the man.
-Roy L Smith (1887 – 1963)

To know how to hide one's ability is great skill.
-François de la Rochefoucauld (1613-80)

Ability is nothing without opportunity.
-Napoleon Bonaparte (1769-1821)

Success is the maximum utilization of the ability that you have.
-Zig Ziglar (1926 – 2012)

You are wholly complete and your success in life will be in direct proportion to your ability to accept this truth about you. *-Dr. Robert Anthony*

A man of ability and the desire to accomplish something can do anything.
-Donald Kircher (1958 – 75)

The ability to convert ideas to things is the secret of outward success.
-Henry Ward Beecher (1813 – 87)

Innovation is the ability to see change as an opportunity - not a threat.
-Anon

It is the ability to choose which makes us human.
-Madeleine L'Engle (1918 – 2007)

Natural ability without education has more often attained to glory and virtue than education without natural ability.
-Cicero (106 BC – 43 BC)

Human beings, who are almost unique in having the ability to learn from the experience of others, are also remarkable for their apparent disinclination to do so.
-Douglas Adams (1952-2001)

The key to success is often the ability to adapt.
-Anthony Brandt (1961 – 2013)

Big jobs usually go to the men who prove their ability to outgrow small ones.
-Theodore Roosevelt (1858-1919)

Leadership is the ability to do, not the ability to state.
-Paul Von Ringelheim (1933 – 2003)

With realization of one's own potential and self-confidence in one's ability, one can build a better world.
-Dalai Lama (1935-)

Lack of will power has caused more failure than lack of intelligence or ability.
-Anon

Those people who develop the ability to continuously acquire new and better forms of knowledge that they can apply to their work and to their lives will be the movers and shakers in our society for the indefinite future.
-Brian Tracy (1944 -)

The superior man is distressed by the limitations of his ability; he is not distressed by the fact that men do not recognize the ability that he has.
-Confucius (551-479 BC)

If there is any one secret of success, it lies in the ability to get the other person's point of view and see things from that person's angle as well as from your own.
-Henry Ford (1863-1947)

It is in the ability to deceive oneself that the greatest talent is shown.
-Anatole France (1844-1924)

For success, attitude is equally as important as ability.
-Harry F. Banks (1876 – 1956)

Ability may get you to the top, but it takes character to keep you there.
-John Wooden (1910 - 2010)

The ability to learn faster than your competitors may be only sustainable competitive advantage.
-Arie de Geus (1930 -)

Don't measure yourself by what you have accomplished, but what you should have accomplished with your ability.
-John Wooden (1910 - 2010)

The single most powerful tool for winning a negotiation is the ability to get up and walk away from the table without a deal.
-Anon

Tact is the ability to describe others as they see themselves.

-Abraham Lincoln (1809-65)

Progress is man's ability to complicate simplicity.
-Thor Heyerdahl (1914-2002)

Ability is a poor man's wealth.
-John Wooden (1910 - 2010)

When I think of vision, I have in mind the ability to see above and beyond the majority.
-Charles R. Swindoll (1934 -)

I claim to be an average man of less than average ability. I have not the shadow of a doubt that any man or woman can achieve what I have, if he or she would make the same effort and cultivate the same hope and faith.
-Mahatma Gandhi (1869-1948)

The difference between a stupid man and a wise one is the stupid man's inability to calculate the consequences of the action. The same goes for government.
-Brian Penton (1904 – 51)

The most talented people are always the nicest.
-James Caan (1940 -)

Chapter 6 The Arts

Actors and Acting

When an actor comes to me and wants to discuss his character, I say, 'It's in the script.' If he says, 'But what's my motivation'? I say, 'Your salary'.
-Alfred Hitchcock (1899 – 1980)

We're actors in our lives, pretendin' to be who we want people to think we are.
-Simone Elkeles (1970 -)

I'll always be there because I'm a skilled professional actor. Whether or not I've any talent is beside the point.
-Michael Caine (1933 -)

We're actors — we're the opposite of people!
-Tom Stoppard (1937 -)

Acting deals with very delicate emotions. It is not putting up a mask. Each time an actor acts he does not hide; he exposes himself.
-Rodney Dangerfield (1921- 2004)

Every writer is a frustrated actor who recites his lines in the hidden auditorium of his skull.
-Rod Serling (1924 – 75)

Show me a great actor and I'll show you a lousy husband. Show me a great actress, and you've seen the devil.
-WC Fields (1880 – 1946)

When you talk about a great actor, you're not talking about Tom Cruise.
-*Lauren Bacall (1924 – 2014)*

When the curtain falls, the best thing an actor can do is to go away.
-*Harold Macmillan (1894 – 1986)*

Any actress who appears in public without being well-groomed is digging her own grave.
-*Joan Crawford (1905 – 77)*

The actor should be able to create the universe in the palm of his hand.
-*Sir Laurence Olivier (1907 – 89)*

All the world's a stage, and all the men and women merely players.
-*William Shakespeare (1564 – 1616)*

I was lousy in school. Real screwed up. A moron. I was antisocial and didn't bother with the other kids. A really bad student. I didn't have any brains. I didn't know what I was doing there. That's why I became an actor.
-*Anthony Hopkins (1937 – 2015)*

Movies are a fad. Audiences really want to see live actors on a stage.
-*Charles Chaplin (1889 – 1977)*

An actor is never so great as when he reminds you of an animal - falling like a cat, lying like a dog, moving like a fox.
-*Francois Truffaut (1932 – 84)*

Acting is behaving truthfully under imaginary circumstances.
-Sanford Meissner (1905 – 97)

The real actor has a direct line to the collective heart.
Sam Rayburn (1882 – 1961)

An actor is a fool for God.
-Geraldine Clark

It is better to be making the news than taking it; to be an actor rather than a critic.
-Winston Churchill (1874 – 1965)

Without wonder and insight, acting is just a business. With it, it becomes creation.
-Bette Davis (1908 – 89)

The basic essential of a great actor is that he loves himself in acting.
-Charlie Chaplin (1889 – 1977)

The best acting is instinctive. It's not intellectual, it's not mechanical, it's instinctive.
-Craig MacDonald

The actor's popularity is evanescent; applauded today, forgotten tomorrow.
-Harrison Ford (1942 -)

Acting should be bigger than life. Scripts should be bigger than life. It should all be bigger than life.
-Bette Davis (1908 – 89)

The better the actor the more stupid he is.
-*Truman Capote (1924 – 84)*

Acting is not about being someone different. It's finding the similarity in what is apparently different, then finding myself in there.
-*Meryl Streep (1949 -)*

The actor becomes an emotional athlete. The process is painful - my personal life suffers.
-*Arthur Helps (1813 – 75)*

An actor has to burn inside with an outer ease.
-*Michael Chekhov (1891 – 1955)*

An actor is a sculptor who carves in snow.
-*Lawrence Barrett (1838 – 91)*

Use what you know. Don't worry about what you don't know.
-*Michael Shurtleff (1920 – 2007)*

When they asked Jack Benny to do something for the Actor's Orphanage - he shot both his parents and moved in.
-*Bob Hope (1903 – 2003)*

Conflict is what creates drama. The more conflict actors find, the more interesting the performance.
-*Michael Shurtleff (1920 – 2007)*

Disney has the best casting. If he doesn't like an actor he just tears him up.
-*Alfred Hitchcock (1899 – 1980)*

If you really do want to be an actor who can satisfy himself and his audience, you need to be vulnerable.
-Jack Lemmon (1925 – 2001)

To grasp the full significance of life is the actor's duty, to interpret it is his problem, and to express it his dedication.
-James Dean (1931 – 55)

Creating relationship is the heart of acting. It is basic. It is essential.
-Michael Shurtleff (1920 – 2007)

Being a star is an agent's dream, not an actor's.
-Robert Duvall (1931 -)

Every scene you will ever act begins in the middle, and it is up to you, the actor, to provide what comes before. -Michael Shurtleff (1920 – 2007)

An actor is a guy who, if you ain't talking about him, he ain't listening.
-Boy George (1961 -)

The first step to a better audition is to give up character and use yourself.
-Michael Shurtleff (1920 – 2007)

Perhaps I'm not a good actor, but I would be even worse at doing anything else.
-Sean Connery (1930 -)

Acting is a masochistic form of exhibitionism, not quite the occupation of an adult.
-Lawrence Olivier (1907 – 89)

I do not regret one professional enemy I have made. Any actor who doesn't dare to make an enemy should get out of the business.
-Bette Davis (1908 -89)

Time has convinced me of one thing: Television is for appearing on--not for looking at.
-Noel Coward (1899 – 1973)

An actor is something less than a man, while an actress is something more than a woman.
-Richard Burton (1925 – 84)

For an actress to be a success, she must have the face of Venus, the brains of a Minerva, the grace of Terpsichore, the memory of a Macaulay, the figure of Juno, and the hide of a rhinoceros.
-Ethel Barrymore (1879-1959)

An actress can only play a woman. I'm an actor, I can play anything.
-Whoopi Goldberg (1955 -)

The only reason I made a commercial for American Express was to pay my American Express bill.
-Peter Ustinov (1921 – 2004)

ART

Creativity is allowing yourself to make mistakes. Art is knowing which ones to keep.
-Scott Adams (1957 -)

Everything you can imagine is real.
-Pablo Picasso (1881 – 1973)

The English public, as a mass, takes no interest in a work of art until it is told that the work in question is immoral.
-Oscar Wilde (1854 – 1900)

Good Artists copy, great artists steal.
-Pablo Picasso (1881 – 1973)

As a work of art, it reminds me of a long conversation between two drunks.
-Clive James (1939 -)

Art is never finished, only abandoned.
-Leonardo da Vinci (1452 – 1519)

Every child is an artist. The problem is how to remain an artist once he grows up.
-Pablo Picasso (1881 – 1973)

Good art is not what it looks like, but what it does to us.
-Roy Adzak (1927 – 87)

Painting is poetry that is seen rather than felt, and poetry is painting that is felt rather than seen.
-Leonardo da Vinci (1452 – 1519)

After a certain high level of technical skill is achieved, science and art tend to coalesce in aesthetics, plasticity, and form. The greatest scientists are always artists as well.
-*Albert Einstein (1879- 1955)*

If you ask me what I came to do in this world, I, an artist, will answer you: I am here to live out loud.
-*Émile Zola (1840 – 1902)*

We have art in order not to die of the truth.
-*Friedrich Nietzsche (1844 – 1900)*

I dream my painting and I paint my dream.
-*Vincent van Gogh (1853 – 90)*

Life is the art of drawing without an eraser.
-*John W Gardener (1912 – 2002)*

You might as well ask an artist to explain his art, or ask a poet to explain his poem. It defeats the purpose. The meaning is only clear thorough the search.
-*Rick Riordan (1964 -)*

Love the art in yourself, not yourself in the art.
-*Konstantin Stanislavsky (1863 – 1938)*

Any fool can be happy. It takes a man with real heart to make beauty out of the stuff that makes us weep.
-*Clive Barker (1952 -)*

It is through Art, and through Art only, that we can realise our perfection.
-*Oscar Wilde (1854 – 1900)*

Paradoxically though it may seem, it is none the less true that life imitates art far more than art imitates life.
-*Oscar Wilde (1854 – 1900)*

Art is not a thing; it is a way.
-*Elbert Hubbard (1856 – 1915)*

A picture is a secret about a secret, the more it tells you the less you know.
-*Diane Arbus (1923 – 71)*

Art is what's left over after you've defined everything else.
-*Michael Vitale*

Painting is just another way of keeping a diary.
-*Pablo Picasso (1881 – 1973)*

Science and art have that in common that everyday things seem to them new and attractive.
-*Friedrich Nietzsche (1844 – 1900)*

Art is the only way to run away without leaving home.
-*Twyla Tharp (1941 -)*

Life is like art. You have to work hard to keep it simple and still have meaning.
-*Charles de Lint (1951 -)*

The aim of every artist is to arrest motion, which is life, by artificial means and hold it fixed so that a hundred years later, when a stranger looks at it, it moves again since it is life.
-*William Faulkner (1897 – 1962)*

Art is the window to man's soul. Without it, he would never be able to see beyond his immediate world; nor could the world see the man within.
-Lady Bird Johnson (1912 – 2007)

Life beats down and crushes the soul and art reminds you that you have one.
-Stella Adler (1901 – 92)

The aim of art is not to represent the outward appearance of things, but their inward significance.
-Aristotle (384 – 322 BC)

It has been said that art is a tryst, for in the joy of it maker and beholder meet.
-Kojiro Tomita (1890 – 1976)

Art is man's nature; nature is God's art.
-Philip James Bailey (1816 – 1902)

I don't paint things. I only paint the difference between things.
-Henri Matisse (1869 – 1954)

It is the spectator, and not life, that art really mirrors.
-Oscar Wilde (1854 – 1900)

An artist cannot fail; it is a success to be one.
-Charles Horton Cooley (1864 – 1929)

There is no must in art because art is free.
-Wassily Kandinsky (1866 – 1944)

Every creator painfully experiences the chasm between his inner vision and its ultimate expression.
-*Isaac Bashevis Singer (1902 – 91)*

Art, like morality, consists in drawing the line somewhere.
-*GK Chesterton (1874 – 1936)*

Art is the stored honey of the human soul, gathered on wings of misery and travail.
-*Theodore Dreiser (1871 – 1945)*

To reveal art and conceal the artist is art's aim.
-*Oscar Wilde (1854 – 1900)*

Painting is easy when you don't know how, but very difficult when you do.
-*Edgar Degas (1834 – 1917)*

You use a glass mirror to see your face; you use works of art to see your soul.
-*George Bernard Shaw (1856 – 1950)*

It is a mistake for a sculptor or a painter to speak or write very often about his job. It releases tension needed for his work.
-*Henry Moore (1898 – 1986)*

All art requires courage.
-*Anne Tucker (1945 -)*

Anyone who says you can't see a thought simply doesn't know art.
-*Wynetka Ann Reynolds (1938 -)*

Art not only imitates nature, but also completes its deficiencies.
-*Aristotle (384 – 322 BC)*

Art consists of limitation. The most beautiful part of every picture is the frame.
-*GK Chesterton (1874 – 1936)*

Art is the lie that enables us to realize the truth.
-*Pablo Picasso (1881 – 1973)*

An artist is someone who produces things that people don't need to have but that he — for some reason — thinks it would be a good idea to give them.
-*Andy Warhol (1928 – 87)*

We all know that Art is not truth. Art is a lie that makes us realize the truth, at least the truth that is given to us to understand.
-*Pablo Picasso (1881 – 1973)*

As far as I am concerned, a painting speaks for itself. What is the use of giving explanations, when all is said and done? A painter has only one language.
-*Pablo Picasso (1881 – 1973)*

The world today doesn't make sense, so why should I paint pictures that do?
-*Pablo Picasso (1881 – 1973)*

Writing is a craft not an art.
-*William Zinsser (1922 -)*

Art is your emotions flowing in a river of imagination.
-*Anon*

There is no abstract art. You must always start with something. Afterward you can remove all traces of reality.
-*Pablo Picasso (1881 – 1973)*

One of the best things about paintings is their silence — which prompts reflection and random reverie.
-*Mark Stevens (1916 – 94)*

Art enables us to find ourselves and lose ourselves at the same time.
-*Thomas Merton (1915 – 68)*

Art disturbs, science reassures.
-*Georges Braque (1882 – 1963)*

Art is pattern informed by sensibility.
-*Sir Herbert Read (1893 – 1968)*

The artist's talent sits uneasy as an object of public acclaim, having been so long an object of private despair.
-*Robert Brault (1963 -)*

I wash my hands of those who imagine chattering to be knowledge, silence to be ignorance, and affection to be art.
-*Kahlil Gibran (1883 – 1931)*

Art is like a border of flowers along the course of civilization.
-*Lincoln Steffens (1866 – 1936)*

In art the hand can never execute anything higher than the heart can inspire.
-*Ralph Waldo Emerson (1803 – 82)*

Works of art are all that survive of incredibly gifted people.
-*Peter C Wilson (1913 – 84)*

What garlic is to food, insanity is to art.
-*Augustus Saint-Gaudens (1848 – 1907)*

Sex is like art. Most of it is pretty bad, and the good stuff is out of your price range.
-Scott Roeben

OPERA

No good opera plot can be sensible, for people do not sing when they are feeling sensible.
-WH Auden (1907 – 73)

The only thing worse than opera is someone who hums along with opera.
-Josh Lanyon

An opera begins long before the curtain goes up and ends long after it has come down. It starts in my imagination, it becomes my life, and it stays part of my life long after I've left the opera house.
-Maria Callas (1923 – 77)

Opera does not call so much for an imaginative ear as for an imaginative eye, an eye which can see beyond little absurdities toward great truths.
-George Marek (1902 – 87)

I don't mind what language an opera is sung in so long as it is a language I don't understand.
-Sir Edward Appleton (1892 – 1965)

I wish the opera was every night. It is, of all entertainments, the sweetest and most delightful. Some of the songs seemed to melt my very soul.
-Fanny Burney (1753 – 1940)

One can't judge Wagner's opera Lohengrin after a first hearing, and I certainly don't intend to hear it a second time.
-Gioacchino Rossini (1792 – 1868)

The opera is like a husband with a foreign title: expensive to support, hard to understand, and therefore a supreme social challenge.
-Cleveland Amory (1917 – 98)

Opera is where a guy gets stabbed in the back, and instead of dying, he sings.
-Robert Burns (1759 – 96)

If a thing isn't worth saying, you sing it. - Pierre
-Beaumarchais (1732 – 1799)

I never was an opera fan - about twenty-five musically supreme masterpieces in this curious medium apart.
-Hans Keller (1919 – 85)

The more opera is dead, the more it flourishes.
-Slavoj Zizek (1949 -)

The taxpayers cannot be relied upon to support performing arts such as opera. As a taxpayer, I am forced to admit that I would rather undergo a vasectomy via Weed Whacker than attend an opera.
-Dave Barry (1947 -)

Every theatre is an insane asylum, but an opera theatre is the ward for the incurables.
-Franz Schalk (1863 – 1931)

People are wrong when they say opera is not what it used to be. It is what it used to be. That is what's wrong with it.
-Noel Coward (1899 – 1973)

Opera in English, is about as sensible as baseball in Italian.
-HL Mencken (1880 – 1956)

Parsifal - the kind of opera that starts at six o'clock and after it has been going three hours, you look at your watch and it says 6:20.
-David Randolph (1914 – 2010)

The opera is to music what a bawdy house is to a cathedral.
-H. L. Mencken (1880 – 1956)

In opera, there is always too much singing.
-Claude Debussy (1862 – 1918)

Going to the opera, like getting drunk, is a sin that carries its own punishment with it.
-Hannah More (1745 – 1833)

I am sure I know of no agony comparable to the listening to an unfamiliar opera.
-Mark Twain (1835 – 1910)

MUSIC

A painter paints pictures on canvas. But musicians paint their pictures on silence.
-*Leopold Stokowski (1882 – 1977)*

Words make you think a thought. Music makes you feel a feeling. A song makes you feel a thought.
-*E. Y. Harburg (1896 – 1981)*

One good thing about music, when it hits you, you feel no pain.
-*Bob Marley (1945 – 81)*

Music is the Voice that tells us that the human race is greater than it knows.
-*Napoleon Bonaparte (1769 – 1821)*

If music be the food of love, play on,
Give me excess of it; that surfeiting,
The appetite may sicken, and so die.
-*William Shakespeare (1564 – 1616)*

Music was my refuge. I could crawl into the space between the notes and curl my back to loneliness.
-*Maya Angelou (1928 – 2014)*

Some people have lives; some people have music.
-*John Green (1977 -)*

Music is ... A higher revelation than all Wisdom & Philosophy.
-*Ludwig van Beethoven (1770 – 1827)*

Music gives a soul to the universe, wings to the mind, flight to the imagination and life to everything.
-*Plato (427 – 347 BC)*

Music is the medicine of the mind.
-*John Logan (1961 -)*

After silence, that which comes nearest to expressing the inexpressible is music.
-*Aldous Huxley (1894 – 1963)*

Those who danced were thought to be quite insane by those who could not hear the music.
-*Angela Monet*

The only escape from the miseries of life are music and cats.
-*Albert Schweitzer (1875 – 1965)*

Without music, life would be a mistake.... I would only believe in a God who knew how to dance.
-*Friedrich Nietzsche (1844 – 1900)*

The only truth is music.
-*Jack Kerouac (1922 – 69)*

Music expresses that which cannot be said and on which it is impossible to be silent.
-*Victor Hugo (1802 – 85)*

Everything in the universe has a rhythm, everything dances.
-*Maya Angelou (1928 – 2014)*

To produce music is also in a sense to produce children. -*Friedrich Nietzsche (1844 – 1900)*

My ambition was to live like music.
-*Mary Gaitskill (1954 -)*

If one hears bad music it is one's duty to drown it by one's conversation.
-*Oscar Wilde (1854 – 1900)*

Songs are as sad as the listener.
-*Jonathan Safran Foer (1977 -)*

You're like a song that I heard when I was a little kid but forgot I knew until I heard it again.
-*Maggie Stiefvater (1981 -)*

Music has a power of forming the character, and should therefore be introduced into the education of the young. *-Aristotle (384 – 322BC)*

Who hears music, feels his solitude peopled at once.
-*Robert Browning (1812 – 89)*

Music produces a kind of pleasure which human nature cannot do without.
-*Confucius (551 – 479 BC)*

Music . . . can name the unnameable and communicate the unknowable.
-*Leonard Bernstein (1918 – 90)*

I have no pleasure in any man who despises music. It is no invention of ours: it is a gift of God. I place it next to theology. Satan hates music: he knows how it drives the evil spirit out of us.
-*Martin Luther (1483 – 1546)*

I just can't listen to any more Wagner, you know...I'm starting to get the urge to conquer Poland.
-*Woody Allen (1935-)*

Music is love in search of a word.
-*Sidonie Gabrielle (1873 – 1954)*

I like beautiful melodies telling me terrible things.
-*Tom Waits (1949 -)*

Music is a moral law. It gives soul to the universe, wings to the mind, flight to the imagination, and charm and gaiety to life and to everything.
-*Plato (428 – 348 BC)*

Jazz isn't dead. It just smells funny.
-*Frank Zappa (1940 - 93)*

Most people live and die with their music still unplayed. They never dare to try.
-*Mary Kay Ash (1915 – 2001)*

He took his pain and turned it into something beautiful. Into something that people connect to. And that's what good music does. It speaks to you. It changes you.
-*Hannah Harrington (1985 -)*

Dancing: The vertical expression of a horizontal desire legalized by music.
-*George Bernard Shaw (1856 – 1950)*

The music is not in the notes, but in the silence between. -*Wolfgang Amadeus Mozart (1756 – 91)*

Music does bring people together. It allows us to experience the same emotions. People everywhere are the same in heart and spirit.
-John Denver (1943 – 97)

My personal hobbies are reading, listening to music, and silence.
-Edith Sitwell (1887 – 1964)

I've never known a musician who regretted being one. Whatever deceptions life may have in store for you, music itself is not going to let you down.
-Virgil Thompson (1896 – 1989)

Beethoven tells you what it's like to be Beethoven and Mozart tells you what it's like to be human. Bach tells you what it's like to be the universe.
-Douglas Adams (1952 – 2001)

How good bad music and bad reasons sound when we march against an enemy.
-Friedrich Nietzsche (1844 – 1900)

Music is the wine that fills the cup of silence.
-Robert Fripp (1946 -)

Music is the soul of language.
-Max Heindel (1865 – 1919)

Pop music often tells you everything is OK, while rock music tells you that it's not OK, but you can change it.
-Bono (1960 -)

Music creates order out of chaos: for rhythm imposes unanimity upon the divergent, melody imposes continuity upon the disjointed, and harmony imposes compatibility upon the incongruous.
-*Yehudi Menuhin (1916 – 99)*

If you cannot teach me to fly, teach me to sing.
-*JM Barrie (1860 – 1937)*

Do I listen to pop music because I'm miserable or am I miserable because listen to pop music?
-*John Cusack (1966 -)*

Why waste money on psychotherapy when you can listen to the B Minor Mass?
-*Michael Torke (1961 -)*

Music is the language of the spirit. It opens the secret of life bringing peace, abolishing strife.
-*Kahlil Gibran (1883 – 1931)*

Music is what feelings sound like.
-*Georgia Cates (1975 -)*

Wagner's music is better than it sounds.
-*Mark Twain (1835 – 1910)*

Music is the poetry of the air.
-*Gerhard Richter (1932 -)*

Music is God's gift to man, the only art of Heaven given to earth, the only art of earth we take to Heaven.
-*Walter Savage Landor (1775 – 1864)*

If I were to begin life again, I would devote it to music. It is the only cheap and unpunished rapture upon earth.
-*Sydney Smith (1771 – 1845)*

When people hear good music, it makes them homesick for something they never had, and never will have.
-*Edgar Watson Howe (1853 – 1937)*

There is nothing in the world so much like prayer as music is.
-*William P Merrill (1867 – 1954)*

When the music changes, so does the dance.
-*African proverb*

Music is the mediator between the spiritual and the sensual life.
-*Ludwig van Beethoven (1770 -1827)*

In memory everything seems to happen to music.
-*Tennessee Williams (1911 – 83)*

Play the music, not the instrument.
-*Anon*

Music is the harmonious voice of creation; an echo of the invisible world.
-*Giuseppe Mazzini (1805 – 1972)*

The Irish gave the bagpipes to the Scots as a joke, but the Scots haven't got the joke yet.
-*Oliver Herford (1863 – 1935)*

Music is audible mathematics.
-*David Osmond (1956 -)*

Country music is three chords and the truth.
-Harlan Howard (1927 – 2002)

Music washes away from the soul the dust of everyday life.
-Berthold Auerbach (1812 – 82)

Music, the mosaic of the air.
-Andrew Marvell (1621 – 78)

Music is the greatest communication in the world. Even if people don't understand the language that you're singing in, they still know good music when they hear it.
-Lou Rawls (1933 – 2006)

Music is the vernacular of the human soul.
-Geoffrey Latham

Music is only love looking for words.
-Lawrence Durrell (1912 – 90)

There is nothing more difficult than talking about music.
-Camille Saint-Saens (1835 – 1921)

The aim and final end of all music should be none other than the glory of God and the refreshment of the soul.
-Johann Sebastian Bach (1685 – 1750)

If a composer could say what he had to say in words he would not bother trying to say it in music.
-Gustav Mahler (1860 – 1911)

I despise a world which does not feel that music is a higher revelation than all wisdom and philosophy.
-Ludwig van Beethoven (1770 – 1827)

Life exists for the love of music or beautiful things.
-GK Chesterton (1874 – 1936)

Music produces a kind of pleasure which human nature cannot do without.
-Confucius (551 – 479 BC)

MOVIES

When I was a kid, if a guy got killed in a western movie I always wondered who got his horse.
-George Carlin (1937 -)

Only thing worse than watching a bad movie is being in one.
-Elvis Presley (1935 – 77)

To grasp and hold a vision, that is the very essence of successful leadership - not only on the movie set where I learned it, but everywhere.
-Ronald Reagan (1911 – 2004)

Life is the movie you see through your own eyes. It makes little difference what's happening out there. It's how you take it that counts.
-Denis Waitley (1933 -)

I used to think as I looked at the Hollywood night, 'there must be thousands of girls sitting alone like me, dreaming of becoming a movie star'. But I'm not going to worry about them. I'm dreaming the hardest.
-Marilyn Monroe (1926 - 62)

I didn't even know my bra size until I made a movie.
-Angelina Jolie (1975-)

If it's a good movie, the sound could go off and the audience would still have a perfectly clear idea of what was going on.
-Alfred Hitchcock (1899 – 1980)

Never judge a book by its movie.

-JW Eagan

I'm not a real movie star. I've still got the same wife I started out with twenty-eight years ago.
-Will Rogers (1879 – 1935)

You know what your problem is, it's that you haven't seen enough movies - all of life's riddles are answered in the movies.
-Steve Martin (1945 -)

It's the movies that have really been running things in America ever since they were invented. They show you what to do, how to do it, when to do it, how to feel about it, and how to look how you feel about it.
-Andy Warhol (1928 – 87)

I don't take the movies seriously, and anyone who does is in for a headache.
-Joseph L. Mankiewicz (1909 – 93)

The whole of life is just like watching a film. Only it's as though you always get in ten minutes after the big picture has started, and no-one will tell you the plot, so you have to work it out all yourself from the clues.
-Terry Pratchett (1948 -)

Give them pleasure. The same pleasure they have when they wake up from a nightmare.
-Alfred Hitchcock (1899 – 1980)

People don't read any more. It's a sad state of affairs. Reading's the only thing that allows you to use your imagination. When you watch films it's someone else's vision, isn't it?
-Lemmy Kilmister (1945 -)

The length of a film should be directly related to the endurance of the human bladder.
-Alfred Hitchcock (1899 – 1980)

The book is a film that takes place in the mind of the reader. That's why we go to movies and say, "Oh, the book is better".
-Paulo Coelho (1947 -)

Academia is the death of cinema. It is the very opposite of passion. Film is not the art of scholars, but of illiterates.
-Werner Herzog (1942 -)

All you need to make a movie is a girl and a gun.
-Jean-Luc Godard (1930 -)

If you watch a scary movie together, then the scariness is cut in half!
-Hidekaz Himaruya (1985 -)

Fairy tales only happen in movies.
-George Melies (1861 – 1938)

It's not what a movie is about, it's how it is about it.
-Roger Ebert (1942 – 2013)

All I need to make a comedy is a park, a policeman, and a pretty girl.
-Charles Chaplin (1889 – 1977)

If you want a happy ending it depends, of course, on where you end the story.
-Orson Welles (1915 – 85)

Films are like an expensive form of therapy to me.
-Tim Burton (1958 -)

Film making is a chance to live many lifetimes.
-Robert Altman (1925 – 2006)

QUOTES IN MOVIES

A boy's best friend is his mother.
-Norman Bates/Anthony Perkins in Psycho (1960)

I love the smell of napalm in the morning.
-Lt. Col. Bill Kilgore/Robert Duvall in Apocalypse Now (1979)

Carpe diem. Seize the day, boys. Make your lives extraordinary.
-John Keating/Robin Williams in Dead Poets Society (1989)

They call me Mister Tibbs!
-Virgil Tibbs/Sidney Poitier in The Heat of the Night (1967)

Did you think I'd be too stupid to know what a eugoogly is?
-Derek Zoolander/Ben Stiller in Zoolander

You've got to ask yourself one question: 'Do I feel lucky?' Well, do ya, punk?
-Harry Callahan/Clint Eastwood in Dirty Harry (1971)

Do I look like someone who cares what God thinks?
-Doug Bradley/Pinhead in Hellraiser (1983)

One morning I shot an elephant in my pajamas. How he got in my pajamas, I don't know.
-Capt. Geoffrey T. Spaulding/Groucho Marx in Animal Crackers (1930)

Gentlemen, you can't fight in here! This is the War Room! *-President Merkin Muffley/Peter Sellers in Dr Strangelove (1964)*

Greed, for lack of a better word, is good.
-Gordon Gekko/Michael Douglas in Wall Street (1987)

Get busy living, or get busy dying.
-*Andy Dufresne/Tim Robbins in The Shawshank Redemption (1994)*

We all go a little mad sometimes.
-*Norman Bates/Anthony Perkins in Psycho (1960)*

He's not the Messiah. He's a very naughty boy!
-*The mother of Brian, a ratbag/Terry Jones in Monty Python's Life of Brian (1979)*

Fat, drunk, and stupid is no way to go through life, son.
-*Dean Wormer/John Vernon in National Lampoon's Animal House (1978)*

Aristotle was not Belgian. The central message of Buddhism is not 'every man for himself.' And the London Underground is not a political movement. Those are all mistakes, Otto. I looked 'em up.
-*Wanda/Jamie Lee Curtis in A Fish Called Wanda (1988)*

Hope. It is the only thing stronger than fear. A little hope is effective. A lot of hope is dangerous. A spark is fine, as long as it's contained.
-*President Snow/Donald Sutherland in The Hunger Games (2012)*

I fart in your general direction. Your mother was a hamster and your father smelt of elderberries.
-*French soldier/John Cleese in Monty Python and the Holy Grail (1975)*

I ate his liver with some fava beans and a nice Chianti.
-*Hannibal Lecter/Anthony Hopkins in The Silence of the Lambs (1991)*

I wanted to see exotic Vietnam, the jewel of Southeast Asia. I, uh, I wanted to meet interesting and stimulating people of an ancient culture, and kill them.
-Private Joker/Matthew Modine in Full Metal Jacket (1987)

I coulda had class. I coulda been a contender. I coulda been somebody.
-Terry Molloy/Marlon Brando in On the Waterfront (1954)

That's what I love about these high school girls, man. I get older, they stay the same age.
-Wooderson/Matthew McConaughey in Dazed and Confused (1993)

If you build it, he will come.
-Shoeless Joe Jackson/Ray Liotta in Field of Dreams (1989)

Dave, this conversation can serve no purpose anymore. Goodbye.
-Hal the computer in 2001 A Space Odyssey (1968)

I'm also just a girl standing in front of a boy asking him to love her.
-Anna Scott/Julia Roberts in Notting Hill (1999)

I'm as mad as hell, and I'm not gonna to take this anymore!
-Howard Beale/Peter Finch in Network (1976)

I'm pretty sure there's a lot more to life than being really, really, ridiculously good looking. And I plan on finding out what that is.
-Zoolander/Ben Stiller in Zoolander (2001)

In Switzerland they had brotherly love – and 500 years of democracy and peace, and what did that produce? The cuckoo clock.
-Harry Lime/Orson Welles in The Third Man (1949)

Infamy, infamy, they've all got it in for me!
-Julius Caesar/Kenneth Williams in Carry On Cleo (1964)

Just keep swimming.
-Finding Nemo (2003)

Love means never having to say you're sorry.
-Jennifer Cavilleri/Ali MacGraw in Love Story (1970)

Life is a box of chocolates, Forrest. You never know what you're gonna get.
-Mrs Gump/Sally Field in Forrest Gump (1994)

After all, tomorrow is another day!
-Scarlett O'Hara/Vivian Leigh in Gone with the Wind (1939)

Life is only on earth, and not for long.
-Justine/Kirsten Dunst in Melancholia (2011)

Man who catch fly with chopstick accomplish anything.
-Mr. Miyagi/Pat Morita in The Karate Kid (1984)

My name is Maximus Decimus Meridius, commander of the Armies of the North, General of the Felix Legions and loyal servant to the true emperor, Marcus Aurelius, father to a murdered son, husband to a murdered wife. And I will have my vengeance, in this life or the next.
-Maximus/Russell Crowe in Gladiator (2000)

Old age. It's the only disease, Mr. Thompson that you don't look forward to being cured of.
-Mr Bernstein/Everett Sloane in Citizen Kane (1941)

That was the most fun I've ever had without laughing.
-Alvy Singer/Woody Allen in Annie Hall (1977)

That's what makes me sad: Life is so different from books.
-Marianne Renoir/Anna Karina in Pierrot Le Fou (1965)

To call you stupid would be an insult to stupid people! -Wanda/Jamie Lee Curtis in A Fish Called Wanda (1988)
To infinity... and beyond.
-Buzz Lightyear/Tim Allen in Toy Story (1995)

Toto, I've a feeling we're not in Kansas anymore.
-Dorothy/Judy Garland in The Wizard of Oz (1939)

Well, what if there is no tomorrow? There wasn't one today.
-Phil Connors/Bill Murray in Groundhog Day (1993)

You're gonna need a bigger boat.
-Brody/Roy Scheider in Jaws (1975)

Chapter 7 Sport

Baseball

There are only two seasons -- winter and Baseball.
-Bill Veeck (1914 – 86)

The Statue of Liberty is no longer saying, "Give me your poor, your tired, your huddled masses." She's got a baseball bat and yelling, "You want a piece of me?
-Robin Williams (1951 – 2014)

You spend a good piece of your life gripping a baseball and in the end it turns out that it was the other way around all the time.
-Jim Bouton (1939 -)

Close don't count in baseball. Close only counts in horseshoes and grenades.
-Frank Robinson (1935 – 56)

A baseball fan is a spectator sitting 500 feet from home plate who can see better than an umpire standing five feet away.
-Anon

Things could be worse. Suppose your errors were counted and published every day, like those of a baseball player.
-Anon

Baseball is like church. Many attend but few understand.
-Wes Westrum (1922 – 2002)

Baseball is ninety percent mental and the other half is physical.
-Yogi Berra (1925 - 2015)

Little League baseball is a very good thing because it keeps the parents off the streets.
-*Yogi Berra (1925 - 2015)*

Boys, baseball is a game where you gotta have fun. You do that by winning.
-*Dave Bristol (1933 -)*

There are three types of baseball players: those who make it happen, those who watch it happen, and those who wonder what happens.
-*Tommy Lasorda (1927 -)*

Baseball was made for kids, and grown-ups only screw it up.
-*Bob Lemon (1920 – 2000)*

Baseball gives every American boy a chance to excel, not just to be as good as someone else but to be better than someone else. This is the nature of man and the name of the game.
Ted Williams (1918 – 2002)

In baseball, my theory is to strive for consistency, not to worry about the numbers. If you dwell on statistics you get short-sighted, if you aim for consistency, the numbers will be there at the end.
-*Tom Seaver (1944 -)*

Playing baseball for a living is like having a license to steal.
-*Pete Rose (1941 -)*

Some people crave baseball - I find this unfathomable but I can easily understand why a person could get excited about playing a bassoon.
-*Frank Zappa (1940 – 93)*

Baseball is a game where a curve is an optical illusion, a screwball can be a pitch or a person, stealing is legal and you can spit anywhere you like except in the umpire's eye or on the ball.
-*Jim Murray (1919 – 98)*

People ask me what I do in winter when there's no baseball. I'll tell you what I do. I stare out the window and wait for spring.
-*Rogers Hornsby (1896 – 1963)*

I think about baseball when I wake up in the morning. I think about it all day and I dream about it at night. The only time I don't think about it is when I'm playing it.
-*Carl Yastrzemski (1939 -)*

Baseball is almost the only orderly thing in a very unorderly world. If you get three strikes, even the best lawyer in the world can't get you off.
-*Bill Veeck (1914 – 86)*

Luck is the great stabilizer in baseball.
-*Tris Speaker (1888 – 1956)*

Baseball is the only field of endeavor where a man can succeed three times out of ten and be considered a good performer.
-*Ted Williams (1918 – 2002)*

Saying that men talk about baseball in order to avoid talking about their feelings is the same as saying that women talk about their feelings in order to avoid talking about baseball.
-*Deborah Tannen (1945 -)*

There are three things you can do in a baseball game. You can win, or you can lose, or it can rain.
-*Casey Stengel (1891 – 1975)*

Baseball is dull only to dull minds.
-Red Barber (1908 -1992)

I know I'm the world's worst fielder, but who gets paid for fielding? There isn't a great fielder in baseball getting the kind of dough I get paid for hitting.
-Dick Stuart (1932 – 2002)

Baseball must be a great game to survive the fools who run it.
-Bill Terry (1898 – 1989)

Okay you guys, pair up in threes.
-Yogi Berra (1925 - 2015)

It took me seventeen years to get three thousand hits in baseball. It took one afternoon on the golf course.
-Hank Aaron

It's getting late early.
-Yogi Berra (1925 - 2015)

Poets are like baseball pitchers. Both have their moments. The intervals are the tough things.
-Robert Frost (1874 – 1963)

Lady, I'm not an athlete. I'm a baseball player.
-John Kruk (1971 -)

Baseball is an island of activity in a sea of statistics.
-Anon

Baseball is the exponent of American Courage, Confidence, Combativeness, American Dash, Discipline, Determination, American Energy, Eagerness, Enthusiasm, American Pluck, Persistency, Performance, American Spirit, Sagacity, Success, American Vim, Vigor, Virility.

-Al Spalding (1850 – 1915)

BOXING

I am the greatest, I said that even before I knew I was.
-Muhammad Ali (1942 -)

I go into the ring with a strategy but as soon as I get punched everything goes out of the window.
-Mike Tyson (1966 -)

The same hand that can write a beautiful poem, can knock you out with one punch - that's Poetic Justice.
-Wayne Kelly (1919 – 2001)

A computer once beat me at chess, but it was no match for me at kick boxing.
-Emo Phillips (1956 -)

Never fight ugly people - they have nothing to lose.
-Wayne Kelly (1919 – 2001)

To me, boxing is like a ballet, except there's no music, no choreography, and the dancers hit each other.
-Jack Handy (1949 -)

I'll beat him so bad he'll need a shoehorn to put his hat on.
-Muhammad Ali (1942 -)

Sure, there have been deaths and injuries in boxing, but none of them serious.
-Alan Minter (1951 -)

Boxers, like prostitutes, are in the business of ruining their bodies for the pleasure of strangers.

-*Wayne Kelly (1919 – 2001)*

All the time he's boxing, he's thinking. All the time he was thinking, I was hitting him.
-*Jack Dempsey (1895 – 1983)*

The question isn't at what age I want to retire, it's at what income.
-*George Foreman (1949 -)*

I wanted to do in boxing what Bruce Lee was able to do in karate. Lee was an artist, and, like him, I try to get beyond the fundamentals of my sport. I want my fights to be seen as plays.
-*Sugar Ray Leonard (1956 -)*

Sure the fight was fixed. I fixed it with a right hand. -*George Foreman (1949-)*

Boxing is a lot of white men watching two black men beat each other up.
-*Muhammad Ali (1942-)*

The fight is won or lost far away from witnesses - behind the lines, in the gym and out there on the road, long.
-*Muhammad Ali (1942 -)*

I am the astronaut of boxing. Joe Louis and Dempsey were just jet pilots. I'm in a world of my own.
-*Muhammad Ali (1942-)*

If you screw things up in tennis, it's 15-love. If you screw up in boxing, it's your ass.
-*Randall Cobb (1950 -)*

Boxing is a celebration of the lost religion of masculinity all the more trenchant for its being lost.
-Joyce Carol Oates (1938 -)

To see a man beaten not by a better opponent but by himself is a tragedy.
-Cus D'Amato (1908 – 85)

A boxing match is like a cowboy movie. There's got to be good guys and there's got to be bad guys. And that's what people pay for - to see the bad guys get beat.
-Sonny Liston (1932 – 70)

Boxing is the toughest and loneliest sport in the world. *-Frank Bruno (1961 -)*

I consider myself blessed. I consider you blessed. We've all been blessed with God-given talents. Mine just happens to be beating people up.
-Sugar Ray Leonard (1956 -)

In boxing you create a strategy to beat each new opponent, it's just like chess.
-Lennox Lewis (1965 -)

I hated every minute of training, but I said, 'Don't quit. Suffer now and live the rest of your life as a champion'.
-Muhammad Ali (1942 -)

Only in America.
-Don King (1931 -)

But it ain't how hard you hit; it's about how hard you can get hit, and keep moving forward.

-Sylvester Stallone (1946 -)

It's just a job. Grass grows, birds fly, waves pound the sand. I beat people up.
-Muhammad Ali (1942 -)

It's not bragging if you can back it up.
-Muhammad Ali (1942 -)

A champion is someone who gets up when he can't.
-Jack Dempsey (1895 – 1983)

You don't understand. I could have been a contender, I could have been a somebody, instead of a bum, which is what I am.
-Marlon Brando (1924 – 2004)

They called me a 'rapist' and a 'recluse.' I'm not a recluse.
-Michael Gerard Tyson (1966 -)

It's like someone jammed an electric light bulb in your face, and busted it. I thought half my head was blowed off…When he knocked me down I could have stayed there for three weeks.
-James J Braddock (1905 -74)

When I was a young fellow I was knocked down plenty. I wanted to stay down, but I couldn't. I had to collect the two dollars for winning or go hungry. I had to get up. I was one of those hungry fighters. You could have hit me on the chin with a sledgehammer for five dollars. When you haven't eaten for two days you'll understand.
-Jack Dempsey (1895 – 1983)

All fighters are prostitutes and all promoters are pimps.
-Larry Holmes (1949-)

Boxing is just show business with blood.
-Frank Bruno (1961 -)

To be a champ you have to believe in yourself when no one else will.
-Sugar Ray Robinson (1921 – 89)

CRICKET

When you play test cricket, you don't give the Englishmen an inch. Play it tough, all the way. Grind them into the dust.
-Don Bradman (1908 – 2001)

Cricket is basically baseball on valium.
-Robin Williams (1951 – 2014)

The English are not very spiritual people, so they invented cricket to give them some idea of eternity.
-George Bernard Shaw (1856 – 1950)

Cricket civilizes people and creates good gentlemen I want everyone to play cricket in Zimbabwe; I want ours to be a nation of gentlemen.
Robert Mugabe (1924 -)

Many Continentals think life is a game; the English think cricket is a game.
-George Mikes (1912 – 87)

I tend to think that cricket is the greatest thing that God ever created on earth - certainly greater than sex, although sex isn't too bad either.
-Harold Pinter (1930 – 2008)

Baseball has the great advantage over cricket of being ended sooner.
-George Bernard Shaw (1856 – 1950)

There is a widely held and quite erroneously held belief that Cricket is just another game.

-Prince Phillip (1921 -)

If there is any game in the world that attracts the half- baked theorist more than Cricket I have yet to hear of it.
-Fred Trueman (1931 – 2006)

Body-line was not an incident, it was not an accident, it was not a temporary aberration. It was the violence and ferocity of our age expressing itself in Cricket.
-CLR James (1901 -89)

He was an admirer of the bullfight, and had once drawn my attention to the fact that only Cricket and bullfighting had inspired any appreciable literature.
-Dal Stivins (1911 – 97)

The British 'Sphere of Influence' the Cricket ball.
-Anon

He revolutionised Cricket. He turned it from an accomplishment into a science.
-K. S. Ranjitsinhji (1872 – 1933) of WG Grace

I was brought up to believe that Cricket is the most important activity in men's lives, the most important thread in the fabric of the cosmos.
-Bernard Hollowood (1910 -81)

Cricket remains for me the game of games, the sans pareil, the great metaphor, the best marriage ever devised of mind and body? For me it remains the Proust of pastimes, the subtlest and most poetic, the most past- and-present; whose beauty can lie equally in days, in a whole, or in one tiny phrase, a blinding split second.
-John Fowles (1926 – 2005)

Cricket is quite a gentle, harmless game, but he's a lucky man who has not to sweat some blood before he's done with it.
-*John Snaith (1876 – 1936)*

If Stalin had learned to play Cricket, the world might now be a better place.
-*Dr. R Downey (1881 – 1953)*

Long ago I discovered that there was more to life than Cricket, and more to Cricket than runs and wickets.
-*David Foot*

Things never turn out in Cricket as one expects.
-*Talbot Baines Reed (1852 – 93)*

A Cricket tour in Australia would be a most delightful period in one's life if one was deaf.
-*Harold Larwood (1904 – 95)*

Personally, I have always looked upon Cricket as organized loafing.
-*William Temple (1881 – 1944)*

Cricket to us was more than play, it was a worship in the summer sun.
-*Edmund Blunden (1896 – 1974)*

Cricket is a most precarious profession; it is called a team game but, in fact, no one is so lonely as a batsman facing a bowler supported by ten fieldsmen and observed by two umpires to ensure that his error does not go unpunished.
-*John Arlott (1914 – 91)*

It (cricket) requires one to assume such indecent postures.
-Oscar Wilde (1854 – 1900)

A cricketer's life is a life of splendid freedom, healthy effort,
endless variety, and delightful good fellowship.
-W.G. Grace (1848 – 1915)

Reading poetry and watching cricket were the sum of my world,
and the two are not so far apart as many aesthetes might believe.
-Donald Bradman (1908 – 2001)

I should like to say that good batsman are born, not made; but my
long experience comes up before me, and tells me that it is not so.
-W.G. Grace (1848 – 1915)

He played a cut so late as to be positively posthumous.
-John Arlott (1914 – 91)

Tufnell! Can I borrow your brain? I'm building an idiot.
-Anon Australian fan

England trained and grass grew at the MCG yesterday, two
activities virtually indistinguishable from each other in tempo.
-Greg Baum (1959 -)

The hallmark of a great captain is the ability to win the toss at the
right time.
-Richie Benaud (1930 – 2015)

I once delivered a simple ball, which I was told, had it gone far
enough, would have been considered a wide.
-Lewis Carroll (1832 – 98)

Being the manager of a touring team is rather like being in charge of a cemetery - lots of people underneath you, but no one listening.
-Wes Hall (1937 -)

I'm confident they play the game in heaven. Wouldn't be heaven otherwise would it?
Patrick Moore (1923 – 2012)

I have prepared for the worst case scenario, but it could be even worse than that.
-Monty Panesar (1982 -)

If God can get me to 25 then I can do the rest.
-Derek Randall (1951 -)

A simple equation for cricketing enjoyment is that the fun had by one side is usually purchased at the expense of the other.
-Rob Gillham

SOCCER

The rules of soccer are very simple, basically it is this: if it moves, kick it. If it doesn't move, kick it until it does.
-Phil Woosnam (1932 – 2013)

I couldn't be more chuffed if I were a badger at the start of the mating season.
-Ian Holloway (1963 -)

If Everton were playing at the bottom of the garden, I'd pull the curtains.
-Bill Shankley (1913 – 81)

Mind you, I've been here during the bad times too - one year we came second.
-Bob Paisley (1919 – 96)

Please don't call me arrogant, but I'm European champion and I think I'm a special one.
-Jose Mourinho (1963 -)

I wouldn't say I was the best manager in the business. But I was in the top one.
-Brian Clough (1935 – 2004)

I know this is a sad occasion but I think that Dixie would be amazed to know that even in death he could draw a bigger crowd than Everton can on a Saturday Afternoon.
-Bill Shankley (1913 – 81)

Some people believe football is a matter of life and death. I'm very disappointed with that attitude. I can assure you it is much, much more important than that.
-*Bill Shankley (1913 – 81)*

I'd have given my right arm to be a pianist.
-*Bobby Robson (1933 – 2009)*

He's always in there looking to miss. By that I mean he's always looking to score, but if he misses he's not afraid of going in there again.
-*Bobby Robson (1933 – 2009)*

If you are first you are first. If you are second, you are nothing.
-*Bill Shankley (1913 – 81)*

It is completely dead out there. I've been phoning myself up and disguising my voice just for a bit of interest.
-*Gerry Francis (1951 -)*

At home they have a few drinks and probably the prawn sandwiches, and they don't realise what's going on out on the pitch. I don't think some of the people who come to Old Trafford can spell football, never mind understand it.
-*Roy Keane (1971 -)*

The best side drew.
-*Bill Shankley (1913 – 81)*

I hope I don't come across as bitter and twisted, but that man (Mick McCarthy) can rot in hell for all I care.
-*Roy Keane (1971 -)*

I knew it wasn't going to be our day when I arrived at Links Park and found that we had a woman running the line. She should be at home making the tea or the dinner for her man who comes in after he has been to the football.
-*Peter Hetherston (1964 -)*

A football team is like a piano. You need eight men to carry it and three who can play the damn thing.
-*Bill Shankley (1913 – 81)*

The man is United - cut him and he bleeds red.
-*Alan Brazil (1959 -)*

Every dog has its day - and today is woof day! Today I just want to bark.
-*Ian Holloway (1963 -)*

The trouble with referees is that they know the rules, but they don't know the game.
-Bill Shankley (1913 – 81)

Without being too harsh on David, he cost us the match.
-*Ian Wright (1963 -)*

They didn't change positions, they just moved the players around.
-*Terry Venables (1943 -)*

That was only a yard away from being an inch-perfect pass.
-*Murdo Macleod (1958 -)*

Not to win is guttering.
-*Mark Noble (1987 -)*

I never make predictions and I never will.

-Paul Gascoigne (1967 -)

Who'll win the league? It's a toss of a coin between three of them.

-Matt le Tissier (1968 -)

It's one of them days when you just say, 'It's one of them days'.

Ian Wright (1963 -)

There's no such thing as a must-win game, and this is one of them.

-Alan Wright (1971 -)

There are some real positives for Wales. Their back four's not bad, sometimes.

-Iain Dowie (1965 -)

We didn't underestimate them. They were just a lot better than we thought.

-Bobby Robson (1933 – 2009)

If you're in the penalty area and don't know what to do with the ball, put it in the net and we'll discuss the options later.

-Bob Paisley (1919 – 96)

You can't say my team aren't winners. They've proved that by finishing fourth, third and second in the last three years.

-Gerard Houllier (1947 -)

Football is a simple game; 22 men chase a ball for 90 minutes and at the end, the Germans win.

-Gary Lineker (1960 -)

I've just watched the replay and there is absolutely no doubt: it's inconclusive.

-*Garth Crooks (1958 -)*

It's looking more and more less likely.

-*Robbie Fowler (1975 -)*

Of course I didn't take my wife to see Rochdale as an anniversary present. It was her birthday. Would I have got married in the football season? Anyway, it was Rochdale reserves.

-*Bill Shankley* (1913 – 81)

Pressure is working down the pit. Pressure is having no work at all. Pressure is trying to escape relegation on 50 shillings a week. Pressure is not the European Cup or the Championship or the Cup Final. That's the reward.

-*Bill Shankley (1913 – 81)*

GOLF

Hockey is a sport for white men. Basketball is a sport for black men. Golf is a sport for white men dressed like black pimps.
-Tiger Woods (1975 -)

Although golf was originally restricted to wealthy, overweight Protestants, today it's open to anybody who owns hideous clothing.
-Dave Barry (1947 -)

The problem with golf is I have to deal with a humiliation factor.
-George W Bush (1946 -)

It took me seventeen years to get three thousand hits in baseball. It took one afternoon on the golf course.
-Hank Aaron (1934 -)

In golf as in life it is the follow through that makes the difference.
-Anon

To find a man's true character, play golf with him.
-P.G. Wodehouse (1881 – 1975)

I'm not feeling very well - I need a doctor immediately. Ring the nearest golf course.
-Groucho Marx (1890 – 1977)

If you drink, don't drive. Don't even putt.
-Dean Martin (1917 – 95)

The secret of good golf is to hit the ball hard, straight and not too often.

I know I am getting better at golf because I am hitting fewer spectators.
-Gerald R. Ford (1914 – 2006)

Golf can best be defined as an endless series of tragedies obscured by the occasional miracle.
-Anon

Golf is like a love affair. If you don't take it seriously, it's no fun; if you do take it seriously, it breaks your heart.
-Arthur Daley

If profanity had an influence on the flight of the ball, the game of golf would be played far better than it is.
-Horace G. Hutchinson (1859 – 1932)

Golf is a fascinating game. It has taken me nearly forty years to discover that I can't play it.
-Ted Ray (1905 – 77)

They say golf is like life, but don't believe them. Golf is more complicated than that.
-Gardener Dickinson (1912 – 98)

Golf is a lot of walking, broken up by disappointment and bad arithmetic.
-Anon

Golf and sex are the only things you can enjoy without being good at them.
-Jimmy DeMaret (1910 – 83)

Golf is a day spent in a round of strenuous idleness.
-*William Wordsworth (1770 – 1850)*

If you are caught on a golf course during a storm and are afraid of lightning, hold up a 1-iron. Not even God can hit a 1-iron.
-*Lee Trevino (1939 -)*

Man blames fate for other accidents but feels personally responsible for a hole in one.
-*Martha Beckman*

An interesting thing about golf is that no matter how badly you play, it is always possible to get worse.
-*Anon*

"Play it as it lies" is one of the fundamental dictates of golf. The other is "Wear it if it clashes."
-*Henry Beard (1945 -)*

I played golf... I did not get a hole in one, but I did hit a guy. That's way more satisfying.
-*Mitch Hedberg (1968 – 2005)*

My swing is so bad I look like a caveman killing his lunch.
-*Lee Trevino (1939 -)*

I played golf... I did not get a hole in one, but I did hit a guy. That's way more satisfying.
-*Thomas Boswell (1947 -)*

A "gimme" can best be defined as an agreement between two golfers, neither of whom can putt very well.
-*Anon*

Golf: A five mile walk punctuated with disappointments.
-Anon

Nothing dissects a man in public quite like golf.
-Brent Musburger (1939 -)

Golf is a game not just of manners but of morals.
-Art Spander (1940 -)

Golf is so popular simply because it is the best game in the world at which to be bad.
-AA Milne (1882 – 1956)

Show me a man who is a good loser and I'll show you a man who is playing golf with his boss.
-Jim Murray (1919 – 98)

He who has the fastest golf cart never has a bad lie.
-Mickey Mantle (1931 – 95)

When I die, bury me on the golf course so my husband will visit.
-Anon

Golf is deceptively simple and endlessly complicated.
-Arnold Palmer (1929 -)

Golf is a game whose aim is to hit a very small ball into an even smaller hole, with weapons singularly ill-designed for the purpose.
-Churchill (1974 – 1965)

The reason most people play golf is to wear clothes they would not be caught dead in otherwise.
-Roger Simon

Golf is like life in a lot of ways - All the biggest wounds are self-inflicted.
-Bill Clinton (1946 -)

The difference in golf and government is that in golf you can't improve your lie.
-George Deukmejian (1928 –)

While playing golf today I hit two good balls. I stepped on a rake.
-Henny Youngman (1906 – 98)

FISHING

Caution is a most valuable asset in fishing, especially if you are the fish.
-Anon

The charm of fishing is that it is the pursuit of that which is elusive but attainable, a perpetual series of occasions for hope.
-John Buchan (1875 – 1940)

He liked fishing and seemed to take pride in being able to like such a stupid occupation.
-Leo Tolstoy (1828 – 1910)

There are two types of fisherman - those who fish for sport and those who fish for fish.
-Anon

Fishing is the sport of drowning worms.
-Anon

Many men go fishing all of their lives without knowing it is not fish they are after.
-Henry David Thoreau (1817 – 62)

This planet is covered with sordid men who demand that he who spends time fishing shall show returns in fish.
-Leonidas Hubbard, Jr. (1872 – 1903)

Time is but the stream I go a-fishing in.
-Henry David Thoreau (1817 – 62)

A bad day of fishing is better than a good day of work.

We used to laugh at Grandpa when he'd head off and go fishing. But we wouldn't be laughing that evening when he'd come back with some whore he picked up in town.
-Jack Handy (1949 -)

All the romance of trout fishing exists in the mind of the angler and is in no way shared by the fish.
-Harold F. Blaisdell

Last year I went fishing with Salvador Dali. He was using a dotted line. He caught every other fish.
-Stephen Wright (1955 -)

The fishing was good; it was the catching that was bad.
-AK Best (1933 -)

There's a fine line between fishing and just standing on the shore like an idiot.
-Stephen Wright (1955 -)

It has always been my private conviction that any man who pits his intelligence against a fish and loses has it coming.
-John Steinbeck (1902 – 68)

Somebody just back of you while you are fishing is as bad as someone looking over your shoulder while you write a letter to your girl.
-Ernest Hemmingway (1899 – 1961)

Give a man a fish and he will eat for a day. Teach him how to fish and he will sit in a boat and drink beer all day.
-Anon

Marta says the interesting thing about fly-fishing is that it's two lives connected by a thin strand. Come on, Marta. Grow up.
-Jack Handy (1949 -)

Bragging may not bring happiness, but no man having caught a large fish goes home through an alley.
-Anon

You know when they have a fishing show on TV? They catch the fish and then let it go. They don't want to eat the fish, they just want to make it late for something.
-Mitch Hedberg (1968 – 2005)

When they go fishing, it is not really fish they are after. It is a philosophic meditation.
-ET Brown

Even if you've been fishing for 3 hours and haven't gotten anything except poison ivy and sunburn, you're still better off than the worm.
-Anon

All fishermen are liars; it's an occupational disease with them like housemaid's knee or editor's ulcers.
-Beatrice Cook

The gods do not deduct from man's allotted span the hours spent fishing.
-Proverb

The best way to a fisherman's heart is through his fly. - Anon
It is to be observed that 'angling' is the name given to fishing by people who can't fish.
-Stephen Leacock (1869 – 1944)

Fishing is a... discipline in the equality of men - for all men are equal before fish.
-Herbert Hoover (1874 – 1964)

Calling fishing a hobby is like calling brain surgery a job.
-Paul Schullery (1948 -)

Three-fourths of the Earth's surface is water, and one-fourth is land. It is quite clear that the good Lord intended us to spend triple the amount of time fishing as taking care of the lawn.
-Chuck Clark

Fishing tournaments seem a little like playing tennis with living balls.
-Jim Harrison (1937 -)

There is no greater fan of fly fishing than the worm.
-Patrick F. McManus (1933 -)

Give a man a fish, and he'll eat for a day. Give a fish a man, and he'll eat for weeks!
-Takayuki Ikkaku

Fishing is a delusion entirely surrounded by liars in old clothes. -Don Marquis (1878 – 1937)

If fishing is a religion, fly fishing is high church.
-Tom Brokaw (1940 -)

No human being, however great, or powerful, was ever so free as a fish.
-John Ruskin (1819 – 1900)

Chapter 8 Pets

Dogs

No matter how little money and how few possessions you own, having a dog makes you rich.
-Louis Sabin

Heaven goes by favor; if it went by merit, you would stay out and your dog would go in.
-Mark Twain (1835 – 1910)

I used to look at (my dog) Smokey and think, 'If you were a little smarter you could tell me what you were thinking,' and he'd look at me like he was saying, 'If you were a little smarter, I wouldn't have to'.
-Fred Jungclaus

One reason a dog is such a lovable creature is his tail wags instead of his tongue.
-Anon

I poured spot remover on my dog. Now he's gone.
Stephen Wright (1955 -)
Everyone needs a dog to adore him, and a cat to bring him back to reality.
-Anon

He is your friend, your partner, your defender, your dog. You are his life, his love, his leader. He will be yours, faithful and true, to the last beat of his heart. You owe it to him to be worthy of such devotion.
-Anon

Money will buy you a fine dog, but only love can make it wag its tail.
-*Richard Friedman*

One dog barks at something and a hundred bark at his sound.
-*Chinese proverb*

My goal in life is to become as wonderful as my dog thinks I am.
-*Anon*

Love me, love my dog.
-*Proverb*

Don't accept your dog's admiration as conclusive evidence that you are wonderful.
-*Ann Landers (1918 – 2002)*

The greatest love is a mother's; then a dog's; then a sweetheart's.
-*Polish proverb*

A dog wags its tail with its heart.
-*Martin Buxbaum (1912 – 91)*

Many years ago when an adored dog died, a great friend, a bishop, said to me, 'You must always remember that, as far as the Bible is concerned, God only threw the humans out of Paradise'.
-*Bruce Foyle*

Dachshund: A half-a-dog high and a dog-and-a-half long. -*Henry Louis Mencken (1880 – 1956)*

One reason a dog can be such a comfort when you're feeling blue is that he doesn't try to find out why.
-*Anon*

Do not call to a dog with a whip in your hand.
-*African proverb*

You can say any foolish thing to do to a dog, and the dog will give you a look that says, 'My God, you're right! I never would've thought of that!'
-*Dave Barry (1941 -)*

Many who have spent a lifetime in it can tell us less of love than the child that lost a dog yesterday.
-*Thornton Wilder (1897 – 1975)*

The bond with a true dog is as lasting as the ties of this earth will ever be.
-*Konrad Lorenz (1903 – 89)*

The dog is a gentleman; I hope to go to his heaven, not man's.
-*Mark Twain (1835 -1910)*

In order to keep a true perspective of one's importance, everyone should have a dog that will worship him and a cat that will ignore him.
-*Dereke Bruce*

If skill could be gained by watching, every dog would become a butcher.
-*Turkish proverb*

Acquiring a dog may be the only opportunity a human ever has to choose a relative.
-*Mordecai Wyatt Johnson (1890 – 1976)*

A dog at play has the mind of a wise martial arts master, a mind capable of perfect focus.

-Anon

I love a dog. He does nothing for political reasons.

-Will Rogers (1879 – 1935)

A dog is the only thing on earth that loves you more than he loves himself.

-Josh Billings (1818 – 85)

Love is the emotion that a woman feels always for a poodle dog and sometimes for a man.

-George Jean Nathan (1882 – 1958)

A dog has the soul of a philosopher.

-Plato (428 – 348 BC)

No one appreciates the very special genius of your conversation as the dog does.

-Christopher Morley (1890 – 1957)

Be on your guard against a silent dog and still water.

-Latin proverb

The dog was created specially for children. He is a god of frolic.

-Henry Ward Beecher (1813 – 87)

From a dog's point of view his master is an elongated and abnormally cunning dog.

-Mabel L Robinson (1874 – 1962)

My dog, she looks at me sometimes with that look, and I think maybe deep down inside she must know exactly how I feel. But then maybe she just wants the food off my plate.
-Anon

I never married because there was no need. I have three pets at home which answer the same purpose as a husband. I have a dog which growls every morning, a parrot which swears all afternoon, and a cat that comes home late at night.
-Marie Corelli (1855 – 1924)

Did you ever notice when you blow in a dog's face he gets mad at you? But when you take him in a car he sticks his head out the window.
-Steve Bluestone

God will prepare everything for our perfect happiness in heaven, and if it takes my dog being there, I believe he'll be there.
-Billy Graham (1918 -)

In order to really enjoy a dog, one doesn't merely try to train him to be semi-human. The point of it is to open oneself to the possibility of becoming partly a dog.
-Edward Hoagland (1932 -)

We are alone, absolutely alone on this chance planet; and amid all the forms of life that surround us, not one, excepting the dog has made an alliance with us.
-Max Depree (1924 -)

Sooner or later we're all someone's dog.
-Terry Pratchett (1948 -)

If a dog will not come to you after having looked you in the face, you should go home and examine your conscience.
-*Woodrow T Wilson (1856 – 1924)*

If you want a friend in Washington, get a dog.
-*Harry S Truman (1884 – 1972)*

Outside of a dog, a book is man's best friend. Inside of a dog it's too dark to read.
-*Groucho Marx (1890 – 1977)*

Happiness is a warm puppy.
-*Charles M. Schulz (1922 – 2000)*

Dogs are our link to paradise. They don't know evil or jealousy or discontent. To sit with a dog on a hillside on a glorious afternoon is to be back in Eden, where doing nothing was not boring--it was peace.
-*Milan Kundera (1929 -)*

If there are no dogs in Heaven, then when I die I want to go where they went.
-*Will Rogers (1879 – 1935)*

All his life he tried to be a good person. Many times, however, he failed. For after all, he was only human. He wasn't a dog.
-*Charles M. Schulz (1922 – 2000)*

Dogs are not our whole life, but they make our lives whole.
-*Roger A. Caras (1928 – 2001)*

Inside every Newfoundland, Boxer, Elkhound and Great Dane is a puppy longing to climb on to your lap.
-*Helen Thomson*

If you pick up a starving dog and make him prosperous, he will not bite you. This is the principal difference between a dog and a man.
-Mark Twain (1835 – 1910)

I hope to be the kind of person my dog thinks I am.
-Anon

There is no psychiatrist in the world like a puppy licking your face.
-Bern Williams (1929 – 2003)

CATS

Always remember, a cat looks down on man, a dog looks up to man, but a pig will look man right in the eye and see his equal.

-Winston Churchill (1874 – 1965)

Cat's motto: No matter what you've done wrong, always try to make it look like the dog did it.
-Anon

Cats are intended to teach us that not everything in nature has a function.
-Garrison Keillor (1942 -)

It's easy to understand why the cat has eclipsed the dog as modern America's favorite pet. People like pets to possess the same qualities they do. Cats are irresponsible and recognize no authority, yet are completely dependent on others for their material needs. Cats cannot be made to do anything useful. Cats are mean for the fun of it.
-PJ O'Rourke (1947 -)

If a dog jumps in your lap, it is because he is fond of you; but if a cat does the same thing, it is because your lap is warmer.
-Alfred North Whitehead (1861 – 1947)

When the mouse laughs at the cat there is a hole nearby.
-Nigerian proverb

If you hold a cat by the tail you learn things you cannot learn any other way.
-Mark Twain (1835-1910)

If toast always lands butter-side down, and cats always land on their feet, what happens if you strap toast on the back of a cat and drop it?
-*Stephen Wright (1955 -)*

Everyone needs a dog to adore him, and a cat to bring him back to reality.
-*Anon*

Who among us hasn't envied a cat's ability to ignore the cares of daily life and to relax completely ?
-*Karen Brademeyer*

God made the cat so that man might have the pleasure of caressing the tiger.
-*Fernand Mery (1897 – 1983)*

If man could be crossed with the cat, it would improve man but deteriorate the cat.
-*Mark Twain (1835 – 1910)*

Never play cat and mouse games if you're a mouse.
-*Don Addis (1935 – 2009)*

One day Alice came to a fork in the road and saw a Cheshire cat in a tree. 'Which road do I take' she asked. 'Where do you want to go' was his response. 'I don't know', Alice answered. Then, said the cat, 'it doesn't matter'.
-*Lewis Carroll (1832 -98)*

As every cat owner knows, nobody owns a cat.
-*Ellen Perry Berkeley*

The cat is above all things, a dramatist.
-*Margaret Benson (1865 – 1916)*

Lettin' the cat outta the bag is a whole lot easier 'n puttin' it back in.
-*Will Rogers (1879 – 1935)*

When I play with my cat, who knows whether she is not amusing herself with me more than I with her.
-*Michel de Montaigne (1533 – 92)*

Anyone who considers protocol unimportant has never dealt with a cat.
-*Robert A Heinlein (1907 -88)*

The dog may be wonderful prose, but only the cat is poetry.
-*French proverb*

Curiosity is the very basis of education and if you tell me that curiosity killed the cat, I say only the cat died nobly.
-*Arnold Edinborough (1922 – 2006)*

Cats are dangerous companions for writers because cat watching is a near-perfect method of writing avoidance.
-*Dan Greenburg (1936 -)*

A cat pours his body on the floor like water. It is restful just to see him.
-*William Lyon Phelps (1865 – 1943)*

The cat is nature's beauty.
-*Proverb*

Your cat will never threaten your popularity by barking at three in the morning. He won't attack the mailman or eat the drapes, although he may climb the drapes to see how the room looks from the ceiling.
-Helen Powers

A cat is a puzzle for which there is no solution.
-Hazel Nicholson

The mice think they are right, but my cat eats them anyways. This is the point, reality is nothing, perception is everything.
-Terry Goodkind (1948 -)

Always remember, a cat looks down on man, a dog looks up to man, but a pig will look man right in the eye and see his equal. -Winston Churchill (1874 – 1965)

In nine lifetimes, you'll never know as much about your cat as your cat knows about you.
-Michel de Montaigne (1533 -92)

If we treated everyone we meet with the same affection we bestow upon our favorite cat, they, too, would purr.
-Martin Delany (1812 -85)

The more people I meet, the more I love my cat.
-Anon

The clever cat eats cheese and breathes down rat holes with baited breath.
-WC Fields (1880 – 1946)

A cat determined not to be found can fold itself up like a pocket handkerchief if it wants to.
-*Louis Camuti (1893 – 1981)*

To bathe a cat takes brute force, perseverance, courage of conviction - and a cat. The last ingredient is usually hardest to come by.
-*Stephen Baker*

A cat will be your friend, but never your slave.
-*Theophile Gautier (1811 – 72)*

A cat has absolute emotional honesty: human beings, for one reason or another, may hide their feelings, but a cat does not.
-*Ernest Hemmingway (1899 – 1961)*

If cats looked like frogs we'd realize what nasty, cruel little bastards they are. Style. That's what people remember.
-*Terry Pratchett (1948 -)*

Cats are connoisseurs of comfort.
-*James Herriot (1916 – 95)*

Cats are intended to teach us that not everything in nature has a purpose.
-*Garrison Keillor (1942 -)*

One day I was counting the cats and I absent-mindedly counted myself.
-*Bobbie Ann Mason (1940 -)*

I would like to see anyone, prophet, king or God, convince a thousand cats to do the same thing at the same time.
-*Neil Gaiman (1960 -)*

What greater gift than the love of a cat.
-Charles Dickens (1812 – 70)

Dogs come when they're called. Cats take a message and get back to you.
-Mary Bly (1962 -)

CHAPTER 9 COUNTRIES

UNITED STATES OF AMERICA

America is the only country that went from barbarism to decadence without civilization in between.
-Oscar Wilde (1854 – 1900)

You can always count on Americans to do the right thing - after they've tried everything else.
-Winston Churchill (1874 – 1965)

Americans have different ways of saying things. They say "elevator", we say "lift"... they say "President", we say "stupid psychopathic git".
-Alexei Sayle (1952 -)

The cost of freedom is always high, but Americans have always paid it. And one path we shall never choose, and that is the path of surrender, or submission.
-John F Kennedy (1917 – 63)

We Americans live in a nation where the medical-care system is second to none in the world, unless you count maybe 25 or 30 little scuzzball countries like Scotland that we could vaporize in seconds if we felt like it.
-Dave Barry (1947 -)

Americans who travel abroad for the first time are often shocked to discover that, despite all the progress that has been made in the last 30 years, many foreign people still speak in foreign languages.
-Dave Barry (1947 -)

I predict future happiness for Americans if they can prevent the government from wasting the labors of the people under the pretense of taking care of them.
-Thomas Jefferson (1762 – 1826)

We can have no "50-50" allegiance in this country. Either a man is an American and nothing else, or he is not an American at all.
-Theodore Roosevelt (1858 – 1919)

Americans play to win at all times. I wouldn't give a hoot and hell for a man who lost and laughed. That's why Americans have never lost nor ever lose a war.
-General George S Patton (1885 – 1945)

Half of the American people have never read a newspaper. Half never voted for President. One hopes it is the same half.
-Gore Vidal (1925 – 2012)

An asylum for the sane would be empty in America.
-George Bernard Shaw (1856 – 1950)

America makes prodigious mistakes, America has colossal faults, but one thing cannot be denied: America is always on the move. She may be going to Hell, of course, but at least she isn't standing still.
-EE Cummings (1894 – 1962)

America's abundance was not created by public sacrifices to "the common good", but by the productive genius of free men who pursued their own personal interests and the making of their own private fortunes.
-Ayn Rand (1905 – 82)

America is a mistake, a giant mistake.
-Sigmund Freud (1856 – 1939)

What the United States does best is to understand itself. What it does worst is understand others.
-*Carlos Fuentes (1928 -)*

America has the longest prison sentences in the West, yet the only condition long sentences demonstrably cure is heterosexuality.
-*Bruce Jackson (1936 -)*

I love America more than any other country in this world, and, exactly for this reason, I insist on the right to criticize her perpetually.
-*James Arthur Baldwin (1924 -87)*

My fellow citizens of the world: ask not what America will do for you, but what together we can do for the freedom of man. John Fitzgerald Kennedy (1917 – 63)
American consumers have no problem with carcinogens, but they will not purchase any product, including floor wax, that has fat in it.
-*Dave Barry (1947 -)*

If there be one principle more deeply rooted than any other in the mind of every American, it is, that we should have nothing to do with conquest.
-*Thomas Jefferson (1762 – 1826)*

America is becoming so educated that ignorance will be a novelty. I will belong to the select few.
-*Will Rogers (1879 – 1935)*

I think the most un-American thing you can say is, 'You can't say that.'
-*Garrison Keillor (1942 -)*

America is the best half-educated country in the world.
-Nicolas Murray Butler (1862 – 1947)

About all I can say for the United States Senate is that it opens with a prayer and closes with an investigation.
-Will Rogers (1879 – 1935)

What's right about America is that although we have a mess of problems, we have great capacity - intellect and resources - to do something about them.
-Henry Ford (1863 – 1947)

The United States was founded by the brightest people in the country - and we haven't seen them since.
-Gore Vidal (1925 – 2012)

What the people want is very simple - they want an America as good as its promise.
-Barbara Jordan (1936 -96)

The cause of America is in a great measure the cause of all mankind.
-Thomas Paine (1737 – 1809)

America was not built on fear. America was built on courage, on imagination, and unbeatable determination to do the job at hand.
-Harry S Truman (1884 – 1972)

I have been thinking that I would make a proposition to my Republican friends... that if they will stop telling lies about the Democrats, we will stop telling the truth about them.
-Adlai Stevenson (1900 -65)

America is great because she is good. If America ceases to be good, America will cease to be great.
-*Alexis de Tocqueville (1805 – 59)*

America did not invent human rights. In a very real sense, it is the other way around. Human rights invented America.
-*Jimmy Carter (1924 -)*

The only foes that threaten America are the enemies at home, and these are ignorance, superstition and incompetence.
-*Elbert Hubbard (1856 – 1915)*

And so, my fellow Americans, ask not what your country can do for you -- ask what you can do for your country.
-*John Fitzgerald Kennedy (1917 – 1965)*

There are those who will say that the liberation of humanity, the freedom of man and mind is nothing but a dream. They are right. It is the American Dream.
-*Archibald MacLeish (1892 – 1982)*

Someday, following the example of the United States of America, there will be a United States of Europe.
-*George Washington (1732 -99)*

The men the American people admire most extravagantly are the most daring liars; the men they detest most violently are those who try to tell them the truth.
-*Henry Louis Menken (1880 -1956)*

Ninety-eight percent of American homes have TV sets, which means the people in the other 2% have to generate their own sex and violence.
-*Franklin P Jones (1887 – 1929)*

Just what is it that America stands for? If she stands for one thing more than another it is for the sovereignty of self-governing people.
-*Woodrow T Wilson (1856 – 1924)*

I hate this "crime doesn't pay" stuff. Crime in the United States is perhaps one of the biggest businesses in the world today.
-*Peter Kirk*

America... just a nation of two hundred million used car salesmen with all the money we need to buy guns and no qualms about killing anybody else in the world who tries to make us uncomfortable.
-*Hunter S Thompson (1937 – 2005)*

The Americans combine the notions of religion and liberty so intimately in their minds that it is impossible to make them conceive of one without the other.
-*Alexis de Tocqueville (1805 -59)*

We Americans have no commission from God to police the world.
-*Benjamin Harrison (1833 – 1901)*

We in America do not have government by the majority. We have government by the majority who participate.
-*Thomas Jefferson (1743 – 1826)*

Most Americans aren't the sort of citizens the Founding Fathers expected; they are contented serfs. Far from being active critics of government, they assume that its might makes it right.
-*Joseph Sobran (1946-)*

America cannot have an empire abroad and a Republic at home.
--*Mark Twain (1835 – 1910)*

It would be some time before I fully realized that the United States sees little need for diplomacy. Power is enough. Only the weak rely on diplomacy ... The Roman Empire had no need for diplomacy. Nor does the United States.
-*Boutros Boutros-Ghali (1922 -)*

From 1945 to 2003, the United States attempted to overthrow more than 40 foreign governments, and to crush more than 30 populist-nationalist movements fighting against intolerable regimes. In the process, the US bombed some 25 countries, caused the end of life for several million people, and condemned many millions more to a life of agony and despair.
-*William Blum (1933 -)*

The Framers of the Bill of Rights did not purport to 'create' rights. Rather, they designed the Bill of Rights to prohibit our Government from infringing rights and liberties presumed to be pre-existing.
-*Justice William J. Brennan (1906 -97)*

When even one American-who has done nothing wrong-is forced by fear to shut his mind and close his mouth-then all Americans are in peril.
Harry S. Truman (1884 – 1972)

The business of America is business.
-*President Calvin Coolidge (1872 – 1933)*

The genius of you Americans is that you never make clear-cut stupid moves, only complicated stupid moves which make the rest of us wonder at the possibility that we might be missing something.
-*Gamal Abdel Nasser (1918 – 70)*

My dream is of a place and a time where America will once again be seen as the last best hope of earth.

-Abraham Lincoln (1809 – 65)

FRANCE

To understand Europe, you have to be a genius - or French.
-Madeleine Albright (1937 -)

If my theory of relativity is proven successful, Germany will claim
me as a German and France will declare that I am a citizen of the
world. Should my theory prove untrue, France will say that I am a
German and Germany will declare that I am a Jew.
-Albert Einstein (1879 – 1955)

France, and the whole of Europe have a great culture and an
amazing history. Most important thing though is that people there
know how to live! In America they've forgotten all about it. I'm
afraid that the American culture is a disaster.
-Johnny Depp (1963 -)

When in 1966 Charles de Gaulle ordered France out of NATO and
American troops off French soil, Secretary of State Dean Rusk
asked him if that included the American soldiers lying dead in the
cemeteries at Normandy and throughout France.
-Charles Krauthammer (1950 -)

In Paris they simply stared when I spoke to them in French; I
never did succeed in making those idiots understand their own
language.
-Mark Twain (1835 -1910)

Hell is a place where the motorists are French, the policemen are
German, and the cooks are English.
-Anon

The French complain of everything, and always.
-Napoleon Bonaparte (1769 – 1821)

French is the language that turns dirt into romance.
-Stephen King (1947 -)

Boy, those French: They have a different word for everything!
-Steve Martin (1945 -)

Escargot is French for 'fat crawling bag of phlegm'.
-Dave Barry (1947 -)

I pity the French Cinema because it has no money. I pity the
American Cinema because it has no ideas.
-Jean-Luc Godard (1930 -)

Bonjoooouuuurrr, ya cheese-eatin' surrender monkeys!
-Ken Keeler/Groundsman Willie (1961 -)

A lot of folks are still demanding more evidence before they
actually consider Iraq a threat. For example, France wants more
evidence. And you know I'm thinking, the last time France wanted
more evidence they rolled right through Paris with the German
flag.
-David Letterman (1947 -)

The reason French roads have trees planted down both sides is
that the Germans like to march in the shade.
-Anon

ENGLAND

The English never draw a line without blurring it.
-*Winston Churchill (1874 – 1965)*

The whole strength of England lies in the fact that the enormous majority of the English people are snobs.
-*George Bernard Shaw (1856 – 1950)*

I speak two languages, Body and English.
-*Mae West (1892 – 1980)*

Once more into the breach, dear friends, once more; Or close the wall up with our English dead!
-*William Shakespeare (1564 – 1616)*

If one could only teach the English how to talk, and the Irish how to listen, society here would be quite civilized.
-*Oscar Wilde (1854 – 1900)*

We have always found the Irish a bit odd. They refuse to be English.
-*Winston Churchill (1874 – 1965)*

English - Who needs that? I'm never going to England!
-*Dan Castellaneta/Homer Simpson (1958 -)*

The English winter, ending in July to recommence in August.
-*Lord Byron (1788 – 1824)*

I tell you Wellington is a bad general, the English are bad soldiers; we will settle this matter by lunch time.
-*Napoleon Bonaparte (1769 – 1821)*

For Heaven's sake discard the monstrous wig which makes the English judges look like rats peeping through bunches of oakum.
-Thomas Jefferson (1762 – 1826)

The only English words I saw in Japan were Sony and Mitsubishi.
-Bill Gullickson (1959 -)

The English are not very spiritual people, so they invented cricket to give them some idea of eternity.
-George Bernard Shaw (1856 – 1950)

Tea to the English is really a picnic indoors.
-Alice Walker (1944 -)

If the English language made any sense, lackadaisical would have something to do with a shortage of flowers.
-Doug Larson (1902 – 81)

England has two books, the Bible and Shakespeare. England made Shakespeare, but the Bible made England.
-Victor Hugo (1802 – 1885)

It was one of those perfect English autumnal days which occur more frequently in memory than in life.
-P.D. James (1920 – 1914)

In England we have such good manners that if someone says something impolite the police get involved.
-Russell Brand (1975 -)

I like the English. They have the most rigid code of immorality in the world.
-Malcolm Bradbury (1932 – 2000)

Hearts at peace, under an English heaven.
-Rupert Brooke (1887 – 1915)

The reason why Englishmen are the best husbands in the world is because they want to be faithful. A Frenchman or an Italian will wake up in the morning and wonder what girl he will meet. An Englishman wakes up and wonders what the cricket score is.
-Barbara Cartland (1901 – 2000)

The British nation is unique in this respect: they are the only people who like to be told how bad things are, who like to be told the worst.
-Winston Churchill (1874 – 1965)

The British do not expect happiness. I had the impression, all the time that I lived there, that they do not want to be happy; they want to be right.
-Quentin Crisp (1908 – 99)

On the Continent people have good food; in England people have good table manners.
-George Mikes (1912 – 87)

What a pity it is that we have no amusements in England but vice and religion!
-Sydney Smith (1771 – 1845)

You never find an Englishman among the under-dogs - except in England, of course.
-Evelyn Waugh (1903 – 96)

There are many things in life more worthwhile than money. One is to be brought up in this our England which is still the envy of less happy lands.
-Lord Denning (1899 – 1999)

In the end it may well be that Britain will be honoured by historians more for the way she disposed of an empire than for the way in which she acquired it.

-Lord Harlech (1918 – 85)

We do not regard the English as foreigners. We look on them only as rather mad Norwegians.

-Halvard Lange (1902 -70)

Remember that you are an Englishman, and have consequently won first prize in the lottery of life.

-Cecil Rhodes (1853 – 1902)

The British are so incestuous. They pass around partners as if they were passing popcorn at a movie.

-Cameron Diaz (1972-)

We have really everything in common with America nowadays except, of course, language.

-Oscar Wilde (1854 – 1900)

I didn't know he was dead; I thought he was British.

-Anon

The English may not like music, but they absolutely love the noise it makes.

-Thomas Beecham (1879 – 1961)

An Englishman, even if he is alone, forms an orderly queue of one.

-George Mikes (1912 -87)

The English are not happy unless they are miserable, the Irish are not at peace unless they are at war, and the Scots are not at home unless they are abroad.
-George Orwell (1903 -50)

The English contribution to world cuisine - the chip.
-John Cleese (1939 -)

Continental people have sex lives; the English have hot-water bottles.
-George Mikes (1912 – 87)

You British plundered half the world for your own profit. Let's not pass it off as the Age of Enlightenment.
-Paddy Chayefsky (1923 – 81)

CANADA

Canada is America's toilet.
-Anon

When I was crossing the border into Canada, they asked if I had any firearms with me. I said, "Well, what do you need?
-Stephen Wright (1955 -)

Canada will be a strong country when Canadians of all provinces feel at home in all parts of the country, and when they feel that all Canada belongs to them.
-Pierre Elliot Trudeau (1919 – 2000)

For some reason a glaze passes over people's faces when you say "Canada". Maybe we should invade South Dakota or something.
-Sandra Gotlieb (1936 -)

A Canadian is sort of like an American, but without the gun.
-Pierre Burton (1920 – 2004)

I've been to Canada, and I've always gotten the impression that I could take the country over in about two days.
-Jon Stewart (1962 -)

I don't even know what street Canada is on.
-Al Capone (1899 – 1947)

God Bless America, but God help Canada to put up with them!
-Anon

We'll explain the appeal of curling to you if you explain the appeal of the National Rifle Association to us.

-Andy Barrie (1945 -)

When I'm in Canada, I feel this is what the world should be like.
-Jane Fonda (1937 -)

The beaver, which has come to represent Canada as the eagle does the United States and the lion Britain, is a flat-tailed, slow-witted, toothy rodent known to bite off its own testicles or to stand under its own falling trees.
-June Callwood (1924 – 2007)

Canada has never been a melting-pot; more like a tossed salad.
-Arnold Edinborough (1922 – 2006)

The Canadian military is like Switzerland's. Without the knife.
-John Wing

Canada is like your attic, you forget that it's up there, but when you go, it's like "Oh man, look at all this great stuff".
-Anon

The Canadian version of Julius Caesar's memoirs? I came, I saw, I coped.
-Clive James (1939 -)

Some countries you love. Some countries you hate. Canada is a country you worry about.
-Robertson Davies (1913 -95)

If some countries have too much history, we have too much geography.
-William Lyon Mackenzie King (1874 – 1950)

Americans are benevolently ignorant about Canada, while Canadians are malevolently well informed about the United States.
-J. Bartlet Brebner (1895 – 1957)

Canada is the only country founded on the relentless pursuit of the rodent.
-Preston Manning (1942 -)

Canada's climate is nine months winter and three months late in the fall.
-Evan Esar (1899 – 1995)

Canadians are arrogant about their own modesty.
-Christopher Molineaux

A Canadian is merely an unarmed American with health care.
-John Wing

Canadians are more polite when they are being rude than Americans are when they are being friendly.
-Edgar Friedenberg (1921 – 2000)

The Canadian kid who wants to grow up to be Prime Minister isn't thinking big, he is setting a limit to his ambitions rather early.
-Mordechai Richler (1931 – 2001)

AUSTRALIA

Don't worry about the world coming to an end today. It is already tomorrow in Australia.
-Charles M Schulz (1922 – 2000)

In America, only the successful writer is important, in France all writers are important, in England no writer is important, and in Australia you have to explain what a writer is.
-Geoffrey Cottrell

God bless America. God save the Queen. God defend New Zealand and thank Christ for Australia.
-Russell Crowe (1964 -)

In Australia, not reading poetry is the national pastime.
-Phyllis McGinley (1905 – 78)

The Australian Book of Etiquette is a very slim volume.
-Paul Theroux (1941 -)

Alone of all the races on earth, they seem to be free from the 'Grass is Greener on the other side of the fence' syndrome, and roundly proclaim that Australia is, in fact, the other side of that fence.
-Douglas Adams (1952 – 2001)

The bigger the hat, the smaller the property.
-Australian proverb

Out in the bush, the tarred road always ends just after the house of the local mayor.
-Australian proverb

There is nothing more Australian than spending time in somebody else's country.
-Anon

There are many non-intellectual countries; Australia is one of the few anti-intellectual ones.
-George Mikes (1912 – 87)

A few years ago we colonised this place with some of our finest felons, thieves, muggers, alcoholics and prostitutes, a strain of depravity which I believe has contributed greatly to this country's amazing vigour and enterprise.
-Ian Wooldridge (1932 – 2007)

At the end of my trial, I was rather hoping the judge would send me to Australia for the rest of my life.
-Jeffrey Archer (1940 -)

Today is your special day, even if today might be tomorrow to an Australian. And even though you're not Australian, it doesn't negate the fact that today may or may not be tomorrow.
-Jarod Kintz (1982 -)

Australia is not very exclusive. On the visa application they still ask if you've been convicted of a felony – although they are willing to give you a visa even if you haven't been.
-P.J O'Rourke (1947 -)

He's got a few roos loose in the top paddock.
-Australian saying

If you find an Australian indoors it's a fair bet that he will have a glass in his hand.
-Jonathan Aitken (1942 -)

New Zealand was colonized initially by those Australians who had the initiative to escape.

-Robert Muldoon (1921 – 92)

GERMANY

One thing I will say about the Germans, they are always perfectly willing to give somebody's land to somebody else.
-Will Rogers (1879 – 1935)

Whenever the literary German dives into a sentence that is the last you are going to see of him until he emerges on the other side of his Atlantic with his verb in his mouth.
-Mark Twain (1835 -1920)

The great virtues of the German people have created more evils than idleness ever did vices.
-Paul Valery (1871 – 1935)

One German makes a philosopher, two a public meeting, three a war.
-Robert D. MacDonald

The East German manages to combine a Teutonic capacity for bureaucracy with a Russian capacity for infinite delay.
-Goronwy Rees (1909 – 79)

There are two kinds of music; German music and bad music.
-Henry Louis Mencken (1880 – 1956)

Free speech isn't dead in Germany and Italy, merely the speakers.
-Bob Hope (1903 – 2003)

An appeal to fear never finds an echo in German hearts.
-Otto von Bismarck (1815 – 98)

East Germany was so total in its totalitarianism that everything was banned which wasn't compulsory.
-P.J. O'Rourke (1947 -)

If I can send the flower of the German nation into the hell of war without the smallest pity for the shedding of precious German blood, then surely I have the right to remove millions of an inferior race that breeds like vermin.
-Adolf Hitler (1889 – 1945)

You can always reason with a German. You can always reason with a barnyard animal, too, for all the good it does.
-P.J. O'Rourke (1947 -)

I speak Spanish to God, Italian to women, French to men and German to my horse.
-Charles V (1500 – 58)

Germany has reduced savagery to a science, and this Great War for the victorious peace of justice must go on until the German cancer is cut clean out of the world body.
-Theodore Roosevelt (1858 – 1919)

Football is a simple game. Twenty-two men chase a ball for 90 minutes and at the end, the Germans always win.
-Gary Lineker (1960 -)

The Schleswig-Holstein question is so complicated only three men in Europe have ever understood it. One was Price Albert, who is dead. The second was a German Professor who became mad. I am the third and I have forgotten all about it.
-Lord Palmerston (1784 – 1865)

German is the most extravagantly ugly language. It sounds like someone using a sick bag on a 747.
-*Willy Rushton (1937 -96)*

The Germans are like women, you can scarcely ever fathom their depths – they haven't any.
-*Friedrich Nietzche (1844 – 1900)*

To walk through the ruined cities of Germany is to feel an actual doubt about the continuity of civilization.
-*George Orwell (1903 – 50)*

Humor is not a mood but a way of looking at things. So if it is correct to say that humor was stamped out in Nazi Germany that does not mean that people were not in good spirits, or anything of that sort, but something much deeper and more important.
-*Ludwig Wittgenstein (1889 – 1951)*

Chapter 10 Occupations

Law and Lawyers

If you don't get a lawyer who knows law then get the one who knows the Judge.
-Anon

It is better to be a mouse in a cat's mouth than a man in a lawyer's hands.
-Spanish proverb

Make crime pay. Become a Lawyer.
-William Rogers (1879 – 1935)

A lawyer with a briefcase can steal more than a thousand men with guns.
-Mario Puzo (1920 – 99)

The good lawyer is not the man who has an eye to every side and angle of contingency, and qualifies all his qualifications, but who throws himself on your part so heartily, that he can get you out of a scrape.
-Ralph Waldo Emmerson (1803 -82)

I busted a mirror and got seven years bad luck, but my lawyer thinks he can get me five.
-Stephen Wright (1955 -)

A jury consists of twelve persons chosen to decide who has the better lawyer.
-Robert Frost (1874 – 1963)

Lawyer: One who protects us from robbers by taking away the temptation.
-*Henry Louis Mencken (1880 – 1956)*

The power of the lawyer is in the uncertainty of the law.
- *Jeremy Bentham (1748 – 1832)*

A lawyer starts life giving $500 worth of law for $5 and ends giving $5 worth for $500.
-*Benjamin H Brewster (1816 – 88)*

A lawyer's primer: If you don't have the law, you argue the facts; if you don't have the facts, you argue the law; if you have neither the facts nor the law, then you argue the Constitution.
-*Anon*

I've never been in love. I've always been a lawyer.
-*Anon*

The lawyer's truth is not Truth, but consistency or a consistent expediency.
-*Henry David Thoreau (1817 – 62)*

He who is his own lawyer has a fool for a client.
-*Proverb*

It is not what a lawyer tells me I may do; but what humanity, reason, and justice tell me I ought to do.
-*Edmund Burke (1729 – 97)*

The minute you read something that you can't understand, you can almost be sure that it was drawn up by a lawyer.
-*Will Rogers (1879 – 1935)*

A lawyer's relationship to justice and wisdom is on a par with a piano tuner's relationship to a concert. He neither composes the music, nor interprets it-he merely keeps the machinery running.
-*Lucille Kallen (1922 – 99)*

LAWYER, n. One skilled in circumvention of the law.
-*Ambrose Bierce (1842 -1914)*

Well, I don't know as I want a lawyer to tell me what I cannot do. I hire him to tell how to do what I want to do.
-*John Pierpont Morgan (1837 – 1913)*

Don't misinform your Doctor nor your Lawyer.
-*Benjamin Franklin (1706 – 90)*

The doctor sees all the weakness of mankind; the lawyer all the wickedness, the theologian all the stupidity.
-*Arthur Schopenhauer (1788 – 1860)*

Law students are trained in the case method, and to the lawyer everything in life looks like a case.
-*Edward Packard Jr. (1931 -)*

No poet ever interpreted nature as freely as a lawyer interprets the truth.
-*Jean Giraudoux (1882 – 1944)*

Never forget that everything Hitler did in Germany was legal.
-*Martin Luther King (1929 – 68)*

The average lawyer is essentially a mechanic who works with a pen instead of a ball peen hammer.
-*Robert Schmitt*

What a holler would ensue if people had to pay the minister as much to marry them as they have to pay a lawyer to get them a divorce.
-Claire Trevor (1910 – 2000)

A good lawyer is a bad neighbor.
-French proverb

A lawyer is never entirely comfortable with a friendly divorce, any more than a good mortician wants to finish his job and then have the patient sit up on the table.
-Jean Kerr (1923 – 2003)

A criminal lawyer, like a trapeze performer, is seldom more than one slip from an awful fall.
-Paul O'Neil (1952 -)

I began wearing hats as a young lawyer because it helped me to establish my professional identity. Before that, whenever I was at a meeting, someone would ask me to get coffee.
-Bella Abzug (1920 – 98)

A lawyer is a learned gentleman who rescues your estate from your enemies and keeps it himself.
-Henry Peter Brougham (1778 – 1868)

The only difference between a dead skunk lying in the road and a dead lawyer lying in the road is that there are skid marks around the skunk.
-Patrick Murray (1956 -)

Difference between law and in-law is you can justify yourself before law but never before in-law.
-Anon

We are all full of weakness and errors; let us mutually pardon each other our follies it is the first law of nature.
-*Voltaire (1694 – 1778)*

Justice that love gives is a surrender, justice that law gives is a punishment.
-*Mahatma Gandhi (1869 – 1948)*

It may be true that the law cannot make a man love me, but it can keep him from lynching me, and I think that's pretty important.
-*Martin Luther King (1929 – 68)*

An individual who breaks a law that conscience tells him is unjust, and who willingly accepts the penalty of imprisonment in order to arouse the conscience of the community over its injustice, is in reality expressing the highest respect for the law.
-*Martin Luther King (1929 -68)*

An unjust law is itself a species of violence. Arrest for its breach is more so.
-*Mahatma Gandhi (1869 – 1948)*

Law of Window Cleaning: It's on the other side.
-*Anon*

Shame may restrain what law does not prohibit.
-*Seneca (4 BC – 65 AD)*

That old law about 'an eye for an eye' leaves everybody blind. The time is always right to do the right thing.
-*Martin Luther King (1929 – 68)*

What is hateful to thyself do not do to another. That is the whole Law, the rest is Commentary.

-Hillel (70 BC -10 AD)

It is the law of nature that woman should be held under the dominance of man.

-Confucius (551 -479 BC)

The best way to get a bad law repealed is to enforce it strictly.

-Abraham Lincoln (1809 – 65)

There is one kind of robber whom the law does not strike at, and who steals what is most precious to men: time.

-Napoleon Bonaparte (1769 – 1821)

Law and justice are not always the same.

-Gloria Steinem (1935 -)

Law school taught me one thing: how to take two situations that are exactly the same and show how they are different.

-Hart Pomerantz

No enactment of man can be considered law unless it conforms to the law of God.

-William Blackstone (1723 – 80)

The law is reason free from passion.

-Aristotle (384 – 322 BC)

Man, when perfected, is the best of animals, but when separated from law and justice, he is the worst of all.

-Aristotle (384 – 322 BC)

The safety of the people shall be the highest law.
-*Cicero (106 – 43 BC)*

Criminals do not die by the hands of the law; they die by the hands of other men.
-*George Bernard Shaw (1856 – 1950)*

The problem with any unwritten law is that you don't know where to go to erase it.
-*Anon*

Hard cases, it is said, make bad law.
-*John Campbell Argyll (1678 – 1743)*

Nothing is more destructive of respect for the government and the law of the land than passing laws which cannot be enforced.
-*Albert Einstein (1879 – 1955)*

There is no crueller tyranny than that which is perpetrated under the shield of law and in the name of justice.
-*Charles de Montesquieu (1689 -1755)*

Obedience of the law is demanded; not asked as a favor. -*Theodore Roosevelt (1858 – 1919)*

The law will never make men free, it is men that have to make the law free.
-*Henry David Thoreau (1817 – 62)*

Law of Probability Dispersal: Whatever it is that hits the fan will not be evenly distributed.
-*Roger Angell (1920 -)*

This is a court of law, young man, not a court of justice.
-*Oliver Wendell Holmes Jr (1841 – 1935)*

We are in bondage to the law so that we might be free.
-*Cicero (106 – 43 BC)*

The state calls its own violence law, but that of the individual crime.
-*Max Stirner (1806 – 56)*

Law and order exist for the purpose of establishing justice and when they fail in this purpose they become the dangerously structured dams that block the flow of social progress.
-*Martin Luther King (1929 – 68)*

Justice is incidental to law and order.
-*J Edgar Hoover (1895 – 1972)*

For the greatest revolutionary changes on this earth would not have been thinkable if their motive force, instead of fanatical, yes, hysterical passion, had been merely the bourgeois virtues of law and order.
-*Adolf Hitler (1889 – 1945)*

Ignorance of the law excuses no man -- from practicing it.
-*Adison Mizner (1872 – 1933)*

A lawsuit is a fruit tree planted in a lawyer's garden.
-*Italian proverb*

Of course people are getting smarter nowadays; they are letting lawyers instead of their conscience be their guides.
-*Will Rogers (1879 – 1935)*

Lawyer: One who defends you at the risk of your pocketbook, reputation and life.
-Eugene E. Brussell

When there is a rift in the lute, the business of the lawyer is to widen the rift and gather the loot.
-Arthur G. Hayes (1881 – 1995)

Litigation is the basic legal right which guarantees every corporation its decade in court.
-David Porter (1941 -)

Some men are heterosexual and some men are bisexual and some men don't think about sex at all … you know, they become lawyers.
-Woody Allen (1935 -)

I used to be a lawyer, but now I am a reformed character.
-Woodrow Wilson (1856 – 1924)

I have come to the conclusion that one useless man is called a disgrace, two men are called a law firm, and three or more become a Congress.
-Peter Stone (1930 – 2003)

Anybody who thinks talk is cheap should get some legal advice.
-Franklin P. Jones (1908 – 80)

A man without money needs no more fear a crowd of lawyers than a crowd of pickpockets.
-R. Rinkle

By all reasonable measures, the American tort system is a disaster. It resembles a wealth-redistribution lottery more than an efficient system designed to compensate those injured by the wrongful actions of others.

-David E. Bernstein (1967 -)

Lawyers are always more ready to get a man into troubles than out of them.

-William Goldsmith (1972 -)

Lawyers are men whom we hire to protect us from lawyers.

-Elbert Hubbard (1856 – 1915)

There is a general prejudice to the effect that lawyers are more honorable then politicians but less honorable than prostitutes. That is an exaggeration.

-Alexander King (1899 – 1965)

Whoever tells the best story wins.

-John Quincy Adams (1767 – 1848)

A man may as well open an oyster without a knife, as a lawyer's mouth without a fee.

-Barten Holyday (1593 – 1661)

Death is not the end. There remains the litigation over the estate.

-Ambrose Bierce (1842 – 1914)

When dictators and tyrants seek to destroy the freedoms of men, their first target is the legal profession and through it the rule of law.

-Leon Jaworski (1905 – 1982)

Judge - A law student who marks his own examination papers.
-*Henry Louis Mencken (1880 -1956)*

I never met a litigator who did not think that he was winning the case right up to the moment when the guillotine came down.
-*William Baxter (1929 – 98)*

There are three sorts of lawyers - able, unable and lamentable.
-*Robert Smith Surtees (1805 – 64)*

Lawyers are the only persons in whom ignorance of the law is not punished.
-*Jeremy Bentham (1748 – 1832)*

Lawyers are like rhinoceroses: thick skinned, short-sighted, and always ready to charge.
-*David Mellor (1949 -)*

A man who never graduated from school might steal from a freight car. But a man who attends college and graduates as a lawyer might steal the whole railroad.
-*Theodore Roosevelt (1858 – 1919)*

In almost every case, you have to read between the lies.
-*Angie Papadakis (1925 -)*

Most lawyers who win a case advise their clients, "We have won," and when justice has frowned upon their cause ... "You have lost."
-*Louis Nizer (1902 – 94)*

In law, nothing is certain but the expense.
-*Samuel Butler (1835 -1902)*

Most attorneys practice law because it gives them a grand and glorious feeling. You give them a grand - and they feel glorious.
-*Milton Berle (1908 -2002)*

The trial lawyer does what Socrates was executed for: making the worse argument appear the stronger.
-*Judge Irving Kaufman (1910 – 92)*

He is no lawyer who cannot take two sides.
-*Charles Lamb (1775 – 1834)*

The reason we can't have the 10 commandments in a courthouse? You cannot post "Thou shall not steal", "Thou shall not commit adultery", and "Thou shall not lie" in a building full of lawyers, judges and politicians. It creates a hostile work environment.
-*George Carlin (1837 – 1908)*

Going to trial with a lawyer who views your whole life as a crime in progress is not a happy prospect.
-*Hunter S Thompson (1937 – 2005)*

Never take less than a guinea for doing anything, nor less than half a one for doing nothing. Among lawyers, moderation would be infamy.
-*Jeremy Bentham (1748 – 1832)*

If everybody left the bulk of their estate to their lawyers, a lot of time would be saved.
-*Anon*

Mercy to the guilty is cruelty to the innocent.
-*Adam Smith (1723 – 90)*

I've never seen anyone rehabilitated by punishment.
-Henry Lawson (1867 – 1922)

Good people do not need laws to tell them to act responsibly, while bad people will find a way around the laws.
-Plato (427-347 B.C.)

JOURNALISM

A news story should be like a mini skirt on a pretty woman. Long enough to cover the subject but short enough to be interesting.
-Anon

I still believe that if your aim is to change the world, journalism is a more immediate short-term weapon.
-Tom Stoppard (1937 -)

I don't think a tough question is disrespectful.
-Helen Thomas (1920 -2013)

Thanks to my solid academic training, today I can write hundreds of words on virtually any topic without possessing a shred of information, which is how I got a good job in journalism.
-Dave Barry (1947 -)

The man who reads nothing at all is better educated than the man who reads nothing but newspapers.
-Thomas Jefferson (1743 – 1826)

Myth is much more important and true than history. History is just journalism and you know how reliable that is.
-Joseph Campbell (1904 – 87)

Rock journalism is people who can't write interviewing people who can't talk for people who can't read.
-Frank Zappa (1940 – 93)

If I want to knock a story off the front page, I just change my hairstyle.
-Hilary Clinton (1947-)

A news sense is really a sense of what is important, what is vital, what has color and life - what people are interested in. That's journalism.
-*Burton Rascoe (1892 – 1957)*

Journalism largely consists in saying "Lord Jones is dead" to people who never knew Lord Jones was alive.
-*GK Chesterton (1874 – 1936)*

People may expect too much of journalism. Not only do they expect it to be entertaining, they expect it to be true.
-*Lewis Lapham (1930 -)*

Better a good journalist than a poor assassin.
-*Jean-Paul Sartre (1905 -80)*

Journalism can never be silent: that is its greatest virtue and its greatest fault. It must speak, and speak immediately, while the echoes of wonder, the claims of triumph and the signs of horror are still in the air.
-*Henry Anatole Grunwald (1922 – 2005)*

If a person is not talented enough to be a novelist, not smart enough to be a lawyer, and his hands are too shaky to perform operations, he becomes a journalist.
-*Norman Mailer (1923 – 2007)*

The difference between literature and journalism is that journalism is unreadable, and literature is not read.
-*Oscar Wilde (1854 – 1900)*

Journalism is organized gossip.
-*Edward Eggleston (1837 – 1902)*

Journalism is the only thinkable alternative to working.
-Jeffrey Bernard (1932 – 97)

The smarter the journalists are, the better off society is. [For] to a degree, people read the press to inform themselves-and the better the teacher, the better the student body.
-Warren Buffet (1930 -)

Journalism is merely history's first draft.
-Geoffrey C Ward (1940 -)

We journalists make it a point to know very little about an extremely wide variety of topics; this is how we stay objective.
-Dave Barry (1947 -)

Today's journalism is obsessed with the kinds of things that tend to preoccupy thirteen-year-old boys: sports, sex, crime, and narcissism.
-Steven Stark

In the real world, nothing happens at the right place at the right time. It is the job of journalists and historians to correct that.
-Mark Twain (1835 – 1910)

Journalists are like dogs, whenever anything moves they begin to bark.
-Arthur Schopenhauer (1788 – 1860)

Reporters are faced with the daily choice of painstakingly researching stories or writing whatever people tell them. Both approaches pay the same.
-Scott Adams (1957 -)

Journalists do not like to report on uncertainties. They would almost rather be wrong than ambiguous.
-*Melvin Maddocks*

Journalism could be described as turning one's enemies into money.
-*Craig Brown (1957 -)*

We journalists... are also extremely impressed with scientists, and we will, frankly, print just about any wacky thing they tell us, especially if it involves outer space.
-*Dave Barry (1947 -)*

In journalism, there has always been a tension between getting it first and getting it right.
-*Ellen Goodman (1941 -)*

Journalists should denounce government by public opinion polls.
-*Dan Rather (1931 -)*

The press, like fire, is an excellent servant, but a terrible master.
-*James Fenimore Cooper (1789 – 1851)*

I hate journalists. There is nothing in them but tittering jeering emptiness. They have all made what Dante calls the Great Refusal. . . . The shallowest people on the ridge of the earth.
-*WB Yeats - (1865 – 1939)*

A free press can be good or bad, but, most certainly, without freedom a press will never be anything but bad.
-*Albert Camus (1913 – 60)*

It is inexcusable for scientists to torture animals; let them make their experiments on journalists and politicians.
-*Henrik Ibsen (1828 – 1906)*

The freedom of the press works in such a way that there is not much freedom from it.
-*Grace Kelly (1929 – 82)*

News is something someone wants suppressed. Everything else is just advertising.
-*Lord Northcliff (1865 – 1922)*

Its failings notwithstanding, there is much to be said in favor of journalism in that by giving us the opinion of the uneducated, it keeps us in touch with the ignorance of the community.
-*Oscar Wilde (1854 – 1900)*

You can't publish a paper on physics without the full experimental data and results; that should be the standard in journalism.
-*Julian Paul Assange (1971 -)*

Exaggeration of every kind is as essential to journalism as it is to dramatic art, for the object of journalism is to make events go as far as possible.
-*Arthur Schopenhauer (1788 – 1860)*

Memory is the personal journalism of the soul.
-*Richard Schickel (1933 -)*

Freedom of the press is limited to those who own one.
-*A. J. Liebling (1904 – 63)*

There can be no higher law in journalism than to tell the truth and to shame the devil - remain detached from the great.
-Walter Lippman (1889 – 1974)

An editor is one who separates the wheat from the chaff and prints the chaff.
-Adlai Stevenson (1900 – 65)

Trying to determine what is going on in the world by reading newspapers is like trying to tell the time by watching the second hand of a clock.
-Ben Hecht (1894 – 1964)

As the saying goes: "If you're not part of the solution, you're a newspaper columnist."
-Dave Barry (1947 -)

You cannot hope to bribe or twist (thank God!) the British journalist. But, seeing what the man will do unbribed, there's no occasion to.
-Humbert Wolfe (1885 – 1940)

It's amazing that the amount of news that happens in the world everyday always just exactly fits the newspaper.
-Jerry Seinfeld (1954 -)

You've only got to be in public life for about a week before you start to question if the newspapers are even giving you today's date with any accuracy!
-Jonathan Lynn & Anthony Jay

Liberals have a quaint and touching faith that truth is on their side and an even quainter faith that journalists are on the side of truth.
-P.J O'Rourke (1947 -)

Doctors and Medicine

Doctors always think anybody doing something they aren't is a quack; also they think all patients are idiots.
-*Flannery O'Connor (1925 – 64)*

Never go to a doctor whose office plants have died.
-*Erma Bombeck (1927 – 96)*

The art of medicine consists of amusing the patient while nature cures the disease.
-*Voltaire (1694 – 1778)*

After you find out all the things that can go wrong, your life becomes less about living and more about waiting.
-*Chuck Palahniuk (1962 -)*

'My doctor says that I have a malformed public duty gland and a natural deficiency in moral fiber,' he muttered to himself, 'and that I am therefore excused from saving Universes'.
-*Douglas Adams (1952 – 2001)*

Doctors?" said Ron, looking startled. "Those Muggle nutters that cut people up"?
-*J.K. Rowling (1965 -)*

There is no medicine like hope, no incentive so great, and no tonic so powerful as expectation of something better tomorrow.
-*Orison Swett Marden (1850 -1924)*

The life so short, the craft so long to learn.
-*Hippocrates (460 -370 BC)*

The superior doctor prevents sickness; the mediocre doctor attends to impending sickness; the inferior doctor treats actual sickness.
-*Chinese proverb*

Each patient carries his own doctor inside him.
-*Norman Cousins (1915 – 90)*

I'm not feeling very well - I need a doctor immediately. Ring the nearest golf course.
-*Groucho Marx (1890 - 1977)*

Doctors are great--as long as you don't need them.
-*Edward E. Rosenbaum (1915 – 2009)*

Philosophy, like medicine, has plenty of drugs, few good remedies, and hardly any specific cures.
-*Sébastien-Roch Nicolas De Chamfort (1741 – 1794)*

The most exquisite pleasure in the practice of medicine comes from nudging a layman in the direction of terror, then bringing him back to safety again.
-*Kurt Vonnegut (1922 – 2007)*

The science of Psychiatry is now where the science of Medicine was before germs were discovered.
-*Malcolm Rogers (1948-)*

Though the doctors treated him, let his blood, and gave him medications to drink, he nevertheless recovered.
-*Leo Tolstoy (1828 – 1910)*

If the doctor told me I had six minutes to live, I'd type a little faster.
-*Isaac Asimov (1920 – 92)*

It should be the function of medicine to help people die young as late in life as possible.
-*Ernst Wynder (1922 – 99)*

Beware of the young doctor and the old barber.
-*Benjamin Franklin (1706 – 90)*

Formerly, when religion was strong and science weak, men mistook magic for medicine; now, when science is strong and religion weak, men mistake medicine for magic.
-*Thomas S. Szasz (1920 – 2012)*

First the doctor told me the good news: I was going to have a disease named after me.
-*Steve Martin (1945 -)*

Every patient is a doctor after his cure.
-*Irish proverb*

I've been poked and prodded in places I'd always prided myself on keeping untouched for that one special doctor who gives me a ring and a promise someday.
-*Libba Bray (1964 -)*

He who studies medicine without books sails an uncharted sea, but he who studies medicine without patients does not go to sea at all.
-*William Osler (1849 – 1919)*

In nothing do men more nearly approach the gods than in giving health to men.

-Cicero (106 – 43 BC)

Excuse me Doctor, I think I know a little something about medicine.

-Dan Castellaneta/Homer Simpson (1958 -)

The greatest mistake in the treatment of diseases is that there are physicians for the body and physicians for the soul, although the two cannot be separated.

-Plato (423 – 347 BC)

Advice after injury is like medicine after death.

-Proverb

In the sick room, ten cents' worth of human understanding equals ten dollars' worth of medical science.

-Martin H. Fischer (1879 – 1962)

My doctor gave me six months to live, but when I couldn't pay the bill he gave me six months more.

-Walter Matthau (1920 -2000)

It is a mathematical fact that fifty percent of all doctors graduate in the bottom half of their class.

-Anon

My doctor tells me I should start slowing it down -- but there are more old drunks than there are old doctors so let's all have another round.

-Willie Nelson (1933 -)

I got the bill for my surgery. Now I know what those doctors were wearing masks for.
-James H. Boren (1925 – 2010)

The death of a child is the single most traumatic event in medicine. To lose a child is to lose a piece of yourself.
-Dr. Burton Grebin (1941 – 2010)

A hospital should also have a recovery room adjoining the cashier's office.
-Francis O'Walsh (1920 – 95)

Dad always thought laughter was the best medicine, which I guess is why several of us died of tuberculosis.
-Jack Handy (1949 -)

You have a cough? Go home tonight, eat a whole box of Ex-Lax — tomorrow you'll be afraid to cough.
-Pearl Williams (1914 – 91)

The best doctor in the world is a veterinarian. He can't ask his patients what is the matter -- he's got to just know.
-Will Rogers (1879 – 1935)

Drugs are not always necessary. Belief in recovery always is.
-Norman Cousins (1915 – 90)

Medicine heals doubts as well as diseases.
-Karl Marx (1818 – 83)

There is no curing a sick man who believes himself to be in health.
-Henri Amiel (1821 – 81)

Medicine, the only profession that labors incessantly to destroy the reason for its existence.
-James Bryce (1838 – 1922)

I recently became a Christian Scientist. It was the only health plan I could afford.
-Betsy Salkind (1963 -)

The doctor must have put my pacemaker in wrong. Every time my husband kisses me, the garage door goes up.
-Minnie Pearl (1912 – 96)

Poisons and medicine are oftentimes the same substance given with different intents.
-Peter Mere Latham (1789 – 1875)

In the nineteenth century men lost their fear of God and acquired a fear of microbes.
-Anon

Advances in medicine and agriculture have saved vastly more lives than have been lost in all the wars in history.
-Dr. Carl Sagan (1934 – 96)

In medicine, as in statecraft and propaganda, words are sometimes the most powerful drugs we can use.
-Dr. Sara Murray Jordan (1904 – 59)

Financial ruin from medical bills is almost exclusively an American disease.
-Roul Turley

I told the doctor I broke my leg in two places. He told me to quit going to those places.
-*Henry Youngman (1906 – 98)*

A great doctor kills more people than a great general.
-*Gottfried Leibniz (1646 – 1716)*

Medicine makes people ill, mathematics makes them sad, and theology makes them sinful.
-*Martin Luther (1483 – 1546)*

God heals and the doctor takes the fees.
-*Benjamin Franklin (1706 – 90)*

Don't misinform your Doctor nor your Lawyer.
-*Benjamin Franklin (1706 – 90)*

A doctor can bury his mistakes but an architect can only advise his clients to plant vines.
-*Frank Lloyd Wright (1867 – 1959)*

It's kinda scary when a doctor asks your price range!
-*Tom Wilson (1959 -)*

The doctor sees all the weakness of mankind; the lawyer all the wickedness, the theologian all the stupidity.
-*Arthur Schopenhauer (1788 – 1860)*

Doctors don't seem to realize that most of us are perfectly content not having to visualize ourselves as animated bags of skin filled with obscene glop.
-*Joe Haldeman (1943 -)*

Finish last in your league and they call you idiot. Finish last in medical school and they call you doctor.
-Abe Lemons (1922 – 2002)

By medicine life may be prolonged, yet death will seize the doctor too.
-William Shakespeare (1564 – 1616)

The doctor is not unfrequently death's pilot-fish.
-George D Prentice (1802 – 70)

The patient is not likely to recover who makes the doctor his heir.
-Thomas Fuller (1608 – 61)

My doctor told me to stop having intimate dinners for four unless there are three other people.
-Orson Welles (1915 – 85)

Doctors are men who prescribe medicines of which they know little, to cure diseases of which they know less, in human beings of whom they know nothing.
-Voltaire (1694 – 1778)

TEACHERS

A teacher must believe in the value and interest of his subject as a doctor believes in health.
-*Gilbert Highet (1906 – 78)*

A gifted teacher is as rare as a gifted doctor, and makes far less money.
-*Anon*

It is the supreme art of the teacher to awaken joy in creative expression and knowledge.
-*Albert Einstein (1879 – 1955)*

The teacher is one who makes two ideas grow where only one grew before.
-*Elbert Hubbard (1856 – 1915)*

Education is the great engine of personal development. It is through education that the daughter of a peasant can become a doctor, that a son of a mineworker can become the head of the mine, that a child of farm workers can become president of a great nation.
-*Nelson Mandela (1918 – 2013)*

Time is the cruelest teacher; first she gives the test, then teaches the lesson.
-*Leonard Bernstein (1918 – 90)*

Teach yourself and you have a fool for a master.
-*Ben Johnson (1572 -1637)*

Teach this triple truth to all: A generous heart, kind speech, and a life of service and compassion are the things which renew humanity.
-Prince Gautama Siddhartha (563-483 BC)

Any teacher that can be replaced by a computer, deserves to be.
-David Thornburg

I have just three things to teach: simplicity, patience, compassion. These three are your greatest treasures.
-Lao Tzu (600 – 531 BC)

The mediocre teacher tells. The good teacher explains. The superior teacher demonstrates. The great teacher inspires.
-William Arthur Ward (1921 – 94)

I try to teach my heart not to want things it can't have.
-Alice Walker (1944 -)

A teacher's day is half bureaucracy, half crisis, half monotony and one-eighth epiphany. Never mind the arithmetic.
-Susan Ohanian

The best teachers teach from the heart, not from the book.
-Anon

Who dares to teach must never cease to learn.
-John Cotton (1856 – 1929)

The years teach much which the days never know.
-Ralph (Waldo Emerson (1802 – 82)

Four thousand volumes of metaphysics will not teach us what the soul is.
-*Voltaire (1694 – 1778)*

I never teach my pupils; I only attempt to provide the conditions in which they can learn.
-*Albert Einstein (1879 – 1955)*

Time is a great teacher, but unfortunately it kills all its pupils.
-*Louis-Hector Berlioz (1803 -69)*

A teacher who is not dogmatic is simply a teacher who is not teaching.
-*GK Chesterton (1874 – 1936)*

If you think in terms of a year, plant a seed; if in terms of ten years, plant trees; if in terms of 100 years, teach the people.
-*Confucius (551 – 479 BC)*

Television! Teacher, mother, secret lover.
-*Dan Castellaneta (Homer Simpson) – (1958 -)*

Good teaching is one-fourth preparation and three-fourths theatre.
-*Gail Goldwin (1937 -)*

What sculpture is to a block of marble, education is to a human soul.
-*Joseph Addison (1672 – 1719)*

No one ever teaches well who wants to teach, or governs well who wants to govern.
-*Plato (428 – 348 BC)*

Education breeds confidence. Confidence breeds hope. Hope breeds peace.
-*Confucius (551 – 479 BC)*

People react to fear, not love - they don't teach that in Sunday School, but it's true.
-*Leonardo da Vinci (1452 – 1519)*

Every child deserves a champion – an adult who will never give up on them, who understands the power of connection and insists that they become the best that they can possibly be.
-*Rita Pierson (1952 – 2013)*

Education can't make us all leaders, but it can teach us which leader to follow.
-*Bel Kaufman (1911 – 2014)*

If someone is going down the wrong road, he doesn't need motivation to speed him up. What he needs is education to turn him around.
-*Jim Rohn (1930 -2009)*

We shouldn't teach great books; we should teach a love of reading.
-*BF Skinner (1904 – 90)*

It must be remembered that the purpose of education is not to fill the minds of students with facts...it is to teach them to think.
-*Robert M Hutchins (1899 – 1977)*

Tell me and I forget. Teach me and I remember. Involve me and I learn.
-*Benjamin Franklin (1706 – 90)*

Education is not preparation for life; education is life itself.
-John Dewey (1859 – 1952)

The function of education is to teach one to think intensively and to think critically... Intelligence plus character - that is the goal of true education.
-Martin Luther King, Jr. (1929-68)

A mind when stretched by a new idea never regains its original dimensions.
-Oliver Wendell Holmes Sr. (1809 – 94)

You can't teach people to be lazy - either they have it, or they don't.
-Murat Bernard Young (1901 – 73)

Education is not filling of a pail but the lighting of a fire.
-WB Yeats (1865 – 1935)

He who knows not and knows not he knows not: he is a fool - shun him. He who knows not and knows he knows not: he is simple - teach him. He who knows and knows not he knows: he is asleep - wake him. He who knows and knows he knows: he is wise - follow him.
Proverb

Children must be taught how to think, not what to think.
-Margaret Mead (1901 – 78)

Give a person a fish and you feed them for a day; teach that person to use the Internet and they won't bother you for weeks.
-Anon

The principal goal of education in the schools should be creating men and women who are capable of doing new things, not simply repeating what other generations have done.
-Jean Piaget (1896 – 1980)

Education is what survives when what has been learned has been forgotten.
-BF Skinner (1904 – 90)

I cannot teach anybody anything, I can only make them think.
-Socrates (470 -399 BC)

Don't just teach your kids to read, teach them to question what they read. Teach them to question everything!
-George Carlin (1937 – 2008)

The wise sceptic does not teach doubt but how to look for the permanent in the mutable and fleeting.
-Ralph Waldo Emerson (1803- 82)

What we learn with pleasure we never forget.
-Alfred Mercier (1816 – 94)

His priority did not seem to be to teach them what he knew, but rather to impress upon them that nothing, not even... knowledge, was fool proof.
-JK Rowling (1965 -)

The beautiful thing about learning is that no one can take it away from you.
-BB King (1925 -)

To waken interest and kindle enthusiasm is the sure way to teach easily and successfully.

-Tryon Edwards (1809 – 94)

Once you have learned to ask questions – relevant and appropriate and substantial questions – you have learned how to learn and no one can keep you from learning whatever you want or need to know.

-Neil Postman (1913 – 2003)

A professor is one who talks in someone else's sleep.

-WH Auden (1907 – 73)

Never offer to teach a fish to swim.

-Anon

Chapter 11 The Human Condition

Happiness

The secret of contentment is knowing how to enjoy what you have, and to be able to lose all desire for things beyond your reach.
-Lyn Yutang (1895 – 1976)

I don't know how to be happy - They didn't teach it in my school.
-Ashleigh Brilliant (1933 -)

Doing what you like is freedom. Liking what you do is happiness.
-Frank Tyger (1929 -)

Be happy with what you have. Be excited about what you want.
-Alan Cohen (1954)

I've learned that people will forget what you said, people will forget what you did, but people will never forget how you made them feel.
-Maya Angelou (1928 – 2014)

We forge the chains we wear in life.
-Charles Dickens (1812 – 70)

There is no such thing as a problem without a gift for you in its hands. You seek problems because you need their gifts.
-Richard Bach (1936 -)

If you want to be happy, set a goal that commands your thoughts, liberates your energy, and inspires your hopes. -Andrew Carnegie (1835 – 1919)

Tension is who you think you should be, relaxation is who you are.
-*Chinese Proverb*

Happiness cannot be travelled to, owned, earned, worn or consumed. Happiness is the spiritual experience of living every minute with love, grace, and gratitude.
-*Denis Waitley (1933 -)*

Happiness is not a station you arrive at, but a manner of travelling.
-*Margaret Lee Runbeck (1905 – 56)*

Thousands of candles can be lit from a single candle, and the life of the candle will not be shortened. Happiness never decreases by being shared.
-*Prince Gautama Siddharta (563-483 B.C.)*

The best remedy for those who are afraid, lonely or unhappy is to go outside, somewhere where they can be quiet, alone with the heavens, nature and God. As long as this exists, and it certainly always will, then there will be comfort for every sorrow, whatever the circumstances may be.
-*Anne Frank (1929 – 45)*

True happiness is not attained through self-gratification, but through fidelity to a worthy purpose.
-*Helen Keller (1880 – 1968)*

Reflect upon you present blessings, of which every man has many--not on your past misfortunes, of which all men have some.
-*Charles Dickens (1812 – 1870)*

When one door of happiness closes, another opens, but often we look so long at the closed door that we do not see the one that has been opened for us.
-Helen Keller (1880 – 1968)

Happiness is not having what you want. It is appreciating what you have.
-Anon

Success is getting what you want. Happiness is wanting what you get.
-Dale Carnegie (1888 – 1955)

Once you do something you love, you never have to work again.
-Willie Hill

The happiness of life is made up of the little charities of a kiss or smile, a kind look, a heartfelt compliment.
-Samuel Taylor Coleridge (1772 – 1832)

Happiness is where we find it, but very rarely where we seek it.
-J. Petit Senn (1792 – 1870)

Look at everything as though you were seeing it either for the first or last time. Then your time on earth will be filled with glory.
-Betty Smith (1896 – 1972)

The secret of happiness is to count your blessings while others are adding up their troubles.
-William Penn (1644 – 1718)

Some cause happiness wherever they go; others whenever they go.
-Oscar Wilde (1854 – 1900)

There is only one happiness in this life, to love and be loved.
-*George Sand (1804 – 76)*

Happiness is like a kiss...you must share it to enjoy it.
-*Bernard Meltzer (1916 – 98)*

For every minute you are angry you lose sixty seconds of happiness.
-*Ralph Waldo Emmerson (1803 -82)*

Happiness is not the absence of problems but the ability to deal with them.
-*Steve Maraboli (1975 -)*

May you have enough happiness to make you sweet, enough trials to make you strong, enough sorrow to keep you human enough hope to make you happy.
-*Anon*

Remember that happiness is a way of travel -- not a destination.
-*Agnes Repplier (1858 – 1950)*

Happiness equals reality minus expectations.
-*Tom Magliozzi (1937 – 2014)*

The greatest happiness of life is the conviction that we are loved - loved for ourselves, or rather, loved in spite of ourselves.
-*Victor Hugo (1802 – 85)*

The pain I feel now is the happiness I had before. That's the deal.
-*CS Lewis (1898 – 1963)*

We find a delight in the beauty and happiness of children that makes the heart too big for the body.
-*Ralph Waldo Emmerson (1803 – 82)*

Happiness is a butterfly, which when pursued, is always just beyond your grasp, but which, if you will sit down quietly, may alight upon you.
-*Nathaniel Hawthorne (1804 – 64)*

There is only one way to happiness and that is to cease worrying about things which are beyond the power of our will.
-*Epictetus (55 -135 AD)*

Sacrificing your happiness for the happiness of the one you love, is by far, the truest type of love.
-*Henry David Thoreau (1817 – 62)*

If a man who enjoys a lesser happiness beholds a greater one, let him leave aside the lesser to gain the greater.
-*Prince Gautama Siddharta (563-483 B.C.)*

There is no happiness; there are only moments of happiness.
-*Spanish proverbs*

While we pursue happiness, we flee from contentment.
-*Hasidic proverb*

There can be no happiness if the things we believe in are different from the things we do.
-*Freya Stark (1893 – 1993)*

Happiness comes of the capacity to feel deeply, to enjoy simply, to think freely, to risk life, to be needed.
-*Storm Jameson (1891 – 1986)*

The moments of happiness we enjoy take us by surprise. It is not that we seize them, but that they seize us.
-*Ashley Montagu (1905 – 99)*

Unless your heart, your soul, and your whole being are behind every decision you make, the words from your mouth will be empty, and each action will be meaningless. Truth and confidence are the roots of happiness.
-*Pietro Aretino (1492 – 1556)*

Don't wait around for other people to be happy for you. Any happiness you get you've got to make yourself.
-*Alice Walker (1944 -)*

Happiness and love are just a choice away.
-*Leo F. Buscaglia (1924 – 98)*

A truly happy person is one who can enjoy the scenery on a detour.
-*Anon*

They say a person needs just three things to be truly happy in this world: someone to love, something to do, and something to hope for.
-*Tom Bodett (1955 -)*

Happiness is the meaning and the purpose of life, the whole aim and end of human existence.
-*Aristotle (384 – 322 BC)*

For me it is sufficient to have a corner by my hearth, a book and a friend, and a nap undisturbed by creditors or grief.
-*Fernandez de Andrada (1575 – 1658)*

A sure way to lose happiness, I found, is to want it at the expense of everything else.

-Bette Davis (1908 – 89)

Happiness is good health and a bad memory.

-Ingrid Bergman (1915 -82)

Success and Failure

If you can meet with Triumph and Disaster
And treat those two impostors just the same.
-Rudyard Kipling(1865 - 1936)

Failure should be our teacher, not our undertaker. Failure is delay, not defeat. It is a temporary detour, not a dead end. Failure is something we can avoid only by saying nothing, doing nothing, and being nothing.
-Denis Waitley (1933 -)

If you don't make things happen then things will happen to you.
-Robert Collier (1885 – 1950)

Winning is not a sometime thing; it's an all-time thing. You don't win once in a while, you don't do things right once in a while, you do them right all the time. Winning is habit. Unfortunately, so is losing.
-Vince Lombardi (1913 -70)

Know where to find the information and how to use it - That's the secret of success.
-Albert Einstein (1879 – 1955)

You were born to win, but to be a winner, you must plan to win, prepare to win, and expect to win.
-Zig Ziglar (1926 – 2012)

Most great people have attained their greatest success just one step beyond their greatest failure.
-Napoleon Hill (1883 – 1970)

The secret of all victory lies in the organization of the non-obvious.
-*Marcus Aurelius (121 – 180)*

Pay no attention to what the critics say; no statue has ever been erected to a critic.
-*Jean Sibelius (1865 – 1957)*

Failure defeats losers, failure inspires winners.
-*Robert T. Kiyosaki (1947 -)*

Success is walking from failure to failure with no loss of enthusiasm.
-*Winston Churchill (1874 – 1965)*

To succeed... You need to find something to hold on to, something to motivate you, something to inspire you.
-*Tony Dorsett (1954 -)*

Forget about the consequences of failure. Failure is only a temporary change in direction to set you straight for your next success.
-*Denis Waitley (1933 -)*

Things work out best for those who make the best of how things work out.
-*John Wooden (1910 – 2010)*

Forget past mistakes. Forget failures. Forget everything except what you're going to do now and do it.
-*William Durant (1861 – 1947)*

Success is doing ordinary things extraordinarily well.
-*Jim Rohn (1930 – 2009)*

Success is liking yourself, liking what you do, and liking how you do it.
-Maya Angelou (1928 – 2014)

It does not matter how slowly you go, so long as you do not stop.
-Confucius (551 – 479 BC)

Success means having the courage, the determination, and the will to become the person you believe you were meant to be.
-George Sheehan (1918 – 93)

I've always believed that one woman's success can only help another woman's success.
-Gloria Vanderbilt (1924 -)

The successful warrior is the average man, with laser-like focus.
-Bruce Lee (1940 -73)

Success is not measured by what you accomplish, but by the opposition you have encountered, and the courage with which you have maintained the struggle against overwhelming odds.
-Orison Swett Marden (1850 - 1924)

Optimism is the faith that leads to achievement. Nothing can be done without hope and confidence.
-Helen Keller (1880 – 1968)

People become really quite remarkable when they start thinking that they can do things. When they believe in themselves, they have the first secret of success.
-Norman Vincent Peale (1898 -1993)

Success is where preparation and opportunity meet.
-Bobby Unser (1934 -)

Success is the sum of small efforts – repeated day in and day out.
-*Robert Collier (1885 – 1950)*

Nothing is particularly hard if you divide it into small jobs.
-*Henry Ford (1863 – 1947)*

Don't let the fear of losing be greater than the excitement of winning.
-*Robert Kiyosaki (1947 -)*

The ladder of success must be set upon something solid before you can start to climb.
-*Voltaire (1694 – 1778)*

The only place where success comes before work is in the dictionary.
-*Vidal Sassoon (1928 – 2012)*

The important thing is not being afraid to take a chance. Remember, the greatest failure is to not try. Once you find something you love to do, be the best at doing it.
-*Debbi Fields (1956 -)*

Success is not the result of spontaneous combustion. You must first set yourself on fire.
-*Fred Shero (1935 – 90)*

Most of the important things in the world have been accomplished by people who have kept on trying when there seemed to be no hope at all.
-*Dale Carnegie (1888 – 1955)*

If you set your goals ridiculously high and it's a failure, you will fail above everyone else's success.
-James Cameron (1954 -)

Success is simple. Do what's right, the right way, at the right time.
Arnold H Glasgow (1905 -98)

Success usually comes to those who are too busy to be looking for it.
Henry David Thoreau (1817 – 62)

If you are not willing to risk the usual, you will have to settle for the ordinary.
-Jim Rohn (1930 – 2009)

Some people dream of success while others wake up and work hard at it.
-Winston Churchill (1874 – 1965)

If you blame others for your failures, do you credit them with your success?
-Anon

Whenever you see a successful person, you only see the public glories, never the private sacrifices to reach them.
-Vaibhav Shah (1984 -)

Success? I don't know what that word means. I'm happy. But success, that goes back to what in somebody's eyes success means. For me, success is inner peace. That's a good day for me.
-Denzel Washington (1954 -)

Try not to become a person of success, but rather try to become a person of value.
-Albert Einstein (1879 – 1955)

To recognize opportunity is the difference between success and failure.
-Anon

It is not the strongest of the species that survive, nor the most intelligent, but the one most responsive to change.
-Charles Darwin (1809 – 82)

The best revenge is massive success.
-Frank Sinatra (1915 – 98)

Failure can be divided into those who thought and never did and into those who did and never thought.
-John Charles Salak (1877 – 1959)

I have not failed. I've just found 10,000 ways that won't work.
-Thomas Edison (1847 – 1931)

A successful man is one who can lay a firm foundation with the bricks others have thrown at him.
-David Brinkley (1920 -2003)

There is much to be said for failure. It is much more interesting than success.
-Sir Max Beerbohm (1872 – 1956)

There are two types of people who will tell you that you cannot make a difference in this world: those who are afraid to try and those who are afraid you will succeed.
-Ray Goforth

Success builds character, failure reveals it.
-*Dave Checkett (1956 -)*

Keep on going, and the chances are that you will stumble on something, perhaps when you are least expecting it. I never heard of anyone ever stumbling on something sitting down. C
-*Charles F. Kettering (1876 – 1958)*

No man is a complete failure until he begins disliking men who succeed.
-*Anon*

All progress takes place outside the comfort zone.
-*Michael John Bobak*

Success comes in cans; failure in cant's.
-*Wilfred Peterson (1900 -95)*

The road to success is always under construction.
-*Lily Tomlinson (1939 -)*

I don't know the key to success, but the key to failure is trying to please everyone.
-*Bill Cosby (1937 -)*

The first step toward success is taken when you refuse to be a captive of the environment in which you first find yourself.
-*Mark Caine*

Successful people do what unsuccessful people are not willing to do. Don't wish it were easier; wish you were better.
-*Jim Rohn (1930 – 2009)*

The ladder of success is never crowded at the top.
-*Napoleon Hill (1883 – 1970)*

We seem to gain wisdom more readily through our failures than through our successes. We always think of failure as the antithesis of success, but it isn't. Success often lies just the other side of failure.
-*Leo F. Buscaglia (1924 – 88)*

The No. 1 reason people fail in life is because they listen to their friends, family, and neighbors.
-*Napoleon Hill (1883 – 1970)*

Success does not consist in never making mistakes but in never making the same one a second time.
-*George Bernard Shaw (1856 – 1950)*

Our greatest fear should not be of failure ... but of succeeding at things in life that don't really matter.
-*Francis Chan (1967 -)*

Nobody ever wrote down a plan to be broke, fat, lazy, or stupid. Those things are what happen when you don't have a plan.
-*Larry Winget (1852 -)*

I couldn't wait for success, so I went ahead without it.
-*Jonathan Miller (1925 -)*

You may have to fight a battle more than once to win it.
-*Margaret Thatcher (1925 – 2013)*

I owe my success to having listened respectfully to the very best advice, and then going away and doing the exact opposite.
-*G. K. Chesterton (1874 – 1936)*

Many of life's failures are people who did not realize how close they were to success when they gave up.
-*Thomas A. Edison (1847 – 1931)*

The greater the artist, the greater the doubt. Perfect confidence is granted to the less talented as a consolation prize.
-*Robert Hughes (1838 – 2012)*

What would you attempt to do if you knew you would not fail?
-*Robert Schuller (1926 -)*

Successful and unsuccessful people do not vary greatly in their abilities. They vary in their desires to reach their potential.
-*John Maxwell (1947 -)*

Success is just a war of attrition. Sure, there's an element of talent you should probably possess. But if you just stick around long enough, eventually something is going to happen.
-*Dax Shepard (1975 -)*

Develop success from failures. Discouragement and failure are two of the suspect stepping stones to success.
-*Dale Carnegie (1888 – 1955)*

Be careful what you water your dreams with. Water them with worry and fear and you will produce weeds that choke the life from your dream. Water them with optimism and solutions and you will cultivate success.
-*Lao Tzu (600 – 531 BC)*

I am not bound to win, I am bound to be true. I am not bound to succeed, but I am bound to live up to the light I have.
-*Abraham Lincoln (1809 – 65)*

The secret of success is this: there is no secret of success.
-*Elbert Hubbard (1856 – 1915)*

Winning needs no explanation, losing has no alibi.
-*Greg Baum (1959 -)*

If you win, you need not have to explain...If you lose, you should not be there to explain!
-*Adolf Hitler (1889 – 1945)*

The only man who never makes mistakes is the man who never does anything.
-*Theodore Roosevelt (1858 – 1918)*

My mother drew a distinction between achievement and success. She said 'achievement is the knowledge that you have studied and worked hard and done the best that is in you. Success is being praised by others. That's nice, too, but not as important or satisfying. Always aim for achievement and forget about success.'
-*Helen Hayes (1900 – 93)*

The road to success is always under construction.
-*Lily Tomlin (1939 -)*

Mistakes are part of the dues one pays for a full life.
-*Sophia Loren (1934-)*

COURAGE

Courage is being scared to death, but saddling up anyway.
-John Wayne (1907 – 1979)

Being deeply loved by someone gives you strength, while loving someone deeply gives you courage.
-Lao Tzu (604 – 531 BC)

The hero and the coward both feel the same thing, but the hero uses his fear, projects it onto his opponent, while the coward runs. It's the same thing, fear, but it's what you do with it that matters.
-Cus D'Amato (1908 – 85)

It takes a great deal of bravery to stand up to our enemies, but just as much to stand up to our friends.
-J.K. Rowling (1965 -)

Live daringly, boldly, fearlessly. Taste the relish to be found in competition – in having put forth the best within you.
-Henry J. Kaiser (1882 – 1967)

It takes courage to grow up and become who you really are.
-E.E. Cummings (1894 – 1962)

All our dreams can come true if we have the courage to pursue them.
-Walt Disney (1901 – 66)

The most courageous act is still to think for yourself. Aloud.
-Coco Chanel (1883 – 1971)

He who is not courageous enough to take risks will accomplish nothing in life.
-Muhammad Ali (1942 -)

I wanted you to see what real courage is, instead of getting the idea that courage is a man with a gun in his hand. It's when you know you're licked before you begin, but you begin anyway and see it through no matter what.
-Harper Lee (1926 –)

Cowardice, as distinguished from panic, is almost always simply a lack of ability to suspend the functioning of the imagination.
-Ernest Hemingway (1899 – 1961)

Some have been thought brave because they were afraid to run away.
-Thomas Fuller (1608 -61)

Fear and courage are brothers.
-Terri Guillemets (1973 -)

Life shrinks or expands in proportion to one's courage.
-Anais Nin (1903 - 77)

One man with courage makes a majority.
-Andrew Jackson (1767 – 1845)

Faced with what is right, to leave it undone shows a lack of courage.
-Confucius (551 – 479 BC)

True courage is not the brutal force of vulgar heroes, but the firm resolve of virtue and reason.
-Alfred North Whitehead (1861 – 1947)

Good character is more to be praised than outstanding talent. Most talents are to some extent a gift. Good character, by contrast, is not given to us. We have to build it piece by piece by thought, choice, courage and determination.
-*H Jackson Brown (1940 -)*

To live with fear and not be afraid is the final test of maturity.
-*Edward Weeks (1980 -)*

Have the courage to live. Anyone can die.
-*Robert Cody (1951 -)*

It is easy to be brave from a safe distance.
-*Aesop (620 – 564 BC)*

Sometimes even to live is an act of courage.
-*Seneca (4 BC – 65 AD)*

I'm not funny. What I am is brave.
-*Lucille Ball (1911 – 89)*

All art requires courage.
-*Anne Tucker (1945 -)*

Courage is fear holding on a minute longer.
-*George S Patton (1885 – 1945)*

You gain strength, courage, and confidence by every experience in which you really stop to look fear in the face... do the thing you think you cannot do.
-*Eleanor Roosevelt (1884 – 1962)*

Courage is tiny pieces of fear all glued together.
-*Terri Guillemets (1973 -)*

He who loses wealth loses much; he who loses a friend loses more; but he that loses his courage loses all.
-*Miguel de Cervantes Saavedra (1547 – 1616)*

Optimism is the foundation of courage.
-*Nicholas Murray Butler (1862 – 1947)*

Those who lack the courage will always find a philosophy to justify it.
-*Albert Camus (1913 – 60)*

Failure is unimportant. It takes courage to make a fool of yourself.
-*Charlie Chaplin (1889 – 1977)*

Often the difference between a successful person and a failure is not one has better abilities or ideas, but the courage that one has to bet on one's ideas, to take a calculated risk - and to act.
-*Andre Malraux (1901 – 76)*

It requires more courage to suffer than to die.
-*Napoleon Bonaparte (1769 – 1821)*

Courage is to feel the daily daggers of relentless steel and keep on living.
-*Douglas Malloch (1877 – 1938)*

Courage is what it takes to stand up and speak; courage is also what it takes to sit down and listen.
-*Winston Churchill (1874 – 1965)*

The test of courage comes when we are in the minority. The test of tolerance comes when we are in the majority.
-*Ralph W. Sockman (1889 – 1970)*

Take chances, make mistakes. That's how you grow. Pain nourishes your courage. You have to fail in order to practice being brave.
-*Mary Tyler Moore (1936 -)*

It takes a lot of courage to show your dreams to someone else.
-*Erma Bombeck (1927- 96)*

War is fear cloaked in courage.
-*Gen William C. Westmoreland (1914 – 2005)*

Untutored courage is useless in the face of educated bullets.
-*General George S. Patton (1885 – 1945)*

Take Courage! Whatever you decide to do, it will probably be the wrong thing.
-*Ashleigh Brilliant (1933 -)*

If I had more skill in what I'm attempting, I wouldn't need so much courage.
-*Ashleigh Brilliant (1933 -)*

Courage is going from failure to failure without losing enthusiasm.
-*Winston Churchill (1874 – 1965)*

Courage is the most important virtue because it makes all others possible.
-*Winston Churchill (1874 – 1965)*

Before you criticize someone you should walk a mile in their shoes. That way, when you criticize them, you're a mile away from them and have their shoes.
-*Jack Handey (1949 -)*

Everyone has talent. What are is rare is the courage to follow it to the dark places it may lead.
-*Erica Jong (1942 -)*

You will never do anything in this world without courage. It's the greatest quality of the mind next to honor.
-*Aristotle (382 – 322 BC)*

Don't be afraid of your fears. They're not there to scare you. They are there to let you know that something is worth it.
-*C. JoyBell C.*

It is curious that physical courage should be so common in the world, and moral courage so rare.
-*Mark Twain (1835 – 1910)*

A ship is safe in harbor, but that is not what ships are for.
-*William GT Shedd*

Courage is simply the willingness to be afraid and act anyway.
-*Dr. Robert Anthony*

With enough courage you can do without reputation.
-*Margaret Mitchell (1900 – 49)*

Courage doesn't always roar. Sometimes courage is the quiet voice at the end of the day saying, 'I will try again tomorrow'.
-*Mary Ann Radmacher*

There is a stubbornness about me that can never bear to be frightened at the will of others. My courage always rises at every attempt to intimidate me.
-*Jane Austen (1775 – 1817)*

Success means having the courage, determination and the will to become a person you were meant to be.
-*George Sheehan. (1918 – 93)*

All happiness depends on courage and work.
-*Balzac (1799 – 1850)*

Courage is the power to let go of the familiar.
-*Raymond Lindquist (1907 – 2001)*

Freedom lies in being bold.
-*Robert Frost (1874 – 1963)*

To dream anything want to dream. That's the beauty of the human mind. To do anything you want to do. That is the strength of the human will. To trust yourself to the limits. That is the courage to succeed.
-*Bernard Edmonds (1951 -)*

Courage is found in unlikely places.
-*J.R.R. Tolkien (1892 – 1973)*

Do you really think it is weakness that yields to temptation? I tell you that there are terrible temptations which it requires strength, strength and courage, to yield to.
-*Oscar Wilde (1854 – 1900)*

No long how long you train someone to be brave, you never know if they are or are not till something real happens.
-*Veronica Roth (1988 -)*

Without courage all virtues lose their meaning.
-*Winston Churchill (1874 – 1965)*

Some people believe that holding on and hanging in there are signs of great strength. However, there are times when it takes more strength to know when to let go and do it.
-*Eppie Lederer (1918 – 2002)*

Success is not measured by what you accomplish, but by the opposition you have encountered, and the courage with which you maintained the struggle with overwhelming odds.
-*Orison Swett Madison (1850 – 1924)*

Courage is grace under pressure.
-*Ernest Hemmingway (1899 – 1961)*

Courage consists of the power of self-recovery.
-*Ralph Waldo Emerson (1803 – 82)*

Keep in mind that many people have died for their beliefs; it's actually quite common. The real courage is in living and suffering for what you believe.
-*Christopher Paolini (1983 -)*

Courage is not simply one of the virtues, but the form of every virtue at the testing point.
-*CS Lewis (1898 – 1963)*

Believe you can and you are halfway there.
-*Theodore Roosevelt (1858 – 1919)*

The paradox of courage is that a man must be a little careless of his life in order to keep it.
-*GK Chesterton (1874 – 1936)*

God give me the courage to not to give up what I think is right even though I think it is hopeless.
-*Chester W Nimitz (1885 1966)*

Speak your mind, even if your voice shakes.
-*Maggie Kuhn (1905 – 95)*

Every man has his own courage, and is betrayed because he seeks in himself the courage of other persons.
-*Ralph Waldo Emerson (1803 – 82)*

God grant me the serenity to accept the things I cannot change, the courage to change things I can, and the wisdom to know the difference.
-*Reinhok Niebuhr (1892 – 1971)*

In the depth of winter, I finally learned that within me there lay an invincible summer.
-*Albert Camus (1913 -60)*

You don't develop courage by being happy in your relationships every day. You develop it by surviving difficult times and challenging adversity.
-*Epicurus (341 – 270 BC)*

Nobody can hurt me without my permission.
-*Mahatma Gandhi (1869 – 1948)*

Life is mostly froth and bubble, two things stand like stone, kindness in another's trouble, courage in your own.
-*Adam Lindsay Gordon (1833 – 70)*

Another word for creativity is courage.
-*Henri Matisse (1869 – 1954)*

Courage is the price that life exacts for granting peace.
-*Amelia Earhart (1897 - 1937)*

Any fool can make things bigger, more complex, and more violent. It takes a touch of genius-and a lot of courage-to move in the opposite direction.
-*Albert Einstein (1879 – 1955)*

It is not because things are difficult that we do not dare; it is because we do not dare that they are difficult.
-*Seneca (4 BC – 65 AD)*

If you could get up the courage to begin, you have the courage to succeed.
-*David Viscott (1938 – 96)*

Do not go where the path may lead, go instead where there is no path and leave a trail.
-*Ralph Waldo Emerson (1803 – 82)*

Most of us have far more courage than we ever dreamed possible.
-*Dale Carnegie (1888 – 1955)*

Only those who will risk going too far can possibly find out how far one can go.
-*TS Eliot (1888 – 1965)*

Man cannot discover new oceans unless he has the courage to lose sight of the shore.
-*Andre Gide (1869 – 1951)*

Take the first step in faith. You don't have to see the whole staircase, just take the first step.
-*Dr. Martin Luther King Jr. (1929 – 68)*

You cannot build character and courage by taking away man's initiative and independence.
-Abraham Lincoln (1809 – 65)

The men who try to do something and fail are infinitely better than those who try to do nothing and succeed.
-Lloyd Jones

Many a man will have the courage to die gallantly, but will not have the courage to say, or even to think, that the cause for which he is asked to die is an unworthy one.
-Bertrand Russell (1872 – 1920)

People are made of flesh and blood and a miracle fiber called courage.
-Mignon McLaughlin (1913 – 83)

The secret of happiness is freedom. The secret of freedom is courage.
-Thucydides (160 – 404 BC)

To me, there is no greater act of courage than being the one who kisses first.
-Janeane Garofalo (1964 -)

Courage follows action.
-Mack R Douglas (1903 – 73)

Courage is the art of being the only one who knows you're scared to death.
-Earl Wilson (1907 – 87)

When will you understand that being normal isn't necessarily a virtue? It rather denotes a lack of courage.
-*Alice Hoffman (1952 -)*

Dream the impossible dream, Fight the unbeatable foe, Strive with your last once of courage to reach the unreachable star.
-*Joe Darion (1917 – 2001)*

It was times like these when I thought my father, who hated guns and had never been to any wars, was the bravest man who ever lived.
-*Harper Lee (1926 -)*

Courage is doing what you're afraid to do. There can be no courage unless you're scared.
-*Edward Vernon Rickenbacker (1890 – 1973)*

A coward is a hero with a wife, kids, and a mortgage.
-*Marvin Kitman   (1929 -)*

Each of us has an inner dream that we can unfold if we will just have the courage to admit what it is. And the faith to trust our own admission. The admitting is often very difficult.
-*Julia Cameron (1948 -)*

If God wanted us to be brave, why did He give us legs?
-*Marvin Kitman (1929 -)*

HOPE

Man can live about forty days without food, about three days without water, about eight minutes without air, but only for one second without hope.
-Hal Lindsay (1929 -)

Yesterday is history, tomorrow is a mystery, today is a gift of God, which is why we call it the present.
-Bil Keane (1922 – 2011)

If at first, the idea is not absurd, then there is no hope for it.
-Albert Einstein (1879 – 1955)

It's really a wonder that I haven't dropped all my ideals, because they seem so absurd and impossible to carry out. Yet I keep them, because in spite of everything, I still believe that people are really good at heart.
-Anne Frank (1929 – 1945)

Love comes to those who still hope even though they've been disappointed, to those who still believe even though they've been betrayed, to those who still love even though they've been hurt before.
-Anon

I like the night. Without the dark, we'd never see the stars.
-Stephenie Meyer (1973 -)

Hope in reality is the worst of all evils, because it prolongs the torments of man.
-Friedrich Nietzsche (1844 – 1900)

It's amazing how a little tomorrow can make up for a whole lot of yesterday.
-*John Guare (1938 -)*

Never let go of hope. One day you will see that it all has finally come together. What you have always wished for has finally come to be. You will look back and laugh at what has passed and you will ask yourself... 'How did I get through all of that?
-*Charles L Allen (1913 – 2005)*

We dream to give ourselves hope. To stop dreaming - well, that's like saying you can never change your fate.
-*Amy Tan (1952 -)*

There is hope in dreams, imagination, and in the courage of those who wish to make those dreams a reality.
-*Jonas Salk (1914 – 95)*

Strange as it may seem, I still hope for the best, even though the best, like an interesting piece of mail, so rarely arrives, and even when it does it can be lost so easily.
-*Daniel Handler (Lemony Snicket) (1970-)*

Hope is important because it can make the present moment less difficult to bear. If we believe that tomorrow will be better, we can bear a hardship today.
-*Thich Nhat Hanh (1926 -)*

When you have lost hope, you have lost everything. And when you think all is lost, when all is dire and bleak, there is always hope.
-*James Frey (1969 -)*

All our lives we search for someone who makes us complete. We choose partners and change partners. We dance the song of heartbreak and hope all the while, wondering if somewhere, somehow there is someone searching for us.
-*Fred Savage (1976 -)*

To do something, however small, to make others happier and better, is the highest ambition, the most elevating hope, which can inspire a human being.
-*John Lubbock (1834 – 1913)*

You can cut all the flowers but you cannot keep spring from coming.
-*Pablo Neruda (1904 -73)*

When things are bad, we take comfort in the thought that they could always be worse. And when they are, we find hope in the thought that things are so bad they have to get better.
-*Malcolm Forbes (1919 – 90)*

I don't think of all the misery, but of the beauty that still remains.
-*Anne Frank (1929 – 45)*

I still believe in Hope - mostly because there's no such place as Fingers Crossed, Arkansas.
-*Molly Ivins (1944 – 2007)*

There is a saying in Tibetan, 'Tragedy should be utilized as a source of strength.' No matter what sort of difficulties, how painful experience is, if we lose our hope, that's our real disaster.
-*Dalai Lama (1935 -)*

Hope is the most exciting thing in life and if you honestly believe that love is out there, it will come. And even if it doesn't come straight away there is still that chance all through your life that it will.
-*Josh Hartnett – (1978 -)*

Hope is a good breakfast, but it is a bad supper.
-*Francis Bacon (1561 – 1626)*

Strong hope is a much greater stimulant of life than any realized joy could be.
-*Friedrich Nietzsche (1844 – 1900)*

The road that is built in hope is more pleasant to the traveller than the road built in despair, even though they both lead to the same destination.
-*Marion Zimmer Bradley (1930 – 99)*

Hope is faith holding out its hand in the dark.
-*George Iles (1852 – 1942)*

Do not spoil what you have by desiring what you have not; remember that what you now have was once among the things you only hoped for.
-*Epicurus (341 – 270 BC)*

Hope is the feeling that the feeling you have isn't permanent.
-*Jean Kerr (1923 – 2003)*

There is a crack in everything.
That's how the light gets in.
-*Leonard Cohen (1934 -)*

In this world you've just got to hope for the best and prepare for the worst and take whatever God sends.
-*Lucy Maud Montgomery (1874 – 1922)*

Shoot for the moon, even if you fail, you'll land among the stars.
-*Cecelia Ahern (1981 -)*

When you do nothing, you feel overwhelmed and powerless. But when you get involved, you feel the sense of hope and accomplishment that comes from knowing you are working to make things better.
-*Albert Einstein (1874 – 1955)*

One lives in the hope of becoming a memory.
-*Antonio Porchia (1885 – 1968)*

Hope is the dream of a soul awake.
-*French proverb*

Remember, Hope is a good thing, maybe the best of things, and no good thing ever dies.
-*Stephen King (1947 -)*

Most of the important things in the world have been accomplished by people who have kept on trying when there seemed to be no hope at all.
-*Dale Carnegie (1888 – 1995)*

For like a shaft, clear and cold, the thought pierced him that in the end the Shadow was only a small and passing thing: there was light and high beauty forever beyond its reach.
-*JRR Tolkien (1892 – 1973)*

What to do if you find yourself stuck in a crack in the ground underneath a giant boulder you can't move, with no hope of rescue. Consider how lucky you are that life has been good to you so far. Alternatively, if life hasn't been good to you so far, which given your current circumstances seems more likely, consider how lucky you are that it won't be troubling you much longer.
-*Douglass Adams (1952 – 2001)*

Where hope would otherwise become hopelessness, it becomes faith.
-*Robert Brault (1963 -)*

Hope never abandons you; you abandon it.
-*George Weinberg (1935 -)*

Once you choose hope, anything's possible.
-*Christopher Reeve (1952 – 2004)*

Hope is a waking dream.
-*Aristotle (384 – 322 BC)*

Hope is the only universal liar who never loses his reputation for veracity.
-*Robert G Ingersoll (1833 - 99)*

Hope arouses, as nothing else can arouse, a passion for the possible.
-*William Sloan Coffin (1924 – 2006)*

Things which you do not hope happen more frequently than things which you do hope.
-*Plautus (254 – 184 BC)*

Hope begins in the dark, the stubborn hope that if you just show up and try to do the right thing, the dawn will come. You wait and watch and work: you don't give up.
-Anne Lamott (1954 -)

Hope is some extraordinary spiritual grace that God gives us to control our fears, not to oust them.
-Vincent McNabb (1868 – 1943)

Hope is the power that gives us the power to step out and try.
-Zig Ziglar (1926 – 2012)

When the world says, "Give up", Hope whispers, "Try it one more time."
-Anon

All human wisdom is summed up in two words - wait and hope.
-Alexandre Dumas Père (1802 -70)

There is nothing so well known as that we should not expect something for nothing — but we all do and call it Hope.
-Edgar Howe (1853 – 1937)

For there is but one problem - the problem of human relations. We forget that there is no hope or joy except in human relations.
-Antoine de Saint-Exupery (1900 – 44)

The sudden disappointment of a hope leaves a scar which the ultimate fulfilment of that hope never entirely removes.
-Thomas Hardy (1840 – 1928)

Of all the forces that make for a better world, none is so indispensable, none so powerful, as hope. Without hope people are only half alive. With hope they dream and think and work.
-*Anon*

Hope is independent of the apparatus of logic.
-*Norman Cousins (1915 -90)*

Hope is knowing that people, like kites, are made to be lifted up.
-*Anon*

Hope rises like a phoenix from the ashes of shattered dreams.
-*SA Sachs (1935 -)*

Hope is the thing with feathers that perches in the soul, and sings the tune without words, and never stops at all.
-*Emily Dickinson (1830 – 86)*

Hope is the physician of each misery.
-*Irish Proverb*

Hope is the pillar that holds up the world.
-*Pliny the Elder (23 – 79 AD)*

God puts rainbows in the clouds so that each of us — in the dreariest and most dreaded moments — can see a possibility of hope.
-*Maya Angelou (1928 – 2014)*

Hope is the denial of reality.
-*Margaret Weis (1948 -)*

Hope deceives more men than cunning does.
-*Luc de Clapiers (1715 – 47)*

What oxygen is to the lungs, such is hope to the meaning of life.
-*Emily Brunner*

To eat bread without hope is still slowly to starve to death.
-*Pearl S. Buck (1892 – 1973)*

Hope is the expectation that something outside of ourselves, something or someone external, is going to come to our rescue and we will live happily ever after.
-*Dr. Robert Anthony*

Hope is grief's best music.
-*Anon*

Hope is not the conviction that something will turn out well but the certainty that something makes sense, regardless of how it turns out.
-*Vaclav Havel (1938 – 2011)*

Never deprive someone of hope — it may be all they have.
-*H Jackson Brown Jr (1940 -)*

Expect to have hope rekindled. Expect your prayers to be answered in wondrous ways. The dry seasons in life do not last. The spring rains will come again.
-*Sarah Ban Breathnach (1947 -)*

Hope is patience with the lamp lit.
-*Tertullian (160 – 200 AD)*

Forgiveness means giving up all hope for a better past.
-*Lily Tomlin (1939 -)*

He who has health, has hope. And he who has hope, has everything.
-*Proverb*

Our imagination is the only limit to what we can hope to have in the future.
-*Charles F Kettering (1876 – 1958)*

The first task of a leader is to keep hope alive.
-*Joe D Batten*

My hopes are not always realized, but I always hope.
-*Ovid (43 BC – 17 AD)*

Everything that is done in the world is done by hope.
-*Martin Luther (1483 – 1546)*

Those who hope for no other life are dead even for this.
-*Johann Wolfgang von Goethe (1749 – 1832)*

Hope and fear are inseparable. There is no hope without fear, nor any fear without hope.
-*François de la Rochefoucauld (1613 – 80)*

Love, we say, is life; but love without hope and faith is agonizing death.
-*Elbert Hubbard (1856 – 1915)*

To hope means to be ready at every moment for that which is not yet born, and yet not become desperate if there is no birth in our lifetime.
-*Emily Dickinson (1830 – 86)*

Hope is the only bee that makes honey without flowers.
-*Robert Green (1833 – 99)*

Hope is not victory.
-*JRR Tolkein (1892 – 1973)*

By accepting you as you are, I do not necessarily abandon all hope of your improving.
-*Ashleigh Brilliant (1933 -)*

The dog is a gentleman; I hope to go to his heaven, not man's.
-*Mark Twain (1835 – 1910)*

To be truly radical is to make hope possible rather than despair convincing.
-*Raymond Williams (1921 – 88)*

Hope is the word which God has written on the brow of every man.
-*Victor Hugo (1802 – 85)*

Hope is a very unruly emotion.
-*Gloria Steinem (1935 -)*

Middle age is when you're sitting at home on a Saturday night and the telephone rings and you hope it isn't for you.
-*Ogden Nash (1902 – 71)*

What makes one heroic? -- Going out to meet at the same time one's highest suffering and one's highest hope.
-*Friedrich Nietzsche (1844 – 1900)*

Hope is the companion of power, and mother of success; for who so hopes strongly has within him the gift of miracles.
-*Samuel Smiles (1812 – 1904)*

Carve a tunnel of hope through the dark mountain of disappointment.
-*Martin Luther King, Jr. (1929 – 68)*

Hope is a bad thing. It means that you are not what you want to be. It means that part of you is dead, if not all of you. It means that you entertain illusions. It's a sort of spiritual clap, I should say.
-*Henry Miller (1891 – 1980)*

There is no medicine like hope, no incentive so great, and no tonic so powerful as expectation of something better tomorrow.
-*Orison Swett Marden (1850 – 1924)*

Hope is the struggle of the soul, breaking loose from what is perishable, and attesting her eternity.
-*Herman Melville (1819 -91)*

Learn from yesterday, live for today, hope for tomorrow. -*Albert Einstein (1879 – 1955)*

When we have lost everything, including hope, life becomes a disgrace, and death a duty.
-*WC Fields (1880 – 1946)*

A man with a grain of faith in God never loses hope, because he ever believes in the ultimate triumph of Truth.
-*Mahatma Gandhi (1869 – 1948)*

The very least you can do in your life is to figure out what you hope for. And the most you can do is live inside that hope.

-Barbara Kingsolver (1955 -)

War is just when it is necessary; arms are permissible when there is no hope except in arms.

-Niccolo Machiavelli (1469 – 1527)

Hope is like a road in the country; there was never a road, but when many people walk on it, the road comes into existence.

-Lyn Yutang (1895 -1976)

 A child's eyes, those clear wells of undefiled thought—what on earth can be more beautiful? Full of hope, love and curiosity, they meet your own.

-Caroline Norton (1808 – 77)

George W Bush

If the terriers and bariffs are torn down, this economy will grow.

You can fool some of the people all the time, and those are the ones you want to concentrate on.

The thing that's wrong with the French is that they don't have a word for entrepreneur.

You teach a child to read, and he or her will be able to pass a literacy test.

Most imports are from outside of the country.

I am mindful not only of preserving executive powers for myself, but for predecessors as well.

In my sentences I go where no man has gone before.

I have a different vision of leadership. A leadership is someone who brings people together.

Well, I think if you say you're going to do something and don't do it, that's trustworthiness.

I just want you to know that, when we talk about war, we're really talking about peace.

There's an old saying in Tennessee - I know it's in Texas, probably in Tennessee...that says, fool me once, shame on...shame on you. Fool me...you can't get fooled again.

I admit it, I am not one of the great linguists.

This case has had full analyzation and has been looked at a lot.

I think we ought to raise the age at which juveniles can have a gun.

It's clearly a budget. It's got a lot of numbers in it

A dictatorship would be a heck of a lot easier, there's no question about it.

The legislature's job is to write law. It's the executive branch's job to interpret law.

See, in my line of work you got to keep repeating things over and over and over again for the truth to sink in, to kind of catapult the propaganda.

When I take action, I'm not going to fire a $2 million missile at a $10 empty tent and hit a camel in the butt. It's going to be decisive.

Our nation must come together to unite.

There's no such thing as legacies. At least, there is a legacy, but I'll never see it.

I want to thank you for taking time out of your day to come and witness my hanging.

One of the common denominators I have found is that expectations rise above that which is expected.

I understand small business growth. I was one.

We don't believe in planners and deciders making the decisions on behalf of Americans.

Natural gas is hemispheric. I like to call it hemispheric in nature because it is a product that we can find in our neighborhoods.

What I'm against is quotas. I'm against hard quotas, quotas that basically delineate based upon whatever. However they delineate, quotas, I think, vulcanize society.

The California crunch really is the result of not enough power-generating plants and then not enough power to power the power of generating plants.

We're concerned about AIDS inside our White House—make no mistake about it.

Redefining the role of the United States from enablers to keep the peace to enablers to keep the peace from peacekeepers is going to be an assignment.

I can hear you, the rest of the world can hear you and the people who knocked these buildings down will hear all of us soon.

We cannot let terrorists hold this nation hostile or hold our allies hostile.

Rarely is the question asked: is our children learning?

It will take time to restore Chaos

One of the great things about books is sometimes there are some fantastic pictures.

If you're sick and tired of the politics of cynicism and polls and principles, come and join this campaign

There's not going to be enough people in the system to take advantage of people like me.

States should have the right to enact... laws... particularly to end the inhumane practice of ending a life that otherwise could live.

I mean, there needs to be a wholesale effort against racial profiling, which is illiterate children.

There's no bigger task than protecting the homeland of our country.

There's no question that the minute I got elected, the storm clouds on the horizon were getting nearly directly overhead.

They want the federal government controlling Social Security like it's some kind of federal program.

This is Preservation Month. I appreciate preservation. It's what you do when you run for president. You gotta preserve.

He can't have it both ways. He can't take the high horse and then claim the low road.

Will the highways on the Internet become more few?"

The most important job is not to be governor, or first lady in my case.

This foreign policy stuff is a little frustrating.

This administration is doing everything we can to end the stalemate in an efficient way. We're making the right decisions to bring the solution to an end.

I know what I believe. I will continue to articulate what I believe and what I believe - I believe what I believe is right.

I love to bring people into the oval office...and say, this is where I office.

Actually, I...this may sound a little West Texan to you, but I like it. When I'm talking about...when I'm talking about myself, and when he's talking about myself, all of us are talking about me.

They misunderestimated me.

I'm honored to shake the hand of a brave Iraqi citizen who had his hand cut off by Saddam Hussein.

More Muslims have died at the hands of killers than - I say more Muslims - a lot of Muslims have died - I don't know the exact count - at Istanbul. Look at these different places around the world where there's been tremendous death and destruction because killers kill.

I think war is a dangerous place.

Secondly, the tactics of our - as you know, we don't have relationships with Iran. I mean, that's - ever since the late '70s, we have no contacts with them, and we've totally sanctioned them. In other words, there's no sanctions - you can't - we're out of sanctions.

First, let me make it very clear, poor people aren't necessarily killers. Just because you happen to be not rich doesn't mean you're willing to kill.

I think anybody who doesn't think I'm smart enough to handle the job is underestimating.

Our enemies are innovative and resourceful, and so are we. They never stop thinking about new ways to harm our country and our people, and neither do we.

Some folks look at me and see a certain swagger, which in Texas is called walking.

Karyn is with us. A West Texas girl, just like me.

You're free. And freedom is beautiful. And, you know, it'll take time to restore chaos and order - order out of chaos. But we will.

Drug therapies are replacing a lot of medicine as we used to know it.

I'm the master of low expectations.

The only things that I can tell you is that every case I have reviewed I have been comfortable with the innocence or guilt of the person that I've looked at. I do not believe we've put a guilty... I mean innocent person to death in the state of Texas.

A tax cut is really one of the anecdotes to coming out of an economic illness.

The problem with golf is I have to deal with a humiliation factor.

I was going to start off tonight by telling some self-deprecating jokes, but then I couldn't think of any mistakes I've made to be self-deprecating about.

I believe if you want to be negative you always can, no matter how hard you try.

I glance at the headlines just to kind of get a flavor for what's moving. I rarely read the stories, and get briefed by people who are probably read the news themselves.

Let me put it to you this way, I am not a revengeful person.

We spent a lot of time talking about Africa, as we should. Africa is a nation that suffers from incredible disease.

I couldn't imagine somebody like Osama bin Laden understanding the joy of Hanukkah.

I know the human being and fish can coexist peacefully.

For every fatal shooting, there were roughly three non-fatal shootings. And, folks, this is unacceptable in America. It's just unacceptable. And we're going to do something about it.

This is an impressive crowd -- the haves and the have mores. Some people call you the elite -- I call you my base.

I call upon all nations to do everything they can to stop these terrorist killers. Thank you. Now watch this drive.

You teach a child to read, and he or her will be able to pass a literacy test.

LAST WORDS

This is the last of earth! I am content.
-John Quincy Adams (1767 – 1848)

No comment.
-Edward Abbey (1927 – 89)

Is it not meningitis?
-Louisa M. Alcott (1832 – 88)

I pray you to bear me witness that I met my fate like a brave man.
-Major John André (1750 -80)

Am I dying or is this my birthday?
-Lady Nancy Astor (1879- 1964)

What is the time? Never mind, it's not important...
-János Arany (1817 – 82)

Codeine . . . bourbon.
-Tallulah Bankhead (1902 – 68)

I've got the bows up... I'm going!
-Donald Campbell (1921 – 67)

How were the receipts today at Madison Square Garden?
-P. T. Barnum (1778 – 1826)

This is not the end of me.
-Henry Campbell-Bannerman (1836 – 1908)

Is everybody happy? I want everybody to be happy. I know I'm happy.
-Ethel Barrymore (1879 – 1959)

I have lived as a philosopher, and die as a Christian.
-*Giacomo Casanova (1725 – 98)*

Die? I should say not, dear fellow. No Barrymore would allow such a conventional thing to happen to him.
-*John Barrymore (1882 – 1942)*

You must pardon me, gentlemen, for being a most unconscionable time a-dying.
-*Charles II (1630 – 85)*

Now comes the mystery.
-*Henry Ward Beecher (1813 – 87)*

There is nothing proper about what you are doing, soldier, but do try to kill me properly.
-*Cicero (106 – 43BC)*

Friends applaud, the comedy is finished.
-*Ludwig van Beethoven (1770 – 1827)*

Thank God. I'm tired of being the funniest person in the room.
-*Del Close (1934 – 99)*

I should never have switched from Scotch to Martinis.
-*Humphrey Bogart (1899 – 157)*

It's better to burn out than to fade away.
-*Kurt Cobain (1967 – 94)*

I am about to -- or I am going to -- die: either expression is correct.
-*Dominique Bouhours (1628 – 1702)*

Since the day of my birth, my death began its walk. It is walking towards me, without hurrying.
-*Jean Cocteau (1889 – 1963)*

Et tu, Brute?
-*Julius Caesar (100 – 44BC)*

What is life? It is the flash of a firefly in the night. It is the breath of a buffalo in the wintertime. It is the little shadow which runs across the grass and loses itself in the sunset.
-*Crowfoot (1830 – 90)*

I am still alive!
-*Caligula (12 – 41 AD)*

That was the best ice-cream soda I ever tasted.
-*Lou Costello (1906 – 59)*

I am dying. I haven't drunk champagne for a long time.
-*Anton Pavlovich Chekhov (1860 – 1904)*

Where is my clock?
-*Salvador Dalí (1904 – 89)*

Swear to make them cut me open, so that I won't be buried alive.
-*Frederic Chopin (1810 -49)*

That guy's got to stop... He'll see us.
-*James Dean (1931 – 55)*

I'm bored with it all.
-*Winston Churchill (1874 – 1965)*

But how the devil do you think this could harm me?
-*Denis Diderot (1713 - 84)*

I'll finally get to see Marilyn.
-*Joe DiMaggio (1914 – 99)*

This time it will be a long one.
-*Georges Clemenceau (1841 – 1929)*

It is nothing... it is nothing...
-Franz Ferdinand Archduke of Austria-Hungary (1863 – 1914)

Nothing soothes pain like human touch.
-Bobby Fischer (1943 – 2008)

I have tried so hard to do the right.
-Grover Cleveland (1837 – 1908)

It was the food! Don't touch the food!
-Richard Harris (1930 – 2002)

Goodnight my darlings, I'll see you tomorrow.
-Noel Coward (1889 -1973)

Children be comforted, I am well.
-Joseph Haydn (1732 – 1809)

Damn it . . . Don't you dare ask God to help me.
-Joan Crawford (1904 – 77)

Goodnight, my kitten.
-Ernest Hemingway (1899 – 1961)

That was a great game of golf, fellers.
-Bing Crosby (1903 – 77)

Maybe I'm dying.
-Jim Henson (1936 – 90)

I am not the least afraid to die.
-Charles Darwin (1809 – 92)

One never knows the ending. One has to die to know exactly what happens after death, although Catholics have their hopes.
-Alfred Hitchcock (1899 – 1980)

My God. What's happened?
-Diana (Spencer), Princess of Wales (1961 – 97)

Oh wow. Oh wow. Oh wow.
-Steve Jobs (1955 – 2011)

It is very beautiful over there.
-Thomas Alva Edison (1847 – 1931)

I should have drunk more Champagne.
-John Maynard Keynes (1883 – 1946)

All my possessions for a moment of time.
-Elizabeth I (1533 – 1603)

The bastards got me, but they won't get everybody.
-Alexander Litvinenko (1962 – 2006)

I've never felt better.
-Douglas Fairbanks, Sr. (1883 – 1939)

Die, my dear? Why, that's the last thing I'll do!
-Groucho Marx (1880 – 1977)

I'd hate to die twice. It's so boring.
-Richard Feynman (1918 – 1988)

We all get the same amount of ice. The rich get it in the summer. The poor get it in the winter.
-Bat Masterson (1853 – 1921)

I've had a hell of a lot of fun and I've enjoyed every minute of it.
-Errol Flynn (109 – 59)

I should have asked for a stunt double!
-Vic Morrow (1929 – 82)

I know you have come to kill me. Shoot coward, you are only going to kill a man.
-*Ernesto "Che" Guevara (1928 – 67)*

The taste of death is upon my lips...I feel something that is not of this earth.
-*Mozart (1756 – 91)*

God will pardon me, that's his line of work.
-*Heinrich Heine (1797 – 1856)*

Tomorrow, I shall no longer be here.
-*Nostradamus (1503 – 66)*

I see black light.
-*Victor Hugo (1802 – 85)*

I am just going outside. I may be some time.
-*Captain Lawrence Oates (1880 – 1912)*

A King should die standing.
-*Louis XVIII (1755 – 1824)*

Aw, no one's gonna shoot at me.
-*Lee Harvey Oswald (1939 – 63)*

The city is fallen and I am still alive.
-*Constantine XI Palaiologos (1405 – 53)*

Why do you weep? Did you think I was immortal?
-*Louis XIV (1638 – 1715)*

Everybody has got to die, but I have always believed an exception would be made in my case. What now?
-*William Saroyan (1908 – 81)*

I am a Queen, but I have not the power to move my arms.
-*Louise, Queen of Prussia (1776 – 1810)*

For God's sake look after our people.
-*Robert Falcon Scott (1868 – 1912)*

Too late for fruit, too soon for flowers.
-*Walter De La Mare (1873 – 156)*

The car seems OK...
-*Ayrton Senna (1960 – 94)*

Go on, get out - last words are for fools who haven't said enough.
-*Karl Marx (1818 – 83)*

I believe we should adjourn this meeting to another place.
-*Adam Smith (1723 – 90)*

Nothing matters. Nothing matters.
-*Louis B. Mayer (1884 – 1957)*

Well, boys, do your best for the women and children, and look out for yourselves.
-*Captain Edward Smith, commander of the RMS TITANIC (1850 – 1912)*

It's all been very interesting.
-*Lady Mary Wortley Montagu (1689 – 1762)*

What is the answer? [no response] In that case, what is the question?
-*Gertrude Stein (1874 -1946)*

I knew it. I knew it. Born in a hotel room - and God damn it - died in a hotel room.
-*Eugene O'Neill (1888 – 1953)*

I'm not afraid of death. I'm going home.
-*Patrick Swayze (1952 – 2009)*

Get my swan costume ready.
-*Anna Pavlova (1881 – 1931)*

It is time for a new direction...
-*Andrei Tarkovski (1932 – 86)*

Here am I, dying of a hundred good symptoms.
-*Alexander Pope (1688 – 1744)*

Oh that press will have me now!
-*Alfred Lord Tennyson (1809 – 92)*

I owe much; I have nothing; the rest I leave to the poor.
-*François Rabelais (1494 – 1553)*

I will not survive this attack. Stalin has finally accomplished the task he attempted unsuccessfully before.
-*Leon Trotsky (1879 – 1940)*

They couldn't hit an elephant at this dist . . . .
-*General John Sedgwick (1813 – 64)*

Go away. I'm all right.
-*H. G. Wells (1866 – 1946)*

Sister, you're trying to keep me alive as an old curiosity, but I'm done, I'm finished, I'm going to die.
-*George Bernard Shaw (1856 – 1950)*

Oh, what's the bloody point?
-*Kenneth Williams (1926 – 88)*

I've had eighteen straight whiskies, I think that's the record . . . - *Dylan Thomas (1914 – 53)*

Don't let it end like this. Tell them I said something.
-Pancho Villa 1878 – 1923)

I have offended God and mankind because my work did not reach the quality it should have.
-Leonardo da Vinci (1452 – 1519)

I die hard but am not afraid to go.
-George Washington (1732 – 99)

Either that wallpaper goes, or I do.
-Oscar Wilde (1854 – 1900)

I am ready.
-Woodrow Wilson (1856 – 1924)

Made in the USA
Middletown, DE
15 April 2023

28909997R00245